The Transformation
of John Foster Dulles

John Foster Dulles converses with some of Union Theological Seminary's students during the 1952 Conference on Ministry. (Photograph is by Alfred Gescheidt, from Black Star. It is the possession of the Burke Library, Union Theological Seminary, and is reprinted with permission.)

The Transformation of John Foster Dulles

From Prophet of Realism to Priest of Nationalism

Mark G. Toulouse

MERCER
MP

ISBN 0-86554-160-4

All books published by Mercer University Press
are produced on acid-free paper
that exceeds the minimum standards set by the
National Historical Publications and Records Commission.

Library of Congress Cataloging in Publication Data
Toulouse, Mark G., 1952–
The transformation of John Foster Dulles.

Bibliography: p. 255
Includes index.
1. Dulles, John Foster, 1888–1959. 2. Statesmen—
United States—Biography. 3. United States—Foreign
relations—1933–1945. 4. United States—Foreign relations
—1945–1953. I. Title.
E748.D868T68   1985   973.921'092'4   85-10467
ISBN 0-86554-160-4 (alk. paper)

Contents

I
The Years of Preparation, 1888-1937

1

2

II
Prophet of Realism:
The Narrative Setting
and the Ideological Framework, 1937-1945

3

4

Dedication

To
Jeffica
source of grace, wisdom, and love

Foreword

To study the ideas of John Foster Dulles, as this book attempts to do, is to come to an understanding of one of the central questions of the twentieth century: war and peace. Despite the remarkable technological advances that have linked all parts of the world more closely together and brought about economic and cultural interchanges among different countries and peoples, these developments have not necessarily brought about a more peaceful international order. Potentially universalizing forces have been helpless to counter trends toward parochialism.

This has been the dilemma of the twentieth century. In this century forces have been marshaled for greater interdependence and internationalism; yet narrow visions and self-centered movements have still spread. In a sense, both these go back to the early modern era, to the sixteenth and seventeenth centuries, when the West opened up vistas of a promised land where all would benefit from scientific and humanistic discoveries. Concurrently Europe divided itself into territorial states, each with its own definition of national interests. Forces of nationalism and internationalism have grown tremendously since, and have penetrated to the rest of the world. War and peace have become dependent on the interplay between these two sets of forces. It would be unrealistic to expect one of them to disappear altogether: peace, therefore, will have to be built on a balance between nationalism and internationalism.

How to achieve such balance is a problem that has fascinated some of this century's best minds and keenest observers. Dulles was one of them. To trace his thoughts is to grasp the meaning of the evolution of America's position in the world, from the turn of the century when the United States entered the world arena as one of the great powers, through mid-century when it was the strongest nation, militarily and economically. How the nation could contribute to the making and keeping of peace, pursuing both its own self-interest and the larger concerns of the world as a whole, fascinated men and women of this generation. To examine his evolving ideas is to comprehend the often tortuous way in which the two sides of America, one internationalist and the other nationalist, entwined and defined policy. Starting out as an internationalist, Dulles in the 1950s ended his career as a "priest of nationalism," to use Mark Toulouse's apt expression. However, as the book shows, the transformation was never simple; his strong, assertive nationalism had a religious, moralistic basis that linked it to the earlier internationalism. On the other hand, his internationalism was steadily transformed as he came to justify the use of force to defend a certain conception of international order.

The study of twentieth-century American diplomacy has been enriched by the opening of archives and private collections and by sustained efforts of historians to go beyond the conventional "diplomatic history" approach. Among the more notable alternatives to this approach has been what may be termed an intellectual history of foreign affairs: to examine ideas, assumptions, psychologies, and mentalities of policymakers and opinion leaders. Through such an approach, we have come to know a great deal about the "ideologies" underlying American foreign policy. This book fits into the new tradition of international/intellectual history, and will make a fine companion volume to such landmarks as Felix Gilbert's *To the Farewell Address*, Sondra Hermann's *Eleven against War*, and Emily Rosenberg's *Spreading the American Dream*. Toulouse, moreover, makes a unique contribution to the literature by examining an important public figure's religious and theological concerns and linking them to his views of world affairs. The result is to establish a connection between American religious history and foreign policy. At a time when the question of the relationship of religion and politics is attracting widespread attention, this book will be of value not merely to specialists but to all those who are interested in that question.

November 1984   *Akira Iriye*
Stein-Freiler Distinguished Service Professor
The University of Chicago

Foreword

From time to time critics and admirers of the United States Constitution and Presbyterianism have called the Constitution a Presbyterian document. One major interpreter, Forrest Macdonald, has written that how one stood in respect to that document when it was being ratified told a great deal about what one believed concerning original sin. Someone must rule. Kings could not, dared not. The people must. Yet they could not be trusted. They elected representatives. They could also not be trusted. There must be an executive branch. A judicial branch would help complete the distribution of powers. Still, one must be vigilant.

The ties between Presbyterianism in its wider covenantal (and thus its nondenominational) sense and the Republic do not begin or end with the suspicious and grand elements of the United States Constitution. Through the two centuries of national life there have been numerous instances when, to borrow columnist George Will's distinction, the soulcraft behind statecraft has been Presbyterian. This dimension of soul in national life demands examination.

Jose Ortega y Gasset argues that every society lives by a rather small if ill-defined set of *creencias*. Creencias he defines as the beliefs that are so deep we do not know we hold them; they are not simply the beliefs we have but the beliefs we *are*. The American sets of creencias, which are always being subtly changed, are not Presbyterian properties. Yet they have taken the shape they have because on this soil there have been respondents to, exemplars of, and traducers of, certain Calvinist-Presbyterian themes: about the initiating and provident power of God; about the vocation and mission and destiny of a nation under God; about the seriousness of moral action on the part of those who govern and direct the nation; about the covenant that holds it together and the transcendent justice that superintends it; about the accountability of its stewards and the righteousness they believe they can effect in the affairs of people.

At its best the Presbyterian covenant impels those who embody and profess it to acts of nobility and sacrifice. They would fulfill the national mission. At its worst the same covenant leads those who claim it to acts of folly and selfishness, denials of the national mission they claim to know so thoroughly. Presbyterianism teaches us to expect the best to live alongside the worst and the worst to be capable of participating in the national mission. We are all mixed cases, package deals.

The men—and one instinctively thinks of self-assured men—who have held public office in this tradition in our time have given observers of the Presbyterian influence much to consider. Thus Woodrow Wilson espoused an idealism that still inspires as much as it puzzles. He professed intentions whose outcomes turned out to be ironic: he was leading Christ's cause of peace in and, he hoped, after World War I; pursuing the war for peace; and committing the denial of democracy that would ensure democracy. More recently, Secretary of State Dean Rusk, schooled at statecraft and a person of many accomplishments, was seen by many to be living out an ethos shaped by Presbyterianism and the craft and mission it inspired. There are others.

Among those others, between Wilson and Rusk, was John Foster Dulles. Those who have read his biography will find credible the notion that there "were John Foster Dulleses." There seem to be two, and they are not easily brought together. There is the pre-World War II ecumenical church leader, admired by seekers of peace and by prophets and ironists alike, who saw in his idealism a profound searching for a national direction among the nations. And there is the post-World War II Cold Warrior, admired by a different set of Americans, who cherished the way that his idealism found expression in a realism that went far beyond Reinhold Niebuhrian impulses and became merely crafty—obsessed with the righteousness of America and its need to be God's instrument against alien forces that had consolidated into a Soviet threat.

The two Dulleses no doubt coexisted all along, but there was also some turning from one to the other. Not all the admirers or critics of the later Dulles could make sense of him in light of the one they had known or read about from prewar days. Cynical biographers—or should they simply be seen as Presbyterian, and hence realist—have seen a switch in Dulles that was occasioned by a thirst for power, a tinge of messianism, and large measures of mere opportunism. Admiring biographers and anthologists—or should they simply be seen as Presbyterian, and hence responsible—have stressed continuity throughout his life. Between them stands Mark Toulouse, who sees both continuity and change, and who wants readers to suspend judgment and entertain the possibility that Dulles was acting in good faith even if it was a faith that—like everyone else's—was not and could not be fulfilled within the boundaries of finitude, the frail limits of history.

How Professor Toulouse makes his case, one that not I alone have found convincing, is now his business; it is the task of a foreword writer to stay out of the way of a plot that should have some suspense. It should be clear from these paragraphs that I consider this work important for understanding Dulles and American foreign policy as it was being set early in the atomic era, when the stakes for preventing both war and ideological dominance by the Soviet Union were first perceived as awesome.

So I confine myself to a last word about the context of ventures like these. Americans, one hears as often as ever and with as much urgency, somehow set out to separate church and state or draw a line of distinction between the rights of the churches and civil authorities, as Jefferson and then Madison would have it. Some citizens who chafe on both sides of such lines occasionally push the liberties that are theirs so far that nothing is left of distinctions. Others claim that the religious outlook dare have no place in statecraft.

John Foster Dulles shows more vividly than most that the people who govern are "package deals." To ask that religious ideals and morality derived therefrom have no part in national and international relations would mean that citizens dare only elect and appoint the nonreligious. This would be a tiny minority of agnostics. In a sophisticated age it would not take experts long to discern quasireligious impulses among them. Religion, if it shapes the deepest values of life, will inevitably play its part in shaping policy. Madison always insisted that just as religion dared not be established or privileged, so religion dare not be a disability for individuals or groups who would make a public case.

The discreet statesperson becomes aware of what his or her religious outlook and values are. Such a person may well exercise restraint in specific expressions of these, being mindful of how they are regarded and tested in a pluralist society, where not all will share them. Yet even the discreet have difficulty knowing what their perspective is, or how to maintain it. Dulles was no exception. It is to the credit of Mark Toulouse that he has patiently tracked this important secretary of state, this churchman and statesman, and let him speak for himself more than have many. Further, he has made the kinds of judgments that guide readers toward their own conclusions without forcing a mold on his subject or them.

I should like to see studies like this, and especially this study, fall into the hands of those who elect, appoint, execute, or are subjects of people who govern. It would be a good exercise in understanding why individuals act as they do in spheres where consequences are so fateful.

November 1984
Martin E. Marty
Fairfax M. Cone Distinguished Service Professor
of Modern Church History
Divinity School
The University of Chicago

Acknowledgments

In the course of completing this study, I have acquired debts too numerous to repay adequately. Acknowledgment in these pages seems insignificant by comparison, yet it does provide a starting point.

Always attentive, responsive, and unbelievably accessible, Martin E. Marty has been an adviser, teacher, frank critic, and warm friend. His influence on me extends far beyond this work. Jerald C. Brauer, through his thoughtful criticism, timely encouragement, and healthy sense of humor, has also had a profound impact on this project. I also wish to thank Professor Akira Iriye for allowing me to join his stimulating seminar on American diplomatic history. Beyond that he set aside time to read the manuscript at each stage of its development and made helpful suggestions along the way.

I must also acknowledge the willing attention that others have given to various portions of this manuscript. John M. Mulder, whose excellent study of Woodrow Wilson helped me form the initial idea for this project, offered suggestions early in the process. John C. Bennett responded to requests for comment by providing generous and valuable insights. Father Avery Dulles carefully read the manuscript and took the time to respond in detail even though he personally disagrees with my portrayal of his father's later years. It should be noted that I exercised the author's prerogative to pick and choose among the many suggestions that were made by all the above individuals and therefore responsibility for the final product rests with me alone.

The topic of civil religion has stimulated lively debate among scholars in recent days. I would like to express my gratitude to the many scholars who have engaged in that debate. Though they receive no particular mention within the text of these pages, their ideas and arguments have certainly helped to inform my own approach to the primary sources utilized in this study.

The library staff of Princeton University was very helpful. I am particularly indebted to Nancy Bressler, Curator of Public Affairs Papers at the Seeley G. Mudd Manuscript Library of Princeton University and to her staff for the careful attention they gave to my requests for aid. Librarians in the John Foster Dulles Wing of the Firestone Library at Princeton University were equally attentive.

I also owe my former colleagues at Illinois Benedictine College in Lisle, Illinois my thanks. By making a computer terminal, a modem, and a telephone line available to me, the college personnel, notably Phil Bean and Eileen Clark, saved me long late-night and early-morning drives in and out of Chicago. My 1975 Ford and I both appreciate that kindness. My thanks also go to the Phillips University Graduate Seminary in Enid, Oklahoma for providing last-minute secretarial services in the person of Donna Lee Holloway. The Seminary also provided support by funding the extremely capable services of Barbara Wilkins Harris for the task of preparing the index.

The staff of Mercer University Press has supported this project in a way that is truly, in my opinion, above and beyond the call of duty. My association with this Press is one that I will long remember with warm appreciation.

I would like to express my gratitude to the management of the *Journal of Presbyterian History* for allowing me to use material from the following article, which originally appeared in their pages: "Working toward Meaningful Peace: John Foster Dulles and the F.C.C.," *Journal of Presbyterian History* 61:4 (Winter 1983): 393-410.

Finally, and most important, I wish to thank my family. First, I am grateful for the fact that my parents provided me early with a home environment conducive to learning. Second, I appreciate beyond measure the so clearly evident support of my academic interests by both my parents and parents-in-law. Most of all, I wish to thank my wife. Without the unending patience and love provided by Jeffica, this project would never have seen completion. She has sacrificed beyond reasonable expectation. The fact that she remains as good-natured as ever is a tribute to her self-giving character. Since this study represents so much of her effort on other fronts, it is only fitting, but hardly payment enough, that it be dedicated to her. I regret that all three of our children, Joshua, Marcie, and Cara, have had to endure the pressure of this research and writing. It pleases both Joshua and me that I can finally answer his often-asked question, "Daddy, aren't you through with that big paper yet?" in the affirmative.

Introduction

The truth is, politics and morality are inseparable. And as mo-rality's foundation is religion, religion and politics are necessarily related. We need religion as a guide.

President Reagan, 1984

President Reagan's remarks, delivered 23 August 1984 at an ecu-menical prayer breakfast in Dallas, Texas shortly after the conclusion of the 1984 Republican Convention, clearly exemplify the common Ameri-can belief that religion and politics are inextricably woven together as one moral fabric in America. Reagan's statement merely reiterates the sen-timents of George Washington's Farewell Address, which referred to re-ligion and morality as the necessary props of political prosperity. This kind of expression is as old as the country itself. Though some might take ex-ception to Reagan's belief that "morality's foundation is religion," and others might take exception to the particular content that Reagan pours into his understanding of the term "religion," few would dispute the fact that questions of religion and morality (however defined) have played an important role in the history of politics in America.

Americans like to think of themselves as a peculiarly moral people. With vocal confidence, Americans have consistently expressed their faith that the American experiment has been a moral one, more so than any of its predecessors on the stage of history. Politicians comfortable with God-language (and all American presidents have been) have character- ized the citizens of America as a "people of God." One of the most com- mon assertions of America's theology has been the affirmation of God's primacy over all human institutions.

Often, politician and citizen alike have elaborated on this affirmation of faith and concluded that standing under God implied an inherent mo- rality, a "chosenness." This places the emphasis on a morality that is im- mediately present in experience rather than on a morality that is demanded. The aspect of the Puritans' covenant theology which empha- sized that chosenness included a large measure of responsibility, and a definite accountability to the One who chooses, has often been conve- niently forgotten. In America, this has somehow been translated into a declaration proclaiming the primacy of a God especially identified with *American* institutions. The "God" of American religious expression be- comes one who is especially interested in the success of the American experiment, one who makes no particular moral demands upon it other than that it continue to succeed and spread that success to the corners of the globe.

Thus the religion that has most often acted as "guide" in America has not been Christianity, though it has most certainly been informed by that historic faith; rather, it is a religion that worships a somewhat deistic God, yet a God who is at least personally concerned enough to have chosen Americans to complete a special mission in history. As the "last best hope of earth," Americans see themselves as *the* collective agent of freedom and equality for God's world. The forces that oppose the mission and success of America are viewed as demonic, anti-God, immoral. Such logic often defended the ever-increasing expansion of the original thirteen col- onies, as today it still stands behind some present arguments on behalf of America's nuclear arsenal.

Americans have therefore displayed a tendency to allow their legiti- mate concern for "morality" to degenerate into "moralism"; that is, the quest for conformity to a universal ideal has often been transformed into a moralistic confidence (self-righteousness) that Americans already embody the universal ideal. This tendency toward an uncritical moralism is still powerfully operative in the diplomacy of our present day.

The whole issue of moralism and its role in the direction of American foreign affairs was raised more vigorously during the Eisenhower period than during any other presidential tenure in modern American history (though the Reagan administration might end up making such a statement obsolete). During the Eisenhower years this moralistic tendency was due in no small measure to the contribution of John Foster Dulles as he tried to define the nation's proper role in world affairs. Several interpreters of the American scene have attempted to make sense of this aspect of John Foster Dulles's character.

Political studies concentrating on the Eisenhower period have been concerned with the question of how Dulles's moralism affected the international political theory practiced during those years. However, none of the diplomatic studies has been directed toward the broader context from which this moralism arises. For Dulles, at least, it grew out of religious roots. On this point, the studies of the Eisenhower/Dulles period are largely silent. Diplomatic historians have not undertaken the task of relating Dulles's distinctive political approach to the religious ideology that lay beneath it. Although most biographers have dealt in some manner with the religious aspect of Dulles's life, they generally miss its significance either because they do not understand the nature of his commitment to religion or because they do not give sufficient attention to it.

The drama that unfolds in the following pages argues that Dulles's moralism did not appear out of nowhere. Rather it resulted from his consistent practice of viewing historical events through a religious lens. His dedication to this task helped to shape the reality in which he lived. As Paul Tillich has expressed: "Reality precedes thought; it is equally true, however, that thought shapes reality."[1] I share Tillich's belief that the two are interdependent.

In trying to discover the relationship between Dulles's religious world view and his political and diplomatic interpretations and actions, I encountered several difficulties. First, there is the inherent difficulty of relating religious theories to actual motivation. What a person says is not

---

[1]Paul Tillich, *A History of Christian Doctrine,* ed. Carl E. Braaten (New York: Simon and Schuster, A Touchstone Book, 1968) xxxvi.

always an adequate indication of what that person actually feels. In Dulles's case, however, this particular problem is less troublesome due to his public and private consistency in painstakingly explaining the principles behind his policies and activities. Nevertheless, as John M. Mulder reminds us, "The task of the historian becomes one of maintaining a tension between sympathetic awareness of the importance of the individual's values and cautious suspicion of his use of them in explaining his own behavior."[2]

A second problem resulted from the presuppositions I entertained when I began this study. As I prepared to examine the years during which Dulles was closely associated with the Federal Council of the Churches of Christ in America, I expected to find the rudiments of his later tendency toward self-righteous explanations of national behavior. Instead, I found his serious condemnation of such explanations. Expecting to find continuity between the early and late Dulles, I found discontinuity. Samuel McCrea Cavert, a noted churchman and intimate acquaintance of Dulles, once expressed confusion regarding whether "the Dulles who was Secretary of State was the same man I had known after 1937 and in the war years."[3]

A closer examination of this discontinuity reinforced my appreciation for the fact that understanding the interaction between religion and politics constitutes a "messy" business, one that is never fully grasped, particularly in the American setting. Yet if one is to understand Dulles properly, the attempt to make sense of this interaction becomes essential.

The thesis explored in the following pages involves tracing the developing discontinuity between the early Dulles and the later Dulles. It is based upon the belief that the discontinuity resulted from a gradual transformation in Dulles's definition of the moral law. Dulles's shift of his

---

[2]John M. Mulder, *Woodrow Wilson: The Years of Preparation* (Princeton: Princeton University Press, 1978) xii.

[3]Samuel McCrea Cavert, oral interview, 39, Dulles Papers, Seeley G. Mudd Library, Princeton University, Princeton, New Jersey. The transcripts of all interviews cited are part of The John Foster Dulles Oral History Collection housed along with the Dulles Papers at Princeton University. All transcripts have been read and approved by the interviewees. Interviews cited hereafter were conducted by Richard Challener in 1965 unless otherwise indicated.

setting, from formulating policies in primarily religious circles to formulating policies in primarily political circles, contributed to this transformation. Yet the center of the shift was fundamentally religious rather than political.

In speaking of a religious shift, one might describe Dulles's transformation in terms of "conversion." Yet "conversion" seems to be a loaded term—one which, because of various theological convictions, is understood in varying ways. In at least one of those ways, however, the term is appropriate in describing what happened to Dulles. William James defined conversion in the following manner:

> Let us hereafter in speaking of the hot place in a man's consciousness, the group of ideas to which he devotes himself, and from which he works, call it *the habitual centre of his personal energy*. It makes a great difference to a man whether one set of his ideas, or another, be the centre of his energy and it makes a great difference, as regards any set of ideas which he may possess, whether they become central or remain peripheral in him. To say a man is "converted" means, in these terms, that religious ideas, previously peripheral in his consciousness, now take a centre place, and that religious aims form the habitual centre of his energy.[4]

Experiences after World War II led Dulles to infuse "the habitual centre of his personal energy" with a new religious meaning. In this way, his transformation might indeed be termed a "conversion." "Transformation," though, is a better descriptive category so long as the reader understands that the transformation was not simply expedient, but rather profoundly existential.

Prophetic Realism

Beginning with the Calvinistic training he received as a young man growing up in a Presbyterian manse, Dulles grew toward a religious understanding which ultimately convinced him that a moral structure existed in the universe to which both individuals and nations should attempt to conform. In the earlier years of his life, those before 1945, he ex-

---

[4]William James, *The Varieties of Religious Experience: A Study in Human Nature* (London: Longmans, Green, and Co., 1906) 196.

pressed this belief from a consistent perspective that I have called "prophetic realism."[5]

The prophetic dimension of this perspective, exemplified by Dulles's effective leadership as a churchman, reminded the American public that a *transcendent* God stands over and above the nation rather than being directly identified with it. In my use of "prophetic," I mean to convey Paul Tillich's understanding of the "Protestant principle" or, as it is termed elsewhere in his writings, "the principle of prophetic protest." The prophetic protest, in Tillich's words, is "to be expressed in every situation as a contradiction to man's permanent attempts to give absolute validity to his own thinking and acting." Further, "it is prophetic judgment against religious pride, ecclesiastical arrogance, and secular self sufficiency and their destructive consequences."[6]

This concept is akin to Max Weber's portrayal of the "ethical prophet." According to Weber, "the legitimation of every distinctly ethical prophecy has always required the notion of a God characterized by attributes that set him sublimely above the world."[7] Therefore, the ethical prophet maintains a transcendent conception of divinity. Commitment to this God who stands above the world leads the prophet to espouse new obligations and break with traditionalism. For the prophet, "the sacredness of a new revelation," Weber explained, "[opposes] tradition."[8] Dulles, through words and action prior to 1945, exemplified concern for these prophetic notions, particularly as he worked toward the creation of a postwar world order. He reminded his hearers that religious loyalty to a transcendent God and his moral law should not be eclipsed by loyalties to any existing state authority.

By "realism" I mean to emphasize Dulles's understanding of the imperfect nature of political institutions and their leaderships. His activities

---

[5]I am aware that biblical scholars question the appropriateness of the prophetic/priestly polarity; my use of these terms is in the sociological sense of the "ideal type" in order to define disparate roles.

[6]Paul Tillich, *The Protestant Era* (Chicago: The University of Chicago Press, Phoenix Books, The Abridged Edition, 1957) 230, 163.

[7]Max Weber, *The Sociology of Religion,* trans. Ephraim Fischoff (Boston: Beacon Press, 1964) 138.

[8]Ibid., 66.

clearly demonstrate that he recognized the necessity for compromising idealistic principles in order to make pragmatic progress in a world populated by imperfect nations and peoples. Accommodation, rather than dogmatism, must characterize interaction between national sovereignties. Such a position recognizes, and allows for, the importance of national-interest considerations while at the same time encouraging people of the world to impress upon their respective national leaders the more general concerns of humanity at large.[9]

Priestly Nationalism

In George Orwell's *1984,* which he finished in 1948, most of the world has been divided into three superstates: Oceania, Eurasia, and Eastasia. These three states are interminably engaged in war with one another, a war that no one of them ever seems capable of winning. The anxiety in the hearts of the citizens only serves to increase the level of their dependence upon the alleged goodness of their respective rulers. To question that is to betray the cause and increase the instability of the situation.

Though events on the world scene in 1948 may not be regarded as the embryonic stage of Orwell's *1984,* they can be considered an inspiration for Orwell's futuristic imagination. After World War II, the advent of the Cold War interrupted American feelings of security and brought with it the anxiety of many crisis situations, the resolutions of which still have ramifications for the present day. In lectures delivered at The University of Chicago in 1951, George F. Kennan, the American ambassador to the Soviet Union at the time, reflected upon the nature of the increased insecurity by comparing the previous feelings of security.

> A half century ago people in this country had a sense of security vis-a-vis their world environment such as I suppose no people had ever had since the days of the Roman Empire. Today that pattern is almost reversed: our national consciousness is dominated by a sense of insecurity greater even than that of many of the peoples of Western Europe who

---

[9]See Kenneth W. Thompson's excellent discussion of the realist perspective in *Ethics, Functionalism, and Power in International Politics: The Crisis in Values* (Baton Rouge: Louisiana State University Press, 1979) esp. 20-27. The later life and thought of Reinhold Niebuhr is generally regarded as the classic example of Christian realism.

stand closer to, and in a position far more vulnerable to, those things that are the main source of our concern. [10]

Beginning in 1945, these new anxieties caused Dulles to begin to transform his concept of the transcendent moral law so that ultimately it became completely identified with the ideals and policies of the Free World. The transformation brought Dulles to a perspective that he enunciated with a consistency equal to that of his earlier perspective. I have termed this later perspective "priestly nationalism."

My use of "priestly" indicates Dulles's later tendency to celebrate American life as representative of God's purposes in human existence. The prophetic reminder of God's transcendence gradually disappeared from Dulles's expression after 1945. In its place came an increasing predilection to minister to the anxieties of a nation locked in cold war by picturing an *immanent* God ever ready to offer divine sanctions for the American policies designed to win that war.

According to Weber, a "distinguishing quality of the priest . . . is his professional equipment of special knowledge, fixed doctrine, and vocational qualifications." Another well-known sociologist of religion, Joachim Wach, further defines the function of the priest:

> The priest is the guardian of traditions and the keeper of the sacred knowledge and of the technique of meditation and prayers. He is the custodian of the holy law, which corresponds to the cosmic moral and ritual order upon which the world, the community and the individual depend. As an interpreter of the law, the priest may function as judge, administrator, teacher, and scholar, formulate standards and rules of conduct and enforce their observance. [11]

By 1952, the year Eisenhower tapped him for the State Department, Dulles had aptly demonstrated his priestly abilities as a "custodian of the holy law." Since by that date he had defined the "cosmic moral and ritual order" by utilizing American distinctions, Dulles viewed the extension of that holy law as an American enterprise, one "upon which the world, the

---

[10]George F. Kennan, *American Diplomacy: 1900-1950* (Chicago: The University of Chicago Press, 1951) 3.

[11]Joachim Wach, *Sociology of Religion* (Chicago: The University of Chicago Press, Phoenix Edition, 1971) 365.

community and the individual depend." As a priest, Dulles's actions exemplified the nationalism he had, as prophet, so carefully and completely
denounced during his earlier years; yet due to the intervening transformation of his world view, he was able to act with integrity. I have yet to
define the term "nationalism." I am using the classic sense of attributing
ultimacy to one's own nation and promoting its culture and interests as
synonymous with what is considered good, just, and righteous for the
human community as a whole.

With the above definitions in mind, the following narrative attempts
to uncover some of the contributing factors leading to Dulles's respective adherence to both prophetic realism and priestly nationalism. Though
this study concentrates primarily on the religious dimensions of Dulles's
life and work, it should not be understood as claiming that nothing else
helped to shape the life and work of the man. I am not offering the reader
a comprehensive intellectual history of Dulles. His religious conception
of the moral law was foundational for his approach to international affairs,
more so than any other single factor since it helped to determine the categories for other influences. Nonetheless, other factors were involved
in making the man who and what he was.

If one were to do a complete intellectual biography of Dulles, certainly the author would need to deal with (to name only a few): the influences of the young Dulles's work with Henri Bergson; his early
involvement in Wilsonian internationalism during World War I; his close
friendship with and heavy dependence upon Lionel Curtis of the Royal
Institute of International Affairs in Great Britain; his international law
practice in the 1920s and early 1930s; and the personal effect of his increasingly comfortable wealth. As one will readily discover, this book does
not completely address these important influences. In truth, relating the
tale of these influences on the written page would easily result in a book
at least matching the size of the present one. I spare the reader this kind
of detail, not because it is unimportant, but merely because it is not essential to a proper understanding of what is related here. The question
this book attempts to answer is one raised in a period different from the
one in which these factors were so formative. Hence these influences
have little to do with the answering of that question.

Primarily, the transformation of Dulles and its religious underpin-
nings necessitate an examination of the interaction between events and
intellectual development after 1937. As will become evident in later pages,

1937 marks an important date in Dulles's religious life. Even though his approach to international affairs is altered considerably at that juncture, some important continuities remain that pertain to the telling of this story. The first section of this study draws attention to these pre-1937 elements so that events of later years will be better understood.

Part 1 of this discussion centers on the "years of preparation."[12] Chapter 1 focuses upon the religious influences of Dulles's early life and his later activity as a Presbyterian layman up to the year 1937, when he became intimately associated with the work of the Federal Council of Churches. The second chapter concentrates on the diplomatic influences of the early years, as well as briefly discussing some of Dulles's involvements in international developments during these years.

Part 2 provides both the narrative setting and the ideological framework of Dulles's involvement with the Federal Council of Churches. Chapters 3 and 4 address the former while chapters 5 through 7 address the latter. The strength of this format lies in its ability to provide a clear chronological history of Dulles's relationship with ecumenical Christianity during this period while at the same time providing a context for the separate discussion of Dulles's ideas. Some repetition results from tracing the same period of time from two related, though slightly different, perspectives.

The third chapter, therefore, details the events leading up to Dulles's participation in the Federal Council of Churches. Chapter 4 describes Dulles's leadership as a prophetic realist attempting to influence and educate the public regarding the issue of establishing postwar international organizations. The fifth chapter explores Dulles's understanding of the problems prohibiting successful implementation of machinery necessary to world peace. The solution he suggested for this problem is examined in chapter 6. Chapter 7 deals with Dulles's role in attempting to implement this solution in San Francisco at The United Nations Organization Conference in the fall of 1945.

The final portion, composed of chapters 8 through 10, attempts to account for the nature of the transformation of Dulles's concept of the moral law. Chapter 8 begins with a discussion of Dulles's prophetic realism at its most fully developed point and progresses by demonstrating

---

[12]This is a phrase borrowed from Mulder. See his *Woodrow Wilson*.

that this posture of accommodation became less flexible. The ninth chapter continues the tracing of this process through to a discussion of Dulles's part in formulating policies designed to prevent the rapid expansion of the Soviet Union. Chapter 10 reveals how events in Asia pushed Dulles to a willingness to sanction use of militaristic force to secure his vision of international peace.

Placing the public utterances and foreign-policy contributions of Dulles in the context of his own personal religious ideology contributes to a much better understanding of the complex world view that lay beneath Dulles's political policy formulations. It also sheds some light on the importance of clerical and lay thought during this period of America's existence. Finally, it may lead us to a deeper understanding of just how religion, recalling Reagan's words, has acted as a "guide" in the general function of American foreign policy, for good and for bad.

A Dulles Album

Shortly after Dulles's death in 1959, Mark Bortman, chairman of the Civic Committee of the People to People Program, sent this picture accompanied by a letter to Mrs. Dulles. The letter began, "I am enclosing a picture of Mr. Dulles which is liked by everyone who has seen it, because in it he is a statesman and a strong, godlike man." The picture was taken on the evening of 11 October 1952 while Dulles was in the pulpit of the Old South Meeting House in Boston, Massachusetts. (Unless otherwise noted, all photos are the property of the Princeton University Library, Princeton, New Jersey.)

John Foster Dulles, Dean Acheson, Shigeru Yoshida, and others at the signing of the Japanese Peace Treaty in September 1951.

Brigadier General Yu Jae Heung (with hand raised), commanding general of the 7th Division at Ouijongbu, explains the tactical situation along the 38th Parallel in Korea on 18 June 1950, just six days before North Korea invaded South Korea.

John Foster Dulles in the United Nations General Assembly, April of 1947.

Colonel and Mrs. John Watson Foster, grandparents of John Foster Dulles. Colonel Foster was secretary of state under President Benjamin Harrison.

John Foster Dulles being sworn in as consultant to the secretary of state to work on broad problems in the field of foreign affairs in April 1950. Alongside him are Dean Acheson and Assistant Chief of Protocol Raymond Muir.

John Foster Dulles and a few delegates to the "International Roundtable of Christian Leaders" convened by the Commission on a Just and Durable Peace in Princeton, New Jersey, in July 1943.

John Foster Dulles and his son, Avery, with a deck-tennis quoit on board the S. S. France *in October 1931.*

Captain John Foster Dulles of the Signal Officers Reserve Corps in the fall of 1917.

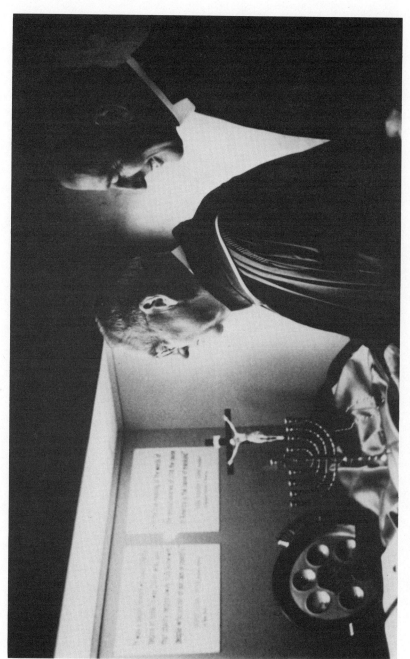

Secretary of State John Foster Dulles and the Reverend Francis Sayre view an exhibit case at the Washington Cathedral, Washington, D.C. Secretary Dulles delivered an address here on 22 June 1958 in support of the European Recovery Plan.

Henry P. Van Dusen and John Foster Dulles listen to a questioner during the 1952 Conference on Ministry held at Union Theological Seminary. (Photograph is by Alfred Gescheidt, from Black Star. It is the possession of the Burke Library, Union Theological Seminary, and is reprinted with permission.)

I

The Years of Preparation,
1888-1937

1

Religious Influences
and Church Involvements

Outside the warm confines of the house located at 1405 I Street, Northwest, in Washington, D.C., one of the heaviest blizzards in the city's history provided an impression of sterility, a perfectly white blanket of newfallen snow. Inside, the occupants of the house worked to provide the actual sterile conditions necessary for the safety and welfare of the baby soon to make an appearance. Mrs. Allen Macy Dulles, the expectant mother, was visiting in the house of her parents, Mr. and Mrs. John W. Foster. The date was 25 February 1888.

The Reverend Allen Macy Dulles, the expectant father, was in the process of moving the family's belongings from Detroit, Michigan, where he had served for several years as pastor of the Trumball Avenue Church, to a parsonage in a small Northern village known as Watertown in the state of New York. He had just accepted the call to serve as the new pastor of the First Presbyterian Church located amidst the tranquil surroundings of that small town. Consequently, he was unable personally to share in the celebrative atmosphere that was building in the modest house on I Street in the nation's capital on that cold, wintry day.

Reverend Dulles's firstborn child, a son, arrived at his grandparents' house without complication. From the perspective of nearly a century later, the birthplace of John Foster Dulles seems symbolic. The greatest portion of his seventy-one years was spent in the city of his birth. During the last seven of those years, he occupied one of the most prestigious offices in the city as the nation's sixty-ninth secretary of state.

Religious Influences

The Influences of the Home. Three months after he was born, young Foster, as he was called by both family and friends, left Washington in the company of his mother to join his father in upstate New York. The next seventeen years were spent in the smalltown atmosphere of Watertown. His minister father and committed Christian mother provided an intensely religious environment for Foster and his siblings, a brother and three sisters. The family ancestors, after all, included numerous ministers and several missionaries to various areas of the world. His paternal grandfather, John Wesley Dulles, dedicated his life to mission service, once traveling in an open boat for 132 days to carry the gospel to Madras.

Foster's father, the Reverend Allen Macy Dulles, was a liberal Protestant minister, one who was greatly influenced by the theological trends of the day. The last two decades of the nineteenth century saw the development of the Social Gospel movement, which claimed a leadership that desired to awaken the social consciousness of the churches. Major figures included Washington Gladden (1836-1918), Francis Greenwood Peabody (1847-1936), Walter Rauschenbusch (1861-1918), and Josiah Strong (1847-1916). Strong's *Our Country: Its Possible Future and Present Crisis* was published in 1885. As probably the most influential book of the nineteenth-century Social Gospel genre, Strong's book represents Protestant liberalism's confidence in applied science and guided evolution. Further, Strong's ideas closely paralleled the political Progressivism developing at the same time.[1]

---

[1]See Dorothea R. Muller, "The Social Philosophy of Josiah Strong: Social Christianity and American Progressivism," *Church History* 28 (1959): 183-201.

On the social side, the older Dulles was deeply influenced by the works of Strong and Rauschenbusch. On the theological side, as his own book *The True Church*[2] bears witness, he was heavily indebted to the work of Ritschl, Harnack, and McGiffert.[3] *The True Church* contrasts the two concepts of the Church, the evangelical and the Catholic, arguing of course that the evangelical concept, "the strength of Protestantism,"[4] can share no common ground with Roman Catholicism.

Though Allen Macy Dulles held what his day saw as an enlightened and literary-critical view of Scripture, he nonetheless stressed the importance of a pious and educated devotion to its principles, both in the home and in the pulpit. Every morning around 7:30 a.m., the Dulles family gathered in the living room of the white clapboard parsonage, usually called to the assembly by Mrs. Dulles's "firm touch on the piano keys" or by the pastor's "tenor voice as he walked down the hall singing joyfully, 'When Morning Gilds the Skies.' "[5] A little pocketbook containing hymns and selections from the Bible served as the sourcebook for morning devotions. It was prepared by Allen Dulles's father, John W. Dulles, for the soldiers of the Civil War.[6] Every member of the family enthusiastically joined in the singing of a hymn, which was then followed by a passage of Scripture either read or recited by one of those assembled. Finally, the morning devotion would end as the whole family knelt while Reverend Dulles prayed.

Committed attendance at every church activity was not just encouraged but expected in the Dulles household. The children not only used their Bibles in Sunday school, but were required to follow carefully the Scripture reading during church, finding and numbering the text for the

---

[2]New York: F. H. Revell, 1907.

[3]See the interesting reflective essay, "The True Church: In Dialogue with Liberal Protestantism" in Avery Dulles, *A Church to Believe In* (New York: Crossroad, 1982), in which the grandson—a Jesuit priest—engages in a dialogue with his liberal Protestant grandfather on the subject of the true church.

[4]Allen Macy Dulles, *The True Church*, 28. Quoted in Avery Dulles, *A Church to Believe In*, 54.

[5]Margaret Dulles Edwards, "Tomorrow's Legacy," *Bible Society Record* (January 1964): 12.

[6]Eleanor Lansing Dulles, *The Last Year* (New York: Harcourt, Brace and World, Inc., 1963) 162.

morning's sermon. All five children regularly attended the Monday evening young people's services, as well as Wednesday night prayer meetings and the preparatory service on Friday night whenever communion was to be served on the following Sunday.[7]

Sunday afternoons were spent participating in carefully planned activities that included either a scholarly introduction to the contents of Scripture, the careful drawing and coloring of maps, or biblical scenes depicting the lives of the heroes in the Old and New Testaments. Memorization of Scripture and of favorite hymns was another important activity for all the Dulles children. Often on Sunday evenings, family and friends gathered on the porch to recite Scripture and sing hymns from memory.

All of this religious activity was not lost on young Foster. In his mother's diary of his early years, she recorded that Foster had a sincere concern for the "blessing" said at mealtime, commenting that he "always said Amen very heartily." He always behaved himself at church and even, as a five-year-old, had what his mother described as a "devotional spirit." In still another entry in her diary, his mother noted that Foster was "reverential to a striking degree. Whenever he sees . . . his father or mother in the attitude of prayer, he will instantly assume the same attitude and so remain until they rise."[8] Letters to his parents, written during his visits to his grandparents, evidence a child who wanted to convey that he was paying proper attention to things religious even when away from home. As a seven-year-old, for example, he wrote, "I went to church and Sunday school. Our lesson was about the Last Supper and the teacher had a little house and some little men for the disciples."[9] Throughout his life, he was a devoted reader of the Bible and consistently carried a small

---

[7]In 1952, on a visit to Watertown, Dulles mentioned that his "family had a rigorous schedule of worship. On thinking back, it seems to me that we averaged over 10 services a week. It is not surprising that that made an impression. It was an impression that was not always enjoyable at the time, but the older I have grown and the wider has been my experience, the more I have appreciated that early religious upbringing and have seen how relevant it is to the far-flung and changing scenes of life" ("Address before the Watertown Chamber of Commerce," 30 April 1952, Dulles Papers, Box 307, Princeton University, Princeton NJ; hereafter referred to as DP).

[8]Diary of Mrs. Allen Macy Dulles, 25 February 1893, DP, Box 603.

[9]John Foster Dulles (hereafter referred to as JFD) to "Mama," 28 April 1895, DP, Box 1.

New Testament with him. At one point, as a teen, he memorized the entire Gospel of John.[10]

Early in their lives all the Dulles children were introduced to the importance of reading the authors of classical literature like Tennyson, Wordsworth, Milton, Shakespeare, and John Bunyan. According to his sister Eleanor, young Foster even "memorized passages of *Pilgrim's Progress.*" Along with his love of these standards of literature, Foster Dulles loved adventure stories. Later in life his craving for adventure stories was satisfied through the reading of detective stories. One incident resulting from his love of adventure stories became the foundation of a much-enjoyed family joke. After he read *The Swiss Family Robinson* "for perhaps the tenth time," his father forbade him to read it again because it was taking "too much time" away from his reading of more significant literature.[11]

This incident serves as an example of just how seriously the Reverend Dulles took the responsibility of introducing his children to serious reflection on the nature of truth and reality. Names like "Berkeley, Schopenhauer, Nietzsche, Hegel, and Bergson grew familiar early."[12] His father's efforts in this direction eventually reaped the desired long-range benefits: all of his children loved education and pursued it through college and beyond. For Foster, the seeds planted at home eventually blossomed into a philosophy major in college and a year's postgraduate study with Henri Bergson at the Sorbonne.

Reverend Dulles believed not only in education, but also in duty. He taught his children a firm belief in the concept of obligation.

> You had to be fair, and you had to pay your way in life, and you had to make things better for living with them. You had to be kind, and you had to be generous, because other people didn't have the opportunities you had.[13]

---

[10]John Robinson Beal, *John Foster Dulles: A Biography* (New York: Harper and Brothers, 1957) 28. See also Lillias Dulles Hinshaw, oral interview conducted by Philip A. Crowl in 1966, 24.

[11]Dulles, *The Last Year*, 161.

[12]Ibid., 127.

[13]Eleanor Lansing Dulles, interview, conducted by Philip A. Crowl, 1965.

Even casual observers of his life can readily see evidence that Foster was heavily influenced by his father's Calvinistic sense of duty. Sometime after his death, his daughter Lillias, herself a graduate of Union Theological Seminary, talked about the strengths and weaknesses of this theological inheritance.

> Its strengths, I think, lie in the feeling that you are given a certain task to perform. And of course, its weakness lies in the reverse of that, that you may make the mistake of feeling that you are God's spokesman.[14]

Both the strengths and weaknesses of his family's Calvinism are obviously present throughout Dulles's life. He was driven by a strong sense of duty, most often characterized by an equally strong belief that what he did would naturally meet with the approval of his maker. Even Foster's choice of a favorite hymn, "Work for the Night is Coming" (Anna L. Coghill, 1854) is indicative of this heritage. As Eleanor pointed out, "It would have been hard to grow up in our home without developing a sense of purpose."[15]

None of the five children of the Dulles family—except perhaps Margaret, who married a Presbyterian minister—ever really developed a conscious and expressed theology. Foster Dulles certainly was not a theologian nor was he interested in reading any serious theological works. As his son Avery has observed, "He didn't enter into questions of a sheerly dogmatic nature."[16] But for Foster, perhaps more than any of the other children, the religious atmosphere of his upbringing contributed to his sincere belief that there existed in the world a "force for good." Eleanor describes the religious influences of their common home life as follows:

> I have never known how much Foster went along with the doctrines of the church—the Apostles Creed, that kind of thing. I've never known. It's hard to know. . . . But there was something about the atmosphere of religion in the family that carried over to us in varying degrees—and to Foster, I think more than the rest of us probably—that there was this force for good, and if it's a force for good, and if you want to be good, you

---

[14]Lillias Dulles Hinshaw, interview.

[15]Dulles, *The Last Year,* 126.

[16]Avery Dulles, interview, conducted by Philip A. Crowl, 1966.

associate yourself with it—and that's going to influence your life. Whatever the formula he adopted, it meant a good deal to him. And I just don't know the terms of this formula. I don't remember that we ever discussed it among ourselves after we were adults.[17]

Even though he had no developed theology, Foster Dulles often commented that the basic Christian principles learned at home had provided him with a sense of direction that significantly shaped his development as an individual. The family environment provided in the Dulles household left an "indelible mark" on all the children. It nurtured "not only a deep faith in central religious truths, but also a sense of the obligation of such a faith toward those distant people who were striving to gain new light and freedom."[18]

The question has often arisen concerning whether Dulles, once he left the religious confines of home to attend college, in 1904, remained active in the church. Some of the speculation that he had nothing to do with religious activities until around 1937 is based upon Thomas Dewey's statement in 1965 that, so far as he knew, Dulles spent many of these years as an atheist.[19] The evidence just does not support Dewey's assumption, however.

As previously indicated, Dulles did not carry with him a specific commitment to all the religious beliefs that meant so much to his father. Such a development is hardly surprising. Even Mrs. Dulles, at least privately, admitted that some of the doctrinal beliefs of the church were "nonsense."[20] A letter written to her son in 1918 presents evidence that Foster lightened somewhat the theological baggage of his heritage. The letter also is interesting from the standpoint of a mother's sincere concern that her son not stray too far from his religious roots.

Father [John W. Foster] said that you said something about not knowing how much religion you had left, and while that is not worrying me I do feel like writing along that line. . . . I presume I taught you some things when you were little that I do not believe now. At any rate, I know

---

[17]Eleanor Lansing Dulles, interview.

[18]Dulles, *The Last Year,* 128.

[19]See Thomas Dewey, interview.

[20]Eleanor Lansing Dulles, interview.

that I let go a great many things I used to believe, but there are two or three things that are very vital to me and I hope to you. . . . God the Father, who knows and loves us, means more and more to me—the reality of a personal being alive and under all this seething world, who will bring order and beauty out of it, and to whom my life and the life of those I love is linked.

Then as I try to live the life that a child of God should live, I feel the need of a perfect life to guide me, a life lived here under our conditions and so the life of Christ becomes a necessity to me. A life that shows us how to live and what is worth living for—and so while I have lost much, God, Christ and duty mean more and more to me.

I hope it is so with you.[21]

Unfortunately, if Dulles replied, he did not keep a duplicate. However, events as they unfolded after this particular letter seem to indicate that he would probably have affirmed his mother's beliefs as characteristic of his own.

The Influences of a Presbyterian Faith. I have already mentioned, in a rather general way, how the Calvinistic sense of duty influenced Dulles; yet Presbyterianism had a much wider impact on the world view of Dulles. Presbyterianism provided Dulles with certain values and unquestioned presuppositions, all of which formed for him a definite posture from which he attempted to solve the various problems he encountered in life. This posture, though it certainly developed as he matured, was rarely subject to intellectual reflection. He simply accepted it. For this reason, it seems reasonable to examine some of the components that make up the Presbyterian "way of life" that exerted such a profound influence in his early years.

Perhaps one of the major influences behind Dulles's renowned self-assurance can be found in his Scottish Presbyterian roots. Calvin, of course, is well known for his dogmatic certainty in matters of both a religious and social nature. Dulles exhibited a similar certainty in these areas. Further, Dulles's ancestral roots were Scottish. As John Mackay indicates, people of Scottish origin often possess a rather passionate temperament.[22] Mackay, a committed Presbyterian leader of Scottish

---

[21]"Mother" to JFD, 1918, DP, Box 2.

[22]Dulles's ancestor, Joseph Dulles, left Scotland in 1776 and settled in Charleston, South Carolina (See Beal, *John Foster Dulles,* 23).

roots himself, once wrote that "there is ground for affirming that some
of the most glorious episodes in the history of Scotch, Irish, and American Presbyterianism, as well as some of the most unhappy, have owed
not a little to the Celtic capacity for passions and extremes." He quotes
Charles Lamb, the famous British essayist, who described the Scottish
temperament in the following manner:

> When once they (Scots) adopt a decided attitude, you never catch the
> Caledonian mind in an undress. The Caledonian never hints or suggests
> anything but unloads his ideas in perfect order and completion. He has
> no falterings of self suspicion. The twilight of dubiety never falls upon him.
> Is he orthodox, he has no doubt. Is he an infidel, he has none either. Be-
> tween the affirmative and the negative there is no border land for him.
> You cannot hover with him upon the confines of truth.[23]

Few people would argue with the assertion that such a description also
fits Foster Dulles.

Dulles's minister father was certainly confident that he could cor-
rectly address the question of the nature of the "true church." His book
by that title is clear evidence of that fact. Yet, in his discussion of that
topic, the elder Dulles was careful to point out that no visible communion
of saints completely embodied the true church. To believe otherwise, he
wrote, would amount to the same exclusivistic concept of the church held
by the Catholic hierarchy. "Christ," he affirmed, "is larger, grander than
any or all the churches." Not even Christianity itself constitutes the true
church, for God's church antedates the movement of Christianity. Jesus
"found a church" and "made it his own."[24]

These fundamental beliefs constitute an important dimension of general Presbyterian reflection on the nature of the Church. As Mackay has
stated, "No Christian Church can fully meet Christ's standards."[25] As a
result of these beliefs, Presbyterians have, for the most part, been ar-
dent supporters of the ecumenical movement. Well before ecumenism

---

[23]John A. Mackay, *The Presbyterian Way of Life* (Englewood Cliffs NJ: Prentice-Hall,
Inc., 1960) 34.

[24]Allen Macy Dulles, *The True Church,* 279, 109. These passages are quoted in Avery
Dulles, *A Church to Believe In,* 58.

[25]Mackay, *The Presbyterian Way of Life,* 212; see also 95-98. The active participation
of Presbyterianism in the ecumenical movement is discussed from 215-20.

gained institutional expression, Reverend Dulles stated his belief that the divided state of Christianity was intolerable. "Hostility among Christians," he wrote, "is a scandal to unbelievers, being a virtual negation of the claims of Christ."[26]

The Presbyterian belief that no earthly church can lay claim to embodying the totality of the true church has led Presbyterians to emphasize that the ideal of the true church should act as a standard by which one can judge the visible manifestations of the Christian Church. As Avery Dulles expressed his grandfather's belief, "The perfected church of the End time becomes . . . a norm for assessing the extent to which an earthly realization of the Church may be called true."[27] This eschatological note is also evident in the Presbyterian notion of society's need for advancement. No social order may be regarded as completely representing the kingdom of God on earth. Thus Presbyterians believe they have a task in society. They must be constantly at work to bring into being a society that more completely fulfills God's will in the world. The moral law, always an important concept in Presbyterian thought, demands a society that has no regard for class, race, nation, or culture. No world order should exalt the interests of any of these categories; rather, the welfare of the "whole people of God" should dictate the actions of humankind in the international arena.

As Mackay expresses the Presbyterian viewpoint, "individual Christians are under obligation, so far as their influence may extend, to bring the whole life of society into harmony with the principles of God's moral government of the world." Calvinism, in this sense, is essentially prophetic.[28] "The Church to be truly the Church," writes Mackay, "must confront culture and civilization and seek their transformation."[29]

This particular dimension of Presbyterian thought is especially evident in Foster Dulles's activities in the civic sphere. Throughout his life he worked to bring society toward a more complete realization of what

---

[26]Allen Macy Dulles, *The True Church,* 56. Quoted in Avery Dulles, *A Church to Believe In,* 58.

[27]Avery Dulles, *A Church to Believe In,* 57.

[28]In using the term *prophetic* here, I am referring to the definition I mentioned in my introduction.

[29]Mackay, *The Presbyterian Way of Life,* 175.

he perceived as the dictates of the moral law. True to Presbyterian expression, he believed that "the welfare of all the people was a primary function of the state." Thus he devoted his life to helping the state fulfill its mission—a mission that resulted from its role as "God's agent in establishing and maintaining order in the world."[30] Obviously, such a high view of the state can assume dangerous characteristics whenever the prophetic belief that no nation, race, class, or culture constitutes the kingdom of God is forgotten. Unfortunately Presbyterians, as well as Christians of other traditions, have all too often suffered a loss of memory in this respect. Dulles was no exception.

The Presbyterian emphasis upon a sovereign God has most often surfaced as the corrective in cases when Presbyterians have suffered such a lapse of memory. The transcendence and sovereignty of God over his creation has always been a dominant emphasis in Presbyterian history. Dulles, throughout his years of intimate association with the churches— especially during his eight-year working relationship with the Federal Council of Churches (1937-1946)—made this belief the cornerstone of his every expression. It was only after he left the work within the churches for a more intensive involvement in civic activities, beginning in 1945, that Dulles's actions and expressions began to take on a decidedly different character.[31]

Another dimension of Presbyterian thought that greatly influenced the life and work of Dulles was the emphasis upon the sinful nature of humankind. From the time of Calvin, the movement later known as Presbyterianism has consistently stressed the fact that human nature possesses a tendency to make humankind "the object of devotion rather than God." Sin, for Calvin and his religious heirs, is embodied in this proclivity to attach ultimacy to personal interest and concerns. Humankind, in the Presbyterian mind, is virtually enslaved to the captivating power of individual and corporate pride. The only hope of escaping it is found by adhering to the person of Christ and passionately desiring to serve his purposes. That is exemplified by active participation in endeavors directed toward bringing about a religious and societal order more fully in line with his will. In this way, as Mackay has so aptly stated, "both in their

---

[30]Ibid., 180, 179.

[31]See chs. 8-10 for an explanation of this development.

theological heritage and their historical witness, Presbyterians have been profoundly Christocentric."[32] As the pages that follow will aptly illustrate, Dulles was profoundly affected by this part of his religious background.

Dulles's great concern for structure and organization was no doubt due in some degree to his Presbyterian upbringing. The Presbyterian emphasis on structure and institutional organization is well known. According to Mackay, "It exists as the servant of the community of Christ to enable the community to function in the most effective way possible." In Presbyterian circles, the General Assembly, representing the Church, deals with those matters "that concern the Church as a whole."[33] Dulles's earnest quest for a United Nations was at least subconsciously informed by this particular dimension of his religious heritage. To read descriptions of his concept of international order prior to the establishment of the United Nations in 1945 is to be impressed by the many ways it resembles the structure of the Presbyterian Church.[34] Certainly it is safe to conclude that Dulles's passion for organization and his dependence upon institutional structure as a prerequisite for any meaningful solution to world problems resulted to some degree from his immense involvement in Presbyterian concerns. Just as Mackay believes that "the structure of the Church is for the life of the Church," Dulles believed that the continued health of all nations depended upon the successful implementation of some type of world order.

At least one other aspect of Presbyterian life is worth mentioning. From the very beginning, Presbyterianism has emphasized the freedom of the individual. The Reverend Dulles was true to this aspect of his faith's tradition when he stressed the priesthood of the individual. Though the Church's structure is important, it has no right to dictate what is acceptable in matters of belief and what is not. Statements of faith can be nothing more than "advisory."[35] Obviously, this belief has implications for life in the state as well. Calvin and his colleagues stood for principles that were

---

[32]Ibid., 67.

[33]Ibid., 116, 118.

[34]See ch. 6 for the discussion of Dulles's concept of a United Nations organization.

[35]Allen Macy Dulles, *The True Church*, 28. Quoted in Avery Dulles, *A Church to Believe In*, 62.

in many ways a factor in helping to defeat the European absolutist state and an aid to the development of democratic governments.[36] Further, Calvin provided for capitalistic enterprise, as is exemplified by his support for the concepts of investment and interest.[37] Whether or not Dulles's commitment to the American system of capitalism was strengthened because of his Presbyterian faith is hard to say for sure. Yet one thing is definite: Dulles's capitalistic leanings were certainly not challenged by his religious heritage. In fact, his commitment to the individual's rights to religious freedom was certainly nurtured during his early years under the careful guidance of his parents, who themselves were conscientiously informed by Presbyterian emphases.

Church Involvements

General Involvements. Throughout the years presently under consideration, Dulles maintained his connections with the church. He served as an elder in the Park Avenue Presbyterian Church, and later in the Brick Presbyterian Church after the two churches merged into one. The pastor, Tertius Van Dyke, a classmate of Dulles's at Princeton, was always deeply appreciative of Foster's active support of his ministry.[38] Occasionally, Dulles even filled the pulpit, an activity that seemed to please him very much.[39]

---

[36]See Mackay, *The Presbyterian Way of Life,* 7. I am well aware that Calvin used his position in Geneva to coerce adherence to his definition of the truth. This is particularly true in the case of Michael Servetus. Yet Geneva must be understood in its historical context. The execution of Servetus was not strange in a time when death was the accepted penalty for heretics refusing to recant. The rigid collectivism of Geneva is easier to understand when one remembers that religious uniformity within any given territory was something taken for granted in the sixteenth century. Calvin's dream for Geneva included his hope that the city would be dedicated to the glory of God. Such a dream could not withstand direct challenges from Servetus or anyone else. Later, the diligence, sobriety, and thrift cultivated in Geneva led to the seventeenth-century Puritan emphasis on individual economic activity without collective restraint.

[37]Ibid., 12.

[38]Tertius Van Dyke to JFD, 6 March 1922, DP, Box 4.

[39]Tertius Van Dyke to JFD, 4 November 1925, and JFD to Tertius Van Dyke, 6 November 1925, DP, Box 7.

Dulles's presence in the church was not limited to his service as an elder in the local congregation. Accepting an invitation in 1921 from Robert E. Speer, the president of the Federal Council of Churches, Dulles began a term of membership on the newly formed Federal Council Commission on International Justice and Goodwill.[40] This association led to a request for legal advice. In 1922 Dulles was called upon to provide "valuable counsel" to the Federal Council of Churches concerning its incorporation.[41]

In 1923 Dulles accepted a commission to serve as a member of the National Conference of the Christian Way of Life. During the course of the same year, the Presbyterian General Assembly named him to membership in the American section of the Universal Christian Conference on Life and Work. A week after this appointment was made, he became an official member of the Presbyterian General Assembly. The next year, the Presbytery of New York elected him a commissioner to the General Assembly to be held in Grand Rapids, Michigan. He was, at the same time, appointed to the presbytery's Committee to Study "War." Throughout the early 1920s he also worked on the Church Extension Committee of the Presbyterian Church.[42]

The international lawyer's reputation as a dedicated worker on church committees brought many interesting requests for service. John D. Rockefeller, Jr., in 1931, asked him to become a member of a traveling commission that would spend six months in Japan, China, and India in order to report on foreign missions in light of current world conditions. Dulles refused the opportunity because, as head of one of New York's most prestigious law firms, he could not afford to be away from the office

---

[40]See exchange of letters, Robert E. Speer to JFD, 28 June 1921, and JFD to Robert E. Speer, undated, DP, Box 4. See also Sidney L. Gulick to JFD, 30 November 1925, DP, Box 7.

[41]A resolution was passed in December 1922 at the annual meeting of the Federal Council expressing formal appreciation for this task. See letter from Samuel McCrea Cavert to JFD, 29 December 1922, DP, Box 4.

[42]See the following letters: E. C. Carter to JFD, 12 December 1923, and JFD to E. C. Carter, 14 December 1923, DP, Box 5; Henry Atkinson, general secretary of the Presbyterian General Assembly, to JFD, 29 May 1923, DP, Box 5; Henry Atkinson to JFD, 1 June 1923, DP, Box 5; H. G. Mendenhall to JFD, 15 April 1924, DP, Box 6; JFD to Theodore F. Savage, 8 January 1933, DP, Box 11.

for that length of time.[43] Support of religious endeavors was not limited to his time alone, however. Quite frequently Dulles could be counted on for financial support of various religious causes. *Christian Work* magazine, which later merged with the *Christian Century,* benefited from his generosity, as did a small Presbyterian church in Seneca Castle, New York when he sent a check to help in the purchase of hymnbooks. Further, he was a consistent contributor to his local church as well as to the Federal Council of Churches.

Specific Involvements. Perhaps the most significant religious involvement of John Foster Dulles during this period came through his contribution to the liberal side of the fundamentalist-modernist controversy as it affected the Presbyterian Church. If Dulles had chosen not to participate in the Presbyterian debates during the 1920s, no doubt their outcome would have differed considerably. That in itself is an interesting realization, particularly as it pertains to the schisms of the next decade. However, my motivation for detailing Dulles's role in the Presbyterian version of the fundamentalist-modernist controversy arises from yet another consideration. His involvement in divisive cases related to this controversy demonstrates that his relationship with the churches was far from casual. Within the context of the extensive legal involvements and commitments required by his law practice during these years, the time-consuming effort he spent defending would-be Presbyterian ministers for no fee becomes that much more impressive.[44]

The Presbyterian controversies heated up in the spring of 1924. Led by William Jennings Bryan, the fundamentalists were pushing the question of whether Harry Emerson Fosdick, the Baptist modernist, ought to be allowed to remain as the pulpit minister of the First Presbyterian Church in New York City. This particular controversy had begun as a reaction to a sermon preached by Fosdick in that pulpit in May of 1922, entitled "Shall the Fundamentalists Win?"

---

[43]Memorandum, JFD to William Nelson Cromwell, 16 June 1931, DP, Box 9.

[44]See Ronald W. Pruessen, *John Foster Dulles: The Road to Power* (New York: The Free Press, 1982) 58-105, for a detailed analysis of Dulles's legal activities during the 1920s. It is worth noting that, in 1926, Dulles became the senior and managing partner of the prestigious Sullivan and Cromwell law firm.

Fosdick claims in his autobiography that the sermon was meant to be a "plea for tolerance" and "goodwill." Stating that the differences dividing the two camps centered "on such matters as the virgin birth of Jesus, the inerrancy of scriptures and the second coming of Christ," Fosdick then made his plea that a "spirit of conciliation" prevail so the evangelical churches would not be torn asunder. [45]

Fosdick, however, did not mince words with the fundamentalists. As his sermon title suggests, he did not intend to sit idly by and allow their victory. In the interest of trying to establish hope in a unified church, he nonetheless denounced the "bitter intolerance" of the fundamentalists. His sermon provided the spark to a potentially volatile situation; the resultant explosion rocked the Presbyterian Church for several years to come.

Clarence Edward McCartney, a fellow minister, led the first attack against Fosdick. Then, in the 1923 General Assembly of the Presbyterian Church, ten Presbyterians brought forth complaints against the heretical preaching of Fosdick. The Committee on Bills and Overtures initially handled the complaints. In filing the majority report, the committee referred the case to the judgment of the New York Presbytery.

However, due to the oratory of William Jennings Bryan, the General Assembly, by a vote of 439 to 359, adopted a minority report which expressed "profound sorrow that doctrines contrary to the standards of the Presbyterian Church" were being preached in the First Presbyterian Church, and further directed the Presbytery of New York City to take whatever action was necessary to "require the preaching and teaching . . . to conform to the system of doctrines taught in the Confession of Faith."[46] The minority report also included a reaffirmation of the so-called "Five Points," a doctrinal deliverance of the General Assembly of 1910 that was reissued in 1916. [47]

In the church season between 1923 and 1924, Dulles became involved in the controversy. Appointed as one of three members of a

---

[45]Harry E. Fosdick, *The Living of These Days* (New York: Harper and Brothers, 1956) 145.

[46]Quoted ibid., 148.

[47]The five points in brief are (1) inerrancy of Scripture; (2) the virgin birth of Jesus; (3) atonement; (4) the bodily resurrection; and (5) the belief in biblical miracles.

"Steering Committee," he was responsible for guiding the liberal side of the argument to be made at the General Assembly meeting in the spring. Two issues, from the viewpoint of the modernists, were of utmost importance. The first related to the Fosdick incident, and the second to the more general question of whether or not doctrinal declarations handed down by the General Assembly were binding on the presbyteries.

The concern of the committee with regard to Fosdick was to convince the General Assembly to recognize the decision of the New York Presbytery in the case. Since it had been ordered by the 1923 General Assembly to pass judgment on the question of Fosdick's orthodoxy, the New York Presbytery hoped that the new General Assembly could be persuaded to accept the recommendation that Fosdick be allowed to remain in the pulpit. The Philadelphia Presbytery, unsatisfied with the New York Presbytery's recommendation, filed a formal request that it be overturned in the General Assembly. To this, the Philadelphia ministers added an "overture" that sought to make it mandatory for all the officials of the church to assent to the "Five Points."

The Philadelphia overture constituted the second issue with which the Steering Committee of the liberals had to contend. Dulles believed the issue was a constitutional matter and therefore should be approached from that perspective. Constitutionally, the presbyteries were seen as responsible for the orthodoxy of their members. Thus any new test of orthodoxy could not be imposed by the General Assembly alone, but must be agreed to by the presbyteries as well. As Dulles expressed it,

> The position which I expect to take . . . is that if the majority of the assembly wish to impose interpretations of the Westminster Confession, which in effect, make new tests of orthodoxy, and if they wish thereby to eliminate a large body of the church, they must certainly go about their task in a constitutional manner and submit to the Presbyteries the new tests of orthodoxy which they propose to impose.[48]

The General Assembly that met in 1924 dealt with both issues. In a letter written to his father, who was teaching at Auburn Theological Seminary,[49] Foster called the meeting "one of the most interesting and exciting weeks" of his life.

---

[48]JFD to Dr. Charles Wood, 13 May 1924, DP, Box 6.

[49]In 1904, Reverend Dulles left Watertown and accepted an appointment as the professor of Theism and Apologetics at Auburn.

I was in the thick of the fight . . . I argued the Fosdick case before the
Judicial Commission and was on the Bills and Overture Committee . . .
Bryan [was] the leading figure for the Conservatives. We succeeded in
wresting control of the committee away from the Fundamentalists and I
was almost daily engaged in controversy with Bryan, all of which was most
interesting. The only way we were able to secure a victory was through
getting the Judicial Commission to assume jourisdiction [*sic*] in the case
of Fosdick and of the Philadelphia Overture, which I do not think they
really had, and then when it came to a question of accepting or reviewing
the decision of the Judicial Commission, the Fundamentalists were, for
the first time, unable to hold their votes in line. The Judicial Commission's report came out Wednesday afternoon about five o'clock. A special train left that evening and all of the delegates had their tickets and
mileage books in their pockets. A review would have meant a delay of
several days, and that was the only thing in the world which prevented
a review of the Judicial Committee's decision in the Fosdick and Philadelphia Overture cases.[50]

Because of the desire on the part of most delegates to leave Grand
Rapids on schedule, the members of the Steering Committee were able
to secure what they believed was an uncontested victory in the Fosdick
case. "Victory" for the Presbyterian friends of Fosdick was defined by
the fact that the New York Presbytery was not commanded to immediately terminate his relationship with the historic First Church in New York
City.

An analysis of the determination made by the Judicial Commission in
the Fosdick case causes one to wonder whether "victory" was a noun
properly applied. The commission found that it was an anomaly for a minister of another denomination to serve as preaching minister for more than
five years in a Presbyterian church. No precedent could be uncovered
for such a practice. The provision pertaining to ministers of other denominations in the Presbyterian "Form of Government" stated that such
ministers "may be employed as occasional supplies."[51] Thus as Dulles
defined it,

---

[50]JFD to Allen Macy Dulles, 2 June 1924, DP, Box 6.

[51]JFD to Thomas Guthrie Speers, 1 April 1925, DP, Box 7. The relevant section of
the "Form of Government" was ch. 21, sec. 1.

the legal effect of the Judicial Commission's decision was to hold that . . . ministers of other denominations might occupy an *"occasional"* relationship to a Presbyterian Church and pulpit, yet there was no provision for such a minister maintaining a *"regular"* relationship over an extended period of years.[52]

On the basis of this reasoning, the Judicial Commission offered Fosdick an opportunity to regularize his position by accepting the doctrinal standards of the church as contained in the Westminster Confession of Faith and thus to become an ordained Presbyterian minister. The invitation seemed gracious enough. Fosdick's Presbyterian friends encouraged him to accept the cordial offer to become a Presbyterian minister and end the controversy. Fosdick, however, saw the thorn on the rose.

Once within the regular ranks of the Presbyterian ministry I could be tried for heresy the first time I uttered a liberal conviction, and obviously many irritated and watchful men were itching for the chance.

Indeed, Cornelius Woelfkin, the minister of Park Avenue Baptist Church, reported that Bryan had said, "We will not have any preacher in our church who is not within reach of our stick."[53] Fosdick offered his resignation to the First Presbyterian Church, to become effective 1 March 1925.

Even though the Fosdick case was finally laid to rest, the divisive forces of Fundamentalism in the Presbyterian Church were only beginning to wage their battles. In the case of the Philadelphia overture, which attempted to enforce uniform adherence to the deliverances of the General Assembly, the first-round victory went to the modernists. The 1924 Judicial Commission ruled that such enforcement was "unconstitutional." As Dulles emphasized to his father shortly afterwards, "The decision . . . is of greater importance" than that of the Fosdick case.[54] He spent the next two years trying to ensure the permanence of the 1924 decision.

The first step taken by Dulles and a few other ministers and laymen of liberal persuasion involved establishing a program to print and distribute pamphlets and sermons by leaders of liberal thought that would concentrate, not on controversial topics, but upon the minister's affirmative

---

[52]Ibid.

[53]Fosdick, *The Living of These Days,* 171.

[54]JFD to Allen Macy Dulles, 2 June 1924, DP, Box 6.

beliefs. These modernists believed that such a distribution would demonstrate to the general Presbyterian public that these leading liberals were actually quite "evangelical" in the essential meaning of that term. Dulles was appointed the chairman of the committee charged with the fundraising needed to underwrite the venture.[55]

The efforts of these men, however, were not immediately successful. Perhaps the major reason for their failure may be attributed to the actions of a concerned group of conservative Presbyterian Church officers in New York. Led by a minister, the Reverend Albert D. Gantz, and a lawyer, James E. Bennett, this group of elders and ministers met in October of 1924 to protest the action of the New York Presbytery in continuing to admit into the ministry candidates who refused to affirm the virgin birth. The group's original complaint was filed in 1923 as a protest against the ordination of Henry P. Van Dusen. The General Assembly of 1924 remanded the complaint to the Synod of New York "for such appropriate actions as the Synod may deem proper."[56]

In October the Synod of New York dismissed the complaint by a vote of 72-20. This decision occasioned the meeting of conservatives in New York City. On the night of 28 October, the conservative elders and ministers met and drafted a complaint, which they filed with the General Assembly scheduled to meet in the spring of 1925.

Dulles prepared the brief representing the Synod of New York for submission to the General Assembly.[57] At the same time, he prepared the response to still another complaint filed by a Walter D. Buchanon and others against the Presbytery of New York for receiving two other candidates into the Presbyterian ministry. It alleged that neither one of the two candidates had affirmed "his faith in the inspiration of the Word of God, or Miracles, or the Virgin Birth or in the actual Resurrection Body."[58]

---

[55]See JFD to John P. Myers, 9 July 1924, DP, Box 6; and JFD to John M. T. Finney, 29 December 1924, DP, Box 6.

[56]Quoted in "Memorandum for Respondent in the Matter of the Complaint of Albert D. Gantz and others against the Synod of New York at the General Assembly, 1925," DP, Box 279. The memorandum was prepared by Dulles.

[57]Henry Sloane Coffin to JFD, 20 March 1925, DP, Box 7.

[58]Quoted in "Memorandum on Behalf of the Presbytery of New York, Respondent," DP, Box 282.

In the eighteen-page brief submitted in the Van Dusen case, Dulles argued three particular points. First, the presbytery is constitutionally guaranteed jurisdiction "to ordain, install, remove and judge ministers." Second, "doctrinal deliverences [*sic*] of the General Assembly do not amend the Constitution and Presbyteries cannot be constitutionally bound thereby." In closing, he argued that "there was no abuse of discretion by the Presbytery of New York" in the licensure of Van Dusen.[59]

The first point, according to Dulles, was constitutionally self-explanatory. The second point was supported by reference to the 1924 Judicial Commission of the 1924 General Assembly, which determined that

> the constitution of our church clearly specifies the doctrinal requirements for ministers and elders and any change in these [such as requiring affirmation of the Virgin Birth] must be by concurrent action of the Assembly and Presbyteries, the only method provided for amendment or modification.[60]

The third point emphasized the fact that the majority of the presbytery was satisfied with the orthodoxy of Van Dusen. Therefore, the licensure was a "sound exercise of discretion" in that it fulfilled the constitutional directive, which states that "if the presbytery is satisfied with his trials, they *shall* then proceed to license him."[61]

In both cases before the General Assembly, Dulles's approach attempted to shift the weight from the single issue of Van Dusen's refusal to affirm the virgin birth to the assertion that part of what a man says cannot constitute all that he says. To one of the leaders of the opposition, Dulles wrote,

> I am more interested in what a man believes than in the matters as to which he may decline to affirm a belief, and . . . it seems to me that the protest . . . does not give a fair or temperate picture of the situation. I believe that an attitude on the part of the church which magnifies an applicant's doubts and ignores his affirmative beliefs, is a greater danger to

---

[59]See "Memorandum in the Matter of the Complaint of Albert D. Gantz," 5, 7, and 13.

[60]Ibid., 9.

[61]Ibid., 16 (italics in original).

the church than any "unbelief" which . . . any . . . individual minister is likely "to spread throughout the denomination."[62]

Despite the tightly reasoned argument presented by Dulles at the General Assembly in 1925, the modernist forces suffered defeat in the Van Dusen case. The Judicial Commission and the General Assembly held that the doctrinal deliverances of the previous General Assemblies were in fact binding on the New York Presbytery in the licensing of new candidates for ministry; therefore the presbytery had erred in licensing Van Dusen.

With regard to the second complaint (the one filed by Buchanon), the General Assembly, since the Synod of New York had not yet heard the case, remanded it to that body for appropriate action. Dulles was appointed by the moderator of the New York Presbytery to represent the presbytery before the Synod of New York in the meeting to be held at Utica in October.

Because of the decision reached in the Van Dusen case, Dulles was forced to change his tactics. He decided to try an approach that averted the theological aspects of the case. The official record in neither one of these two cases, he argued, revealed anything with reference to the beliefs, disbeliefs, or doubts of either candidate. Official transcripts of the examination for ordination were not required for ordination. Thus "the action of the presbytery can not, on appeal to a higher judicatory, be held erroneous in the total absence of any record showing what, in fact, were the beliefs of the candidates."[63]

The complainants, argued Dulles, do not contend that there was any failure to follow scrupulously the prescribed constitutional procedure. Rather, they claim only that the examination disclosed that the candidates were not clear enough in their affirmation of doctrines deemed essential according to the ruling in the Van Dusen case. Dulles pointed out that the record showed only a minority of the members of the Committee on Examination of Candidates felt that this was the case.

Since the purpose of examining the candidates was to "satisfy" the presbytery and, once "satisfied," the presbytery was to license the can-

---

[62]JFD to James E. Bennett, 19 November 1924, DP, Box 6.

[63]"Memorandum on Behalf of the Presbytery of New York," 5.

didates, the criteria for licensing these two candidates were fully met. Any change in the accepted examination procedure, such as requiring the presence of an official stenographer, would revolutionize the process of licensing and ordaining candidates for ministry in the Presbyterian Church. Emphasis would be placed upon the form of statements made by the candidates, thus creating "a purely ritualistic procedure" and effectively destroying "the spiritual element in induction into our ministry."[64]

In January of 1926, the Synod of New York decided in favor of Dulles and his argument. The whole matter, as far as the Church's hierarchy was concerned, was put to rest when the General Assembly of 1926 concurred with the finding of the synod. Over the course of the next decade, three secessionist moves on the part of the conservatives were effected, which brought the Westminster Seminary, an independent foreign missions board, and the Orthodox Presbyterian Church into existence.

Praise of Dulles's brief came from all directions. That of Henry Sloane Coffin was typical of the others: "The decision of the Judicial Committee is a great triumph for you. It . . . practically embodied your entire brief. I cannot thank you enough nor tell you how sincerely I admire the masterly way you prepared that brief."[65] According to his pastor, Tertius Van Dyke, Dulles "made a genuine contribution to the living history of the Presbyterian Church" during this period.[66]

Dulles was not a pious individual. Nor did he, at this time, make any meaningful contribution to the church in a theological sense. However, neither of these statements detracts in any way from the overall picture—that Dulles's service to the church during these years was significant and emanated from a dedicated and mature religious faith originally nurtured in a small Watertown Presbyterian manse.

Throughout these early years, religious influences and practices formed Dulles's character in significant ways. In coming years, he would often exemplify his Presbyterian roots through his optimistic, somewhat

---

[64]Ibid., 7.

[65]Henry Sloane Coffin to JFD, 15 October 1926, DP, Box 7; for other notes of praise, see William Adams Brown to JFD, 8 January 1926, and Tertius Van Dyke to JFD, 25 January 1926, DP, Box 7. See also Tertius Van Dyke to JFD, 7 October 1935, DP, Box 14.

[66]Tertius Van Dyke to JFD, 25 January 1926.

social-gospel viewpoint. His Presbyterianism led him to a sincerely ecumenical outlook that was tempered by a dual emphasis on the sovereignty of God and the naturally human tendency toward sin. The former becomes evident during his association with the Federal Council of Churches as he, time and time again, warns against the deification of the state. The latter is demonstrated by his realistic assessment of the claims of national power and sovereignty in the international arena. The activities of these years, as well as those of later years, clearly demonstrate his religious commitments as a caring Presbyterian churchman.

Diplomatic Influences
and International Involvements

Religious influences, though many and varied, did not of themselves constitute the total environment within which young Foster Dulles reached maturity. Among other activities in the Dulles household, the vigorous commitment to outdoor activities stands out as a primary one. During the summers Edith Dulles would carry her children off to her parents' summer home in Henderson Harbor, twenty-five miles south of Watertown, on the shores of Lake Ontario. There the family engaged in camping, serious fishing, long hiking, swimming, and competitive as well as recreational sailboating.

A seemingly natural, energetic, and lusty outdoorsman, young Foster flourished in the surroundings of Henderson Harbor. He became a superb sailor, excellent swimmer, and first-rate fisherman. All these activities helped to teach him the importance of careful planning, self-reliance, and the patience to see a task through to the desired end.

The summers afforded young Foster Dulles with ample opportunity to spend unusually large blocks of time with his maternal grandfather, John W. Foster, after whom he was named. A great storyteller, his grandfather captivated him for hours at a time reminiscing about his colorful past. He appeared to possess an unlimited repertory of entertaining anecdotes. One thing the older Foster loved to talk about was his family heritage. He took seriously the dying words of his father: "Don't let the little ones forget." He did his part to make sure that they remembered their roots. John W. Foster was the third son of Matthew Foster. Matthew immigrated to America with his parents from England in 1815 at the age of fifteen. In 1817 he left northern New York on foot and walked to Vincennes, Indiana, where he staked a claim to eighty acres of timberland, built a log cabin, and then, once again on foot, returned to New York to bring his parents back with him. An enterprising character, Matthew grew quite affluent.[1]

Born in 1836, John W. Foster spent his childhood on an Indiana farm. He attended Indiana University and entered the practice of law. During the Civil War, he served as a colonel in the 65th Indiana Volunteers. Emerging from the war as a brigadier general, he rose to prominence when he became chairman of the Republican State Committee and helped to swing Indiana toward support of President Grant's reelection in 1872. President Grant rewarded him for his efforts by appointing him minister to Mexico. Later he became the minister to Russia (1880) and then the minister to Spain (1882). When James G. Blaine resigned as Benjamin Harrison's secretary of state in order to make a final run for the presidency, Harrison named Foster to become the forty-ninth secretary of state. He served in this post during the last eight months of Benjamin Harrison's administration in 1892-1893.

After Harrison's loss to Grover Cleveland, Foster served the new president in negotiations over Canadian questions with Britain. His public service continued under Presidents McKinley and Roosevelt. For McKinley, he worked on problems related to the Bering Sea. For Roo-

---

[1]Further information on Matthew Foster is available in Mildred Comfort, *John Foster Dulles: Peacemaker* (Minneapolis: T. S. Denison and Company, Inc., 1960) 10-13. More information on John W. Foster is available in the recently published book by Michael J. Devine entitled *John W. Foster: Politics and Diplomacy in the Imperial Era, 1873-1917* (Athens: Ohio University Press, 1981).

sevelt, he became a general adviser to the State Department, doing particularly valuable work on the Alaskan boundary dispute. Upon his
retirement from public service and his Washington law practice, he became a legal adviser to the Imperial Government of China, specifically
appointed to assist in negotiating the Sino-Japanese peace treaty. The
picture commemorating the signing of the Treaty of Shimonoseki was later
proudly hung in his grandson's study.[2]

Grandfather Foster was devoted to his grandchildren, particularly to
the eldest grandson, young John Foster Dulles. Some evidence suggests
that the relationship between grandfather and grandson sometimes ri-
valed the relationship between father and son.[3] Some of the early cor-
respondence between the two was kept by young Foster's mother. Even
when the grandson was merely three years old, "grandpapa" Foster was
writing to him asking, "When are you coming to Washington?"[4]

When young Foster was five, his grandfather sent a letter from the
steamer *Rameses* on the Nile River in Egypt. He and his wife were tour-
ing the churches and houses built thousands of years earlier by the Egyp-
tian for whom the steamer was named.

> When the boat stops, we all get on little ponies called donkeys and ride
> to the churches to see them. The donkeys are funny creatures and every
> little while they throw some of us over their heads. Grandmama has tum-
> bled off three times and says she does not like donkeys.[5]

These early exchanges between grandfather and grandson indicate a very
close relationship. In early 1895, when the elder Foster was invited by
Viceroy Li Hung Chang to remain in China as a government adviser, he
declined by stating: "I have made an engagement with and a promise to
my seven year old grandson that I would come home in time to go a-fish-
ing with him that summer and that it would destroy all his esteem and

---

[2]See Ronald W. Pruessen, *John Foster Dulles: The Road to Power,* (New York: The
Free Press, 1982) 5-6. See also John W. Foster, *Diplomatic Memoirs* (Boston: Houghton
Mifflin Co., 1909) 2:156-57, 281-302.

[3]See Eleanor Lansing Dulles, interview conducted by Philip A. Crowl. See John Robinson Beal, *John Foster Dulles: A Biography* (New York: Harper and Brothers, 1957) 27.

[4]John W. Foster to JFD, 27 December 1891, DP, Box 1.

[5]John W. Foster to JFD, 2 December 1893, DP, Box 1.

confidence in me if I failed in my promise."[6] The elder Foster's world seemed, at times, to revolve around his namesake.

John Foster Dulles spent the entire spring semester of 1895 at the Washington home of his grandmother and grandfather. His maternal aunt and uncle were also residing in the house. "Uncle Bert," Robert Lansing, was an attorney in Washington. The only Democrat in the Republican clan, he was the husband of Foster's Aunt Eleanor. A few years later, from 1915-1920, "Uncle Bert" was to serve as the fifty-seventh secretary of state under President Woodrow Wilson. Thus young Foster Dulles was intimately acquainted with two relatives who held the post of secretary of state for the United States.

Diplomatic and International Influences

These early years spent in the company of his grandfather and his uncle, both prominent statesmen, influenced the young Foster Dulles beyond measure. Often, during the summer months, the three of them would fish and sail all day long together. In 1906, the elder Foster gave his grandson a small sailboat that became known as the "Number Five" after the number painted on its side. It was probably the only small rig of its kind to have carried, all at once, three men of the same family who all served as American secretaries of state.

The Dulles children were simply born into a family circle immersed in an international tradition. Their ancestry on the Dulles side consisted of several missionaries, an envoy, and a merchant in the China tea trade. The Foster side, of course, was dominated by their grandparents' diplomatic experiences.[7] Art objects from the Far East and from all over Europe graced the living quarters of the stately Foster townhouse in Washington. The town home also served as a gathering place for visiting dignitaries from all over the world. The young Dulles children were often able to talk with ambassadors, missionaries, and other very important persons who dropped in quite frequently to visit with the grandparents. Stays at the Washington address also offered other advantages for the

---

[6]Foster, *Diplomatic Memoirs*, 2:156.

[7]Eleanor Lansing Dulles, *The Last Year* (New York: Harcourt, Brace and World, Inc., 1963) 61.

young Dulles children. For instance, at the tender age of four, Foster made his first visit to the White House when invited to the birthday party of five-year-old Benjamin Harrison Mckee, President Harrison's grandson.[8]

Foster Dulles loved the exciting atmosphere of Washington. He seemed destined to a long association with members of the prestigious political and diplomatic circles of the city. Of all the Dulles children, he seemed more influenced by the international tradition of his family and the stimulating environment in which they lived. On those numerous fishing and sailing outings with his grandfather and uncle, he listened attentively to the two elder statesmen as they discussed international affairs. Together—one a Republican mostly remembered as a nationalist and the other a Democrat and committed internationalist—they instilled in him a love for diplomacy. Perhaps Dulles's love for bipartisan politics began on those fishing jaunts. One thing is certain, the two politicians definitely affected the future of their young protégé. Years later, Foster Dulles reflected on the fact that these conversations served as the foundation for his future. "It became my ambition to go forward in that way."[9] One can only wonder whether Dulles was beginning to view the secretary of state's office as a family heirloom.

Another major factor in developing young Foster's international awareness was his parents' commitment to broadening the perspectives of their children. Allen and Edith Dulles took family vacations to Europe whenever possible. In the fall of 1903, Edith, on her own, took Foster and his sister Margaret to France. By living with a Swiss painter and his family, the children had an excellent opportunity to gain some expertise in French.[10]

Following another family tradition, Dulles entered Princeton University in the fall of 1904, at the age of sixteen. His father, as well as several of his uncles, had graduated from Princeton. At the time of his entrance

---

[8]Pruessen, *The Road to Power,* 8.

[9]JFD, "Faith of Our Fathers," in *The Spiritual Legacy of John Foster Dulles,* ed. Henry P. Van Dusen (Philadelphia: The Westminster Press, 1960) 6. See also Dulles, *The Last Year,* 167.

[10]Dulles, *The Last Year,* 63.

to Princeton, Foster's uncle Joseph Dulles was the librarian at the Princeton Theological Seminary.

Dulles found the rigorous academic setting at Princeton somewhat disconcerting at first. In one of his first writing assignments, one that contains numerous misspellings, he confessed,

> It is hard to write five hundred words on one's preperation in English when one has not spent five hundred minutes preparing it. . . . As to compositions and essays I have written very few, as the present writing will testify. In fact I am surprized that I was ever allowed to enter the college, as far as English preperation is concerned. . . . I have memorized, and forgotten several short poems of Longfellow, Tennyson, and Whittier, but am not so thoroughly acquainted with those books which are required for enterance into most Universities as those who have studied and dissected them with an eye, more directly, toward the examination.[11]

Dulles worked hard to compensate for his age and deficiencies in preparation. He was not much for socializing at Princeton, probably due to the insecurities of his younger age. Any social contacts he had made generally came through his interest in the game of chess or his membership in the debating Whig Society. He became an accomplished debater, eventually winning the Junior Debate Prize.

He must have dramatically improved his talent in debating during his first two years at Princeton. In what must be an early (undated) debate preparation, again one that contains numerous misspellings, Dulles argued that Lincoln deserved to stand higher in the estimation of his countrymen than George Washington because

> Lincoln's religious nature was very deep. He was a sincere Christain. He believed in the Bible and in prayer. The Bible was one of the few books he had when a boy and he knew it thoroughly. He constantly quoted and refered to it in his speeches. He never swore or allowed others to do so in his presence.

One might argue that Dulles, given his early understanding of Lincoln, chose him as a role model for his public speaking.[12]

---

[11]JFD, "My Prep in English," 1904, DP, Box 279.

[12]See paper entitled "Resolved," undated, 6, DP, Box 279.

As a philosophy major, Dulles experienced great success. He worked closely with the renowned Professor John Grier Hibben. In addition, he took an occasional course under the president of the university, Woodrow Wilson. As a junior, he was awarded the Dickinson Prize for an essay in logic. As a graduate, he earned the highest honors bestowed by the Philosophy Department. His senior thesis brought him the Chancellor Green Mental Science Fellowship, which was accompanied by a year of study at the Sorbonne. Even though he graduated second in his class, he was named valedictorian at his graduation.[13]

In the spring of 1907, Dulles's junior year was interrupted by an incident that proved highly influential in his ultimate decision to become a lawyer. His grandfather, due to his years of association with the Chinese government, was invited to serve as a delegate for the Imperial Government of China to the Second Hague Peace Conference. He invited his grandson to accompany him. Nineteen-year-old Foster made arrangements to take his final exams early the next fall and on 31 May he sailed with his grandfather to The Hague. While attending the conference, he was made a secretary to the Chinese delegation.[14]

His favorite remembrance of this conference involved his role in helping to solve a "protocol" crisis that arose when none of the delegates wanted to place his nation in the lesser position associated with making the primary courtesy calls. The conference could not begin until the courtesy calls were made. Finally, as Dulles humorously recounts it, a solution was reached.

> It was finally decided to cut the Gordian knot by fixing an appointed hour at which each person in attendance at the conference would arrange to have his cards left upon each other member of the conference. Accordingly, at four o'clock on a given afternoon, all of the secretaries, of which I was one, set out in automobiles loaded with about two hundred cards of each of the other members of his delegation, which were then left at the hotels where the other members were residing. In this way the conference was able to get off to an orderly start and the world war was deferred for nearly seven years.[15]

---

[13]Dulles, *The Last Year,* 125.

[14]Foster, *Diplomatic Memoirs,* 2:212.

[15]JFD, "Remarks Introducing Mr. Huber at a Bar Association Luncheon," 3 June 1931, DP, Box 10.

For Dulles, The Hague offered heady experiences. The diplomatic hobnobbing afforded by this opportunity surely made an immense impression on a young man who was struggling to make a decision about a career. His parents, throughout his college years, evidently assumed he was heading toward a future in the ministry. Foster seemed unsure himself whether he would become a minister or an international lawyer. At least, he did not make his decision public until after his year at the Sorbonne.

While in Paris studying with Bergson, Dulles also took some coursework in international law. One of his notebooks, preserved in his papers, contains notes taken mostly in French concerning the question of international fishing rights.[16] By the time he returned from the Sorbonne, his mind was made up. He informed his parents that he had decided to go into law. By all family accounts, his parents were extremely supportive of his decision.[17] However, a letter written nearly thirty years later indicates that his mother was perhaps at the time subtly apprehensive of her son's decision.

> I remember that after graduation, when you told me that you were going into the law and not the ministry, that you said you thought you could do just as much good in that field, and you are proving it, for your reputation gives weight to all you say.
>
> I know the temptation to selfishness in the busy New York life and it makes me very happy that you are willing to sacrifice something for the real need of the world.[18]

The fall following his college graduation, Dulles entered George Washington University Law School. During the two years it took him to complete the program, he lived with his grandfather in Washington. William Howard Taft was president during those years. According to Foster Dulles's diary, he spent a good portion of his time socializing with the Taft children, Robert (the future Ohio Senator and presidential candidate), Charles, and Helen. On 25 November 1910, his diary records that he

---

[16]Townsend Hoopes, *The Devil and John Foster Dulles* (Boston: Little, Brown and Co., 1973) 23.

[17]See Dulles, *The Last Year,* 127, and Margaret Dulles Edwards, interview, 5.

[18]"Mother" to JFD, 21 May 1937, DP, Box 16.

"sent Miss [Helen] Taft a corsage of orchids . . . which she wore to the theatre following [dinner together]." The next day he had "tea at the White House with Mrs. Taft, Helen Taft, and [the] Dutch Minister." On 1 December he attended "Miss [Helen] Taft's coming out tea." Numerous other diary entries during the next several months mention evenings spent dancing at the White House.[19]

Dulles left the law school without formally receiving the degree. George Washington had a three-year residency requirement and since Dulles completed the work in two years, he was refused the degree. The injustice he suffered because of this technicality was finally corrected twenty-one years later when it became advantageous for the university to recognize him as one of its graduates. Cloyd H. Marvin, president of the university, informed Dulles by letter that George Washington University wanted to confer the degree retroactively dated 1912, the year his entering class was graduated.[20]

During the summer after he left the law school, Dulles crammed for the New York State bar exam. Whenever he took a break from his studies, he was generally in the company of a young woman named Janet Avery. Evidently, on the evening of the day the law exam was scheduled, Dulles had a date with Janet. According to Townsend Hoopes, Dulles practiced his first application of "brinksmanship" when he calculated the number of questions he needed to answer on the exam to pass and then left the remainder blank in order to catch the train back to Auburn from Rochester so he would be on time for his date.[21] He married Janet a short time later.

As early as the February before Dulles's last semester in law school, his grandfather was hard at work utilizing his relationship with William Nelson Cromwell, of the impressive Wall Street law firm of Sullivan and Cromwell, to provide a job for his grandson. Cromwell was willing to take

---

[19]See the following dates in the Dulles Diary: 25 November 1910, 26 November 1910, 1 December 1910, 3 December 1910, 30 December 1910, 10 January 1911, 18 January 1911, 1 February 1911, DP, Box 278. These entries are typical of the social activities recorded during these years. It is also interesting to note that every Sunday a notation about attendance at church is recorded.

[20]Cloyd H. Marvin to JFD, 3 June 1932, DP, Box 11.

[21]Hoopes, *The Devil,* 25; see also Beal, *John Foster Dulles,* 54-55.

a chance on the young lawyer for the sake of an "old association."[22] Dulles was offered a job as a law clerk for a fifty-dollar-per-month salary.

Grandfather Foster continued to advise the young lawyer whenever he could. Shortly after he began his work at the law firm, Dulles wrote to his grandfather complaining of the routine of being a law clerk. The elder statesman wrote back that he would be in New York shortly and he might be able to take the time to stop in "to say a word of benefit" on the young man's behalf. Yet he reminded Foster that it was "steady, good, hard work" that would determine his "advancement."

> You must not allow yourself to tire of the druggery [sic] of the office—that is what the new clerks have to go through, I suppose. But your work of that kind is not as bad as what I had to go through in my first year in a law office—I was janitor. . . . Was it not the Apostle Paul or someone else who impressed upon us to "despise not the doing of small things?"[23]

Three years later, when Foster was offered a lucrative position with the corporate offices of Grace and Company, his grandfather warned him not to do anything that would take him out of law.[24] Dulles heeded the advice of his grandfather and reaped enormous benefits. At the very young age of thirty-two, he was made a partner at Sullivan and Cromwell. Seven years later, he was chosen to head the prestigious law firm.

Diplomatic and International Involvements

Immediately after his graduation from law school, Foster Dulles urgently sought ways to fulfill his immense interest in international affairs. Clerking at Sullivan and Cromwell was incredibly boring work. To him, it seemed that the time would never come when he would demonstrate his abilities as an international lawyer. Circumstances, however, would soon provide him with that opportunity.

During World War I, Dulles applied for active service. His application was turned down because of his defective eyesight. Consequently, he

---

[22]John W. Foster to W. N. Cromwell, 15 February 1911, DP, Box 1; see also Beal, *John Foster Dulles*, 55.

[23]John W. Foster to JFD, 20 August 1911, DP, Box 1.

[24]John W. Foster to JFD, 9 April 1914, DP, Box 1.

served as a captain with Military Intelligence, and later as a liaison officer between the War Trade Board and the War Department.[25] While with the War Trade Board, he worked out an intricate scheme that enabled about eighty-seven Dutch ships tied up in U.S. ports to be added to the American merchant fleet without compromising the neutrality of Holland. By July of 1918, he had proven himself a very capable and persistent negotiator; he was promoted to the position of personal assistant to Vance McCormick, the chairman of the War Trade Board. In the fall, just before he was honorably discharged in order to go to Versailles with Wilson's entourage, he was awarded the rank of major.[26]

As a result of Dulles's expert work on economic matters with the War Trade Board during the war, he was able to secure a job as a legal adviser to Bernard Baruch, the United States representative on the Reparations Committee at Versailles. As head of the War Industries Board during World War I, Baruch was impressed by the abilities Dulles exemplified in carrying out his duties with the War Trade Board. During his eight months in Paris, beginning in January of 1919, Dulles concerned himself with the work of the Reparations Committee. His work there proved to be quite significant.

Dulles was involved in the American effort to counteract British and French demands for reimbursement of all war costs. The Allies wanted Germany to bear the cost of replacing *all* monies expended in fighting the war, as well as the cost of replacing damaged or destroyed properties. Dulles reminded the Allies of the reparations portions of the Pre-Armistice Agreement with Germany signed in November 1918. In the agreement, the Allies committed Germany to the repayment of only those damages done to "the civilian population of the Allies and their property by the aggression of Germany by land, by sea, and by air." Dulles argued that this agreement constituted a contract.

> Gentlemen, we have here an agreement. It is an agreement which cannot be ignored, and I am confident that no one here would propose to ignore it. I know that I have the full concurrence of all in the proposition

---

[25]See letter from John Biddle, secretary of war, to Vance McCormick, chairman of the War Trade Board, 12 March 1918, DP, Box 2.

[26]Pruessen, *The Road to Power,* has an extended and interesting discussion of Dulles's War Board activities on 24-28.

that if this agreement constitutes a limitation upon our right to demand reparation of the enemy, that limitation will be respected.

And can there be any question that this agreement does constitute a limitation[?][27]

In a later statement, he made an even more emotional plea.

In a material sense we stand to gain, gain greatly, by the defeat of our proposition. But we did not make war for material interests. We do not make peace for material interests. We have sacrificed and today again stand ready to sacrifice our material interests for principles which we have espoused. I stand here today honestly convinced that we are bound by the agreement and that no other course is honorably open to us than that which I have proposed.[28]

The ideological argument briefly sketched above carried little weight with the British and French delegates. Only the most practical arguments made any sense to them. Dulles, therefore, also argued that "to demand the gigantic total of war costs would . . . be to jeopardize securing that specific reparation as to which Germany must recognize her liability, and the satisfaction of which will tax her resources to the limit."[29] The force of this practical argument finally won the dissenting Allies over to the American position. However, the Allies pushed the discouraged and frustrated Americans to the acceptance of a clause in the agreement laying total responsibility for all damages and losses on the enemy states even though, due to practical limitations, they could not repay these damages. This notorious "war guilt" clause provided the Allies with the psychological sop necessary to satisfy "bitter voters and politicians at home."[30]

Victory regarding the limitation of reparations was the single achievement for the Americans in the reparations talks and it would later be wiped out by the Senate's unwillingness to ratify the treaty. In other

---

[27]JFD, "Reparation Commission: Statement on Behalf of the American Delegation," 13 February 1919, 3, DP, Box 289.

[28]JFD, "Reparation Commission: Statement on Behalf of the American Delegates, 9th Meeting," 19 February 1919, 14, DP, Box 289.

[29]Ibid.

[30]See Pruessen, *The Road to Power,* 37.

reparation issues in Versailles, the Allies won expressions that reflected their positions. Wilson, over the very vocal and logically presented objections of Dulles, agreed to include the pensions of servicemen in the agreement.[31] Americans also lost on questions of setting a fixed sum of reparations to be paid, of setting a time limit for those payments to be made, and of limiting the powers of the postconference reparations commission.[32]

Dulles resigned his position at Versailles in August. Popular speculation attributed his resignation to the fact that Congress had refused to appoint an American member to the postconference reparations commission.[33] The newspaper reports concerning his resignation, whether accurate or not, at least illustrate the widespread knowledge of Dulles's unhappiness with the way the reparations talks were progressing and his dissatisfaction with the isolationism that was surfacing in America at the time.

Returning to his law practice in New York, Dulles continued to publicly comment on the question of reparations. When, in 1921, the Allied Reparation Commission set Germany's total reparations responsibility at thirty-three billion dollars, Dulles issued a statement regarding Germany that later proved to be quite an accurate assessment.

> It is safe to conclude that Germany today is among the most pacific of the nations of the world. It is, of course, possible that this situation may not always prevail but if there is a change it will be only because the German people are so goaded by impossible economic conditions of peace that in desperation they will seek a change of rulers.[34]

---

[31]See the memo of the high-level meeting of the American delegation, 1 April 1919, DP, Box 289. Dulles continued to publicly criticize Wilson for his stance on this issue. See the exchange between Vance McCormick and JFD where McCormick chastises Dulles for talking about the specifics of the 1 April meeting in public. Dulles mentioned this incident in his speech before the Council of Foreign Relations on 19 December 1922. Dates of the letters are 22 December 1922 and 26 December 1922, DP, Box 4. See also JFD, "Draft Speech," 28 April 1926, 7, delivered to Foreign Policy Association in New York, DP, Box 289; and JFD, "The Christian Forces and a Stable Peace," 25 January 1941, DP, Box 20.

[32]See Pruessen, *The Road to Power,* 38-44.

[33]See Lincoln Eyre, "Resignation of Dulles Affects U.S. Interests," *Standard,* 14 August 1919; see also *The New York World,* same date.

[34]JFD, "Eve of Washington Conference: A Draft," 21 November 1921, 9, DP, Box 289.

In December he told a luncheon discussion group held under the auspices of the Foreign Policy Association that the "tragic condition of inflation" in the world economy was a direct result of the irrational reparations demands made upon Germany.[35]

Less than fifteen months after the final reparations amount was set, Germany defaulted. In the fall, Dulles argued in an article published in the first issue of the now-prominent *Foreign Affairs,* that the Allied debts should be cancelled altogether.[36] Later, responding to a letter requesting clarification of his position, Dulles wrote,

> From an economic standpoint, I believe that it would enhance the general good if these debts were cancelled. The greater part of them will, in no event, be paid, but their existence and such sporadic efforts as may be made to pay or to compel payment will merely retard the general recovery.[37]

During the 1924 presidential campaign, Dulles left the Republican party to support an old friend, John W. Davis, the Democratic nominee. He even served as the candidate's foreign policy adviser during the campaign. He was particularly upset with the Republican party's attempt to claim credit for helping to work out the Dawes Plan. To Davis, he wrote,

> It borders upon the ludicrous that the Republican party should now, after the event, so eagerly seek to take credit unto itself for a course of action which it neither initiated nor officially aided; which was taken despite of [*sic*] and in a manner to circumvent its oft repeated policy of aloofness; and the result of which constitutes a complete demonstration of the stupidity of that policy.[38]

Hoover's nomination as a Republican in 1928 brought Dulles's permanent return to that party. He had worked closely with Hoover in Paris and believed that his foreign policy stance made him a desirable presidential candidate. In 1931, when Hoover declared the one-year moratorium on

---

[35]JFD, "An Association of Nations," in *News Bulletin of the Foreign Policy Association* (30 December 1921), DP, Box 289.

[36]JFD, "The Allied Debts," *Foreign Affairs* 1 (September 1922).

[37]JFD to Mrs. A. J. Boulton, 5 December 1923, DP, Box 5.

[38]JFD to John W. Davis, July 1924, DP, Box 6.

debt repayment, Dulles wrote to Hoover commending him for taking that action.[39]

During the remainder of the 1920s, Dulles was heavily involved in his legal work, mostly as an adviser to large American corporations. Putting his knowledge of the world economy to good use, Dulles advised corporations and banks on loans to Germany. He also represented the New York Life Insurance Company and other insurance companies in their efforts to retrieve the massive losses of their life insurance reserve funds, which were invested in Russia prior to the Bolshevik revolution. Those reserves were seized and nationalized after the Soviets came to power. These activities gained Dulles quite a reputation. He quickly became one of the highest-paid international lawyers on the American scene. As *Fortune* magazine noted, by 1931 Dulles was an important figure in corporate law.[40]

Dulles's world view throughout this period was progressive, even liberal, when compared to the desire among most Americans to be repaid every penny of the war debts owed to them. Throughout the war, he shared completely the Wilsonian hope for a new international order that would make hard negotiation between countries a reality and the potential for peace more than merely a passing fancy. He consistently called for reform in the sphere of international affairs, reforms that the American people were not quite ready to accept. Dulles urged practical measures that would insure, at least in part, responsible action in the world arena.[41]

----

[39]JFD to President Hoover, 22 June 1931, DP, Box 10.

[40]*Fortune* 3 (January 1931): 62. See the excellent discussion of Dulles's legal involvements during these years in Pruessen, *The Road to Power*, 58-75.

[41]Pruessen criticizes Dulles for not being more radical in action. I think the criticism is, in the main, unfair, particularly since Congress refused to even ratify the Versailles Treaty or to become a participating member of the League of Nations. Dulles wanted to get as much of the loaf as possible, especially since he realized the whole loaf was an impossibility given the American climate. Intense pressure was exerted upon American leadership to lead the country back into isolationism. Dulles did what he felt he could to reach his desired end—American participation in the League. Therefore, Pruessen's criticism that Dulles "stopped far short of advocating profound dislocations in the international order" is not really a substantive one. As a realist, Dulles worked for reform he thought could possibly gain acceptance. Due to adverse public opinion, even those modest reforms were rejected. It seems unnecessary to criticize him for not advocating even more radical solutions. (See Pruessen, *The Road to Power*, 56-57, 103-105, and 504-505.)

Dulles, as an "internationalist" rather than an "isolationist," tried to pursue policy that was in the American national interest from within the context of consciously attempting to understand the needs of the other peoples in the world. For him, such a position was one of "enlightened self-interest."[42] In assuming this posture, Dulles represents what Kenneth W. Thompson describes as the "realist" perspective in international affairs.

> International politics, as politics within national communities, is lived at the point of convergence of particular and universalistic interests. If this is something less than abstract love and justice, it is more than a totally self-centered narrow nationalism. Sometimes, in politics, as in life, enlightened self-interest is man's highest moral attainment.[43]

This commitment to an internationalist understanding during these years is the foundation for the progressive views Dulles consistently expressed. Out of this commitment to enlightened self-interest, he argued that excessive reparations constituted a "gaping wound . . . draining the vitality of modern civilization."[44] He did not attempt to cloak his concern for national interests with simple moralizing, as he was prone to do in later years. Rather, he argued that

> moral distinctions, though pleasing to those who draw them, are hard to sustain in fact, and I know of no historic reasons to justify our approaching these problems of international relations with the complacent assumption that we are party to a clashing of the forces of good and evil, and that solution is to be found in the moral regeneration of those who hold views contrary to our own.[45]

---

[42]This was one of his favorite expressions. See, for example, *The Six Pillars of Peace: A Study Guide* (New York: The Commission on a Just and Durable Peace, 1943) 30. For a particular example of how he applied this idea to policy, see JFD to Hamilton Fish Armstrong, 18 March 1940, DP, Box 19.

[43]Kenneth W. Thompson, *Ethics, Functionalism, and Power in International Politics: the Crisis in Values* (Baton Rouge: Louisiana State University Press, 1979) 22.

[44]JFD, "The Reparation Problem," *The New Republic* 26 (30 March 1921): 133.

[45]Quoted in Pruessen, *The Road to Power,* 102, this excerpt is from an address entitled "The Relation of France to a Program of World Reconstruction," undated, but probably in 1924. See also JFD to L. L. Summers, 5 January 1921, DP, Box 4.

Concern for peoples in other nations of the world originated for Dulles out of the milieu provided by his family. His family circle, since it included both missionaries and diplomats, often attracted visitors from faraway places like Beirut, China, Korea, and India. The Dulles children listened attentively as their distinguished visitors told stories of people less fortunate than themselves. As Eleanor L. Dulles remembers it, she and her brothers and sisters "did not think of these peoples in terms of foreign policy, but we did grow to understand the life, the poverty, the superstitions, and the eager hopefulness of those with whom the missionaries dealt."[46]

The remnants of both the religious and diplomatic influences exerted by Dulles's early familial surroundings are unmistakably present in his later life. From the Presbyterian manse he inherited moral commitments coupled with a Calvinistic sense of duty, both of which profoundly contributed to the shaping of his world view. From his grandfather and his uncle, his predecessors in the State Department, he learned that he had an individual responsibility to put that sense of duty to work by attempting to transform his moral commitments into practical realities. Though these influences are evidenced in nearly all of his involvements in the international arena, historical contingencies and personal experiences of later years were to bring significant change to the way he understood and utilized them.

---

[46]Dulles, *The Last Year,* 62; see also 167.

Prophet of Realism:
The Narrative Setting
and the Ideological Framework,
1937-1945

3

The Great Enlightenment

Beginning in 1937, Dulles was called upon to translate both his prophetic Protestantism and his international political realism into practical service performed on behalf of the Church. Events resulting from his participation in the 1937 Oxford Ecumenical Church Conference led to his involvement with the Federal Council of Churches of Christ in America. In order to better understand the ways in which the prophetic and realistic dimensions of his world view influenced his later years, it is now appropriate to look more closely at his immense involvement in church circles during the years 1937-1945.

Of the countless words written about John Foster Dulles, none have substantively or accurately considered his connection with the Federal Council of Churches.[1] No published narrative has yet described the de-

---

[1]Albert Keim, in his dissertation entitled "John Foster Dulles and the Federal Council

tails either of how this connection began or the manner in which it continued over approximately eight years. Nor has any interpreter really considered how this association brought Dulles to a new appreciation of his Presbyterian heritage and taught him how to utilize that heritage effectively as a leader in the Protestant search for a meaningful peace during the war years.[2]

Too often, critics of Dulles have misunderstood his early life, especially his activities in religious circles, because they have interpreted the earlier years through the lens of his later activities as secretary of state.[3] These interpretations are inadequate because Dulles's approach to international affairs underwent a profound transformation prior to the time that he occupied the secretary's office in the State Department. As years passed and relations worsened between the Soviet Union and the United

---

of Churches, 1937-1949" (Ohio State University, 1971), has dealt with these years. Yet I disagree with his conclusion that Dulles's "contribution was strategic rather than substantive. It was not the ideas he expressed, but who he was which was important. His position as a leader of the American foreign policy establishment gave church pronouncements an authority they could not have otherwise enjoyed" (253). Though the latter statement is more than likely true, the former statement is not. As the following pages indicate, I believe that Dulles was fundamentally a shaper of the ideas as well and that it was in this area that he made his greatest contribution.

[2]Ronald Pruessen's biography of Dulles entitled *John Foster Dulles: The Road to Power* (New York: The Free Press, 1982) has recently appeared in print. It is the most complete critical and scholarly evaluation of Dulles's early life. A welcome and exceedingly significant contribution to the Dulles literature, this volume is the first to reveal, even partially, the philosophical flexibility of Dulles's earlier years. However, when Pruessen discusses Dulles's involvement with the churches, he underestimates both the realistic trend of Protestant thought concerning the international issues at the time, and Dulles's sincere participation therein (see particularly 178-217, 254-58, 291-97, and 499-509). A more extensive evaluation of Pruessen's interpretation of Dulles may be found in my review of his book. See the *Christian Century* 99 (6 October 1982): 994-95.

[3]John M. Mulder's article, "The Moral World of John Foster Dulles," *Journal of Presbyterian History* 49 (Summer 1971), represents an example of this particular interpretation. The other major critical biography of Dulles (Townsend Hoopes, *The Devil and John Foster Dulles* [Boston: Little, Brown and Company, 1973]) is also representative of this viewpoint. Neither Mulder nor Hoopes allows the context of Dulles's involvement with the Federal Council to speak for itself. Hoopes particularly interprets Secretary of State Dulles's contribution to intensifying the Cold War as the natural culmination of a consistent character pattern. (See the insightful review of Hoopes's book written by Charles West and published in the *Journal of Presbyterian History* 53 [Spring 1975]: 67-69.) Of the 505 pages of Hoopes's book, only about five pages are devoted to this period of Dulles's life.

States, Dulles became one of the more forceful representatives of the nationalist viewpoint he had so completely criticized during his tenure with the churches. This later nationalist viewpoint has led many observers to the conclusion that Dulles was not really committed to, nor even substantially in agreement with, the approach of the churches during the years of his association with them.[4] I contend, however, that no contradiction of substance exists between the Dulles of the religious sphere and the Dulles of the political arena.

At least before events began to harden Dulles's attitude toward the Soviets beginning in late 1945, he accurately represented the thinking of Protestant realists like Reinhold Niebuhr and John C. Bennett, the two well-known Protestant theologians.[5] For various reasons, events and circumstances after 1945 caused Dulles to transform his position from a Protestant prophetic realism stressing the interdependence of nations to a more private notion of religion linked to the democratic ideology of the Free World.[6]

What follows is a concise and faithful narrative accounting that explores the context of these years.[7] During the years 1937-1945, Dulles was vitally connected with the Federal Council of the Churches of Christ in America. A faithful narrative must speak of the origins of his involvement and of his eventual work as chairman of the Commission to Study

---

[4]Mulder, for instance, tries to surmise why Dulles and men like Reinhold Niebuhr and John C. Bennett, the "consummate political realists," could work together (see "The Moral World," 168). Pruessen also uses this interpretation to conclude that Dulles was essentially a businessman who saw religious terminology and expression as an effective way to further the traditional pursuit of American self-interest (see particularly, *The Road to Power*, 295-97).

[5]Van Dusen notes that Niebuhr and Dulles "had a great respect for each other. . . . I don't think that we felt, in the context in which we saw him, that Dulles was conservative at all. I would say he was a moderate liberal. . . . Among his closest legal colleagues, he was regarded as, if not a radical, a liberal" (Henry P. Van Dusen, interview, 41, 43).

[6]See chs. 8-10 below for an accounting of how this transformation occurs.

[7]An article published in 1975 provides occasional narrative detail of Dulles's activities during this period, though its focus is specifically pointed in another direction. See Dennis L. Tarr, "The Presbyterian Church and the Founding of the United Nations," *Journal of Presbyterian History* 53 (Spring 1975): 3-32. Nearly all the detail of my narrative is gleaned from sources such as the *Federal Council Bulletin, Christian Century, Christianity and Crisis*, personal letters, and speeches delivered close to the events themselves.

the Bases of a Just and Durable Peace. The contribution of the commission during this period to the life of the American Protestant Church is a
very important one. As Henry P. Van Dusen stated when he reflected
on the activities of the Dulles Commission, "The American church talked
more powerfully, both in terms of intrinsic wisdom and in terms of influence, at that particular period [1940-1945] than before or since."[8]

Origins: The "Great Enlightenment"

Immediately prior to the ecumenical Oxford Conference of 1937,
Dulles was in Paris presiding over the biennial meeting of the Institute of
Intellectual Cooperation, the International Studies Conference, held under the auspices of the League of Nations. This meeting of intellectuals,
politicians, and economists proved to be a great disappointment to Dulles.
In fact, as he reflected upon it sometime later, he viewed it as a complete
waste of time. In his words, "I saw the impossibility of bringing the delegates present even to discuss the agreed topic of 'peaceful change' lest
it might be inferred that their own nations admitted the possibility of
change to its disadvantage."[9]

When the conference came to its conclusion, Dulles left Paris for Oxford in the company of his wife Janet. While the trip across the Channel
from the continent of Europe to the British Isles is a short one, that dis-
tance hardly signifies the momentous change in the way Dulles framed
solutions to international problems after making the trip.

The Oxford Conference was sponsored by the Universal Christian
Council for Life and Work. According to Samuel McCrea Cavert, it was
the conference that most directly led to the formation of the World Council of Churches.[10] The conference was convened because the prospects
for continued world peace looked bleak. Churchmen were anxious to
stress their continuing bonds of unity in spite of the widening rift between the nations. Perhaps through the common fellowship of their faith,

---

[8]Van Dusen, interview, 53.

[9]John Foster Dulles, "The Churches and World Order," in *The Spiritual Legacy of John Foster Dulles*, ed. Henry P. Van Dusen (Philadelphia: The Westminster Press, 1960) 23.

[10]Samuel McCrea Cavert, interview, 24.

they could become a redeeming influence in the world that would help to preserve the precarious peace. At least this was their hope.

It is important to understand the background of Dulles's involvement with the Oxford Conference, as it sheds light on just how he was regarded by American churchmen at the time. In 1936 Dr. Joseph Oldham, a distinguished British layman and organizing secretary of the Oxford Conference, visited the United States. His purpose in making the trip was to solidify preparations for the upcoming conference. Oldham was most "anxious" to meet Dulles. Sometime earlier, Henry P. Van Dusen had mentioned to Dr. Oldham that Dulles was a prominent international lawyer who also happened to be an elder in the Presbyterian church. Here was a man, said Van Dusen, "they ought not to miss."[11]

Oldham came away from his meeting with Dulles vastly impressed with his knowledge of international affairs. He immediately invited him to write one of the preparatory papers for Oxford. As Roswell Barnes later commented, "It was a natural selection."[12] Dulles readily agreed to attend the conference because "it seemed to me that I might there find the answer to certain questions which perplexed me."[13] Chief among these perplexing questions was his concern over just what role the church would be able to play in overcoming the national selfishness exhibited just prior to Oxford at the Paris Conference.

The topic at the Oxford Conference was "Church, Community, and State." Dulles participated in the section entitled "The Universal Church and the World of Nations." The chairman of that section, President of Princeton Theological Seminary John Mackay, recalls that Dulles, "in view of his known caliber and interests," was made chairman of a subcommittee which was asked to deal with the question of Christianity and war. In the discussions of the section as a whole, "Dulles played a very important part."[14]

Dulles was immediately struck by the atmosphere of brotherly love— "irrespective of national or racial differences"—that governed the pro-

---

[11] Ibid., 2. See also John Mackay, interview conducted by Philip A. Crowl, 1965.

[12] Roswell Barnes, interview conducted by Philip A. Crowl, 1964, 24.

[13] JFD, "As Seen by a Layman," *Religion in Life* 7 (Winter 1938): 36.

[14] Mackay, interview, 4.

ceedings. This was indeed far different from the "distrustful atmosphere of national competition" that made agreement impossible at Paris.[15] The environment at Oxford, Dulles concluded, was much more conducive to solving the pressing international problems of the day.

As Dulles later tried to explain the significance of what he called his "great enlightenment" at Oxford, he came to the realization that the whole of the last thirty years of his work to secure international peace represented an "experience with futility."[16] Dulles often reiterated that the major cause of conference failures in the past was the "hatreds and prejudice" that "impaired clear thinking." Conference after conference broke down because both sides "closed their minds to facts which did not support a consideration of self-interest; because hypocrisy and self-righteousness destroyed the very basis for mutual understanding."[17]

The spirit at Oxford was entirely different and this difference profoundly affected Dulles. He was very much impressed by the conception of the church as a community that transcended the boundaries of any particular nation. Largely due to the influence of his father's socially progressive outlook, Dulles grew up believing that the church should always strive to project that conception of itself to the world. However, shortly before Oxford, Dulles began to feel that the church was altogether too lax in its attempt to fulfill this responsibility. In his address to the conference, entitled "The Problem of Peace in a Dynamic World," Dulles—true to his belief in the necessity of adhering to what Paul Tillich has called the "Protestant principle"[18]—asserted that the main obstacles to peace were created by pride and selfishness. These traits could only be offset

by replacing them [with] some sentiment more dominant and gripping and

---

[15]JFD, "Faith of Our Fathers," in *The Spiritual Legacy*, 6.

[16]JFD, "The Churches and World Order," 23-24.

[17]*Federal Council Bulletin* 24 (January 1941): 6.

[18]According to Tillich, the Protestant principle "is the theological expression of the true relation between the unconditional and the conditioned or, religiously speaking, between God and man. . . . It is the guardian against the attempts of the finite and conditioned to usurp the place of the unconditional in thinking and acting" (see Paul Tillich, *The Protestant Era*, abr. ed. [Chicago: The University of Chicago Press, Phoenix Books, 1957] 163). This Protestant principle is also referred to as the "prophetic protest" of Protestantism (see ibid., 230).

which would contain in it the elements of universality as against partic-
ularity. . . . What of the democratic nations? What of the so-called Christian nations? They boast of high ideals, but have they the spiritual fire
with which to drive out petty instincts which bind them to a system which
spells their doom[?]][19]

The fact that, at Oxford, the discussions were built upon something
deeper and more enduring than national self-interest gave Dulles a renewed hope in the possibility of "creating an international ethos which
would be essential as a foundation for any lasting political structure."[20]
Dulles left Oxford with the distinct impression that the only hope for driving out the "petty instincts" lay with the churches. The Oxford experience made Dulles realize how he could put his belief in the prophetic
nature of Protestantism to work in the international arena. Such an understanding could contribute to successfully overcoming the temptation
to self-righteousness so evident among the nations of the world. Opening an address in 1939 before the United Christian Convention, he defined the problem to which the church needed to direct its attention.

For upwards of thirty years I have devoted myself to international problems. Throughout most of this time I have believed that the attainment
of a peaceful world was exclusively a political problem. As I have studied
more deeply I have come to realize that this is not the case. Of course
political devices are indispensible [sic]. But such devices will not be
adopted or, if adopted, will not work so long as millions of people look
upon State, rather than God, as their supreme ideal.[21]

The influence of the Oxford Conference upon Dulles is undeniable;
the evidence for it is extensive.[22] Oxford obviously brought Dulles to a

---

[19]JFD, "The Problem of Peace in a Dynamic World," *Religion in Life* 6 (Spring 1937):
207.

[20]Cavert, interview, 5.

[21]JFD, "The Churches' Contribution toward a Warless World," *Religion in Life* 9
(Winter 1940): 31. Further discussion relating to Dulles's thoughts on the deification of
the state is found in ch. 5.

[22]Dulles discusses the influence of the conference upon him in each of the following
addresses: "As Seen by a Layman"; "The Churches' Contribution"; "The Churches and
World Order"; and "Faith of Our Fathers." See also *Federal Council Bulletin* 24 (January

renewed appreciation of his past, and this caused him to reevaluate his perspective in international affairs. As the theologian Bennett expressed it, after Oxford Dulles "went back to his heritage to a certain extent, and there was a certain continuity."[23] More than a decade later, Dulles recounted the Oxford experience for the congregation in the Watertown church where he had been baptized as a child. He told his listeners that it was "then [at Oxford] I began to understand the profound significance of the spiritual values that my mother and father had taught."[24] In other words, Oxford taught Dulles the importance of trying to transform his inherited spiritual values into practical contributions in the political sphere.

The churches, Dulles later wrote, could see the broad picture because "in the eyes of God, all men are equal, and their welfare is of equal moment." "Only through an approach of such universality" can there be "any promise of a solution." Thus Dulles dedicated himself, for a time, to work with the churches so "that the spirit of Oxford should not lie down but be projected through the membership—particularly the lay membership" of all the churches.[25]

Increasing Involvement
in the Federal Council

In an editorial published in the January 1940 edition of the *Federal Council Bulletin*, the question of America's role in the future peace was

---

1941): 6. Both Lillias Dulles Hinshaw and Avery Dulles, his daughter and son, emphasize the impact of Oxford upon his life. See their respective interviews in the Oral History Collection. E. Raymond Platig, in his dissertation, goes so far as to view Dulles's involvement with the churches after Oxford as the result of a recent "conversion" to Christianity. According to Platig, this conversion was a natural outgrowth of Dulles's previous commitment to a utilitarian ethic. Dulles became a professing Christian, writes Platig, because after Oxford he came to feel that "Christianity was socially useful" (see E. Raymond Platig, "John Foster Dulles: A Study of His Political and Moral Thought Prior to 1953 with Special Emphasis on International Relations" [dissertation, University of Chicago, 1957] 130). Platig's terminology is insufficient; it dismisses the sincerity of Dulles's previous religious attachments.

[23]John C. Bennett, interview, 22.

[24]JFD, "Faith of Our Fathers," 6.

[25]JFD, "As Seen by a Layman," 18-19, 22. See also "The Churches' Role," 8: "I am anxious that the remainder of my life shall more effectively serve the cause of international peace than has the past. Therefore, I have increasingly sought the fellowship of Christians, believing that practical results can best be achieved by the cooperation of those who possess the spiritual qualities Christ taught."

raised. "We want America to stay out of the war," wrote the editor, "we cannot be content that America should stay out of the peace." The editorial continued, commenting very affirmatively on "the contribution which is being made to Christian thinking along this line by John Foster Dulles . . . one of America's foremost students of international affairs."[26]

Dulles's initial involvement with the churches in this regard was minimal. However, as time passed his participation became increasingly extensive. In August 1939 he served as a delegate in the International Conference of Lay Experts and Ecumenical Leaders convened by the Provisional Committee of the World Council of Churches in Geneva. He impressed many of those present as he debated Sir Alfred Zimmern on the implications of the Versailles Peace Treaty for what happened in Germany, particularly the rise of Hitler. Because of his participation in Geneva, Dulles's attention to the role of the churches in the crisis between the nations was greatly deepened. The potential influence of an educated world Christian community for cultivating peace was beginning to become clear in his mind. He wanted to make use of the potential for bringing about the kind of peace he envisioned.

The delegates of the Geneva Conference recommended that the churches, on a worldwide basis, study the peace and war problems with a view toward taking a responsible Christian position on the perplexing problems raised by the war. American concerns for implementing this recommendation led to the National Study Conference on the Churches and the International Situation, which was held on 27-29 February 1940, in Philadelphia. The conference was sponsored by the Federal Council's Department of International Justice and Goodwill in collaboration with the Foreign Missions Conference of North America; 285 delegates from across the country attended it. Dulles delivered the keynote address.[27]

As a direct outgrowth of his participation in the conference at Philadelphia, Dulles was asked by the Department of International Justice and Goodwill to serve as chairman of a fifteen-man Commission on the American Churches and the Peace and War Problem. It was one of two study committees working on problems of this sort for the Federal Council. The

---

[26]*Federal Council Bulletin* 23 (January 1940): 2. The *Federal Council Bulletin* is the monthly voice of the Federal Council of Churches of Christ in America.

[27]JFD, "The United States and the World of Nations," 27 February 1940, DP, Box 19.

other committee, composed of seventy members, was jointly chaired by
Professor John C. Bennett, of the Pacific School of Religion, and Edwin
E. Aubrey, of the Divinity School at the University of Chicago.

Dulles's committee studied memoranda on the postwar situation ex-
changed by church groups from all over the world through the office of
the Provisional Committee of the World Council of Churches in Geneva.
The committee's task was to analyze the documents and present regular
reports to the Federal Council. In this way, the leaders in the American
church hoped that the Christian forces in the country might be put in a
position to make an educated contribution to the establishment of a world
order built on enduring peace.

On the evening of 4 October 1940, Dr. Walter W. Van Kirk, the secretary of the Department of International Justice and Goodwill, hosted a
dinner meeting. Dulles was asked by those present to draft a statement
that would serve both to emphasize and to preserve the essential unity
of the churches in the face of divisive issues. An earlier attempt in June
to draft a common statement to embody the views of both pacifists and
just-war advocates, as well as American Christians and Christians of other
countries, failed to win support due largely to the criticism of Dulles.

The rejected statement, entitled "A Statement on the Present Opportunity and Duty of Christians," was drafted principally by Van Kirk
and Dr. William Adams Brown of Union Theological Seminary for submission to the Federal Council's Executive Committee. In the main,
Dulles's criticism of the document centered around his view that the
statement presented the Allies uncritically, as if they represented the
completely moral side of the conflict, and described the Axis powers as
evil personified. He elaborated this view in a personal letter to Van Kirk.

> I am struck by the fact that history shows that in every so-called "Chris-
> tian" country, in time of war or international stress, the church has uni-
> formally [sic] become the hand-maiden of national politics. The church
> leaders then see the moral issue as identical with the national issue and
> call upon church members as a matter of religious duty to support its [sic]
> own national leaders as being "right." I think one of the great weak-
> nesses of the church is that Christians are thus split by their national in-
> terests into opposing and hostile groups, hating each other, and that this
> is destructive of unity and power in the church. I greatly hoped that in
> the present crisis the Christian church in this country could avoid con-
> centrating upon the admitted evils elsewhere, slurring over the admitted

evils at home and thereby becoming, in my judgment, hypocritical and unChristian.[28]

Two weeks to the day after Dulles was asked to draft the proposed unity statement, on 18 October, he circulated for comment and criticism a draft that came to be entitled "The American Churches and the International Situation."[29] The statement urged Christians to rise above the hatreds of war in order to maintain fellowship with one another on a worldwide basis. Chief among the thoughts presented in the statement was the plea that Christians recognize the need for repentance, humility, avoidance of hatred and hypocrisy, and the spiritual supremacy of God rather than the state.[30] Dulles presented the statement to the 600 delegates of the biennial meeting of the Federal Council held at the Hotel Dennis on 10-13 December in Atlantic City. The program of the meeting centered around the relation of the churches to the international situation.

Dulles's role in Atlantic City was particularly influential. In addition to his work on the statement, Dulles was directly involved in leading discussion as the chairman of the major seminar dealing with the churches and international affairs. His hard work was well rewarded. The biennial meeting officially adopted Dulles's statement, "characterized by many church leaders . . . as one of the most significant pronouncements of recent years,"[31] and then proceeded to distribute it widely to the heads of the various denominations, city and state councils of churches, ministerial associations across the country, officers of the World Council of Churches, and the National Christian Councils of China, Japan, India, and elsewhere.

---

[28]JFD to W. W. Van Kirk, 13 June 1940, DP, Box 19.

[29]This statement is not to be confused with another by the same title that was released on 22 January 1940 over the signatures of several churchmen including Dulles. See n. 64 in ch. 5 for further information regarding this other statement.

[30]For further information, see *Federal Council Bulletin* 24 (January 1941); *Biennial Report of the Federal Council of the Churches of Christ in America* (hereafter referred to as *Biennial Report*), (1940); and "Policy during the War Urged on Churches," *New York Times,* 11 December 1940.

[31]*Federal Council Bulletin* 23 (January 1940): 2.

One of the most important actions to emerge from Atlantic City was one of the least heralded at the time. The Executive Committee decided to appoint a commission to be known as the Commission to Study the Bases of a Just and Durable Peace.[32] As described in the minutes of the committee, this commission was to be broadly representative of the communions holding membership in the Federal Council.[33] Because it was appointed by the Federal Council as a special commission, it was not organically related to any one department of the Council and its Committee of Direction reported directly to the Executive Committee. The directives of the commission were outlined as follows:

> First, to clarify the mind of our churches regarding the moral, political and economic foundations of an enduring peace; second, to prepare the people of our churches and of our nation for assuming their appropriate responsibility for the establishment of such a peace; third, to maintain contacts with the Study Department of the World Council of Churches (now in process of formation); fourth, to consider the feasibility of assembling as soon as practicable after the armistice has been declared in any of the wars now being waged, for the purpose of mobilizing the support of all lands in the making of a peace consonant with Christian principles.[34]

Dulles was the natural selection for chairman of the commission. By this time, he was the principle layman associated with the Federal Council.[35] His impressive work as chairman of the Commission on the American Churches and the Peace and War Problem had culminated in the important contributions in Atlantic City. He had gained support among

---

[32]The phrase, "a just and durable peace," was Dulles's. On 16 November 1943, upon request of the commission, a vote was taken to change the name to read simply "Commission on a Just and Durable Peace" (*Annual Report of the Federal Council of the Churches of Christ in America* [1943] 153. Hereafter referred to as *Annual Report*).

[33]Representatives from each of the following bodies were "invited to become members of the commission: the International Council of Religious Education, the Foreign Missions Conference of North America, the Home Mission Councils, the National Council of Church Women and the United Stewardship Council, the Church Peace Union and the World Alliance for International Friendship through the Churches" (*Biennial Report* [1940] 214).

[34]*Annual Report* (1941) 94.

[35]Richard Fagley, interview conducted by Richard D. Challener, 1964, 27.

leaders of both the interventionist and noninterventionist factions of the church. Therefore, his leadership could provide the council with the unified front it needed in order to make a significant contribution to the attainment of a just and durable peace.

4

The Commission
on a Just
and Durable Peace

John Foster Dulles's Calvinist heritage emphasized that a Christian should serve others. In Dulles's mind the best path to meaningful service at this time in history involved attempting to make an important contribution to the reformation of the machinery of international relations. Through the plan to appoint a commission to study the peace issue, the Federal Council of Churches had suggested that the churches should be educated regarding the potential components of international order after the war. Yet Dulles was not satisfied with merely being knowledgeable about the shape of world order in years to come. For this reason, he hesitated before actually accepting the assignment as chairman of the newly formed commission. He was concerned about whether or not the work of the commission would simply be that of a study group; he wanted it to make an impact on actual policy decisions by educating public opinion on important issues. He wanted a commission that would be dedicated to

implementing the liberal Christian version of world order, one that reminded nations of their finite status while concentrating upon fulfilling the
social-gospel imperatives concerned with the needs of the less fortunate.
In his view, the commission should direct its energies toward the implementation of the Protestant principle of prophetic protest; that is, he felt
the commission should bring a judgment upon the present situation, which
evidenced the pride and self-righteousness of human institutions.

Approximately one month after the Federal Council's announcement
of the commission's formation, Dulles accepted the chairmanship. Obviously, he was satisfied that the commission could make a significant
contribution toward the shaping of public opinion as it pertained to world
order after the war. Dulles informed his good friend Lionel Curtis of Oxford, England of his decision to work with the commission. The phrasing
of the letter is indicative of Dulles's feelings about the work.

> I have just agreed to become the Chairman of a Committee being orga-
> nized by the Federal Council of Churches to study the basis for durable
> peace. This now seems a long way off. But some day it will come and I
> am fearful that this country will be the greatest obstacle in the way of
> then doing what ought to be done. On this account *I am anxious* to start
> some work of education which will permit the church influence to be mo-
> bilized effectively when the moment comes (emphasis added). [1]

In a more public expression of his reasons for accepting the position,
Dulles stated,

> I have assumed this responsibility firstly, because I believe it is imper-
> ative that our nation should become generally conscious of the underly-
> ing moral and social forces which are at work and that we should come
> into harmony with them; secondly, because I believe that Christians,
> above all others, should be able to bring about this result. [2]

The first of these reasons for involvement belies the Presbyterian presupposition regarding the moral law's demand upon societies to conform
to the general interests of humanity. The second emphasizes the Presbyterian social-gospel confidence that Christians can and should help to

---

[1] JFD to Lionel Curtis, 28 February 1941, DP, Box 20.

[2] JFD, "Christianity in This Hour," 21 April 1941, 19, DP, Box 20. This speech was
delivered before a meeting of the Federation of Churches and Council of Church Women,
held at Rochester, New York.

bring the demands of the moral law into being. In an attempt to guarantee "this result," the commission embarked on a campaign to educate the Christian public concerning the issues. Publication and distribution played a key role in this process.

The Printed Words

Foster Dulles's work as chairman of the commission has been described by those who worked with him as "masterly" and "effective," one of "tremendous zeal and concern."[3] He was an extremely diligent worker. "It wasn't easy to be a staff worker with him," Roswell Barnes recounted, "because he drove himself relentlessly."[4] Dulles's extraordinary ability as an organizer, his puritanical zeal, and his seemingly endless vitality made him a tremendous leader but a very difficult associate. On several occasions, he hid out with four or five members of the commission at his home on Long Island and spent the entire day discussing issues that he or someone else formulated. At other times, Dulles conducted business more routinely by calling a meeting of the commission's Committee of Direction, which consisted of between twenty and twenty-five members.[5]

His method of working with this smaller committee was to use a yellow legal pad. He was never without it. Before most every meeting of the committee, Dulles scribbled a rough draft of some pronouncement he felt the commission should issue. Nearly every one of the countless documents produced by the commission over the years originated on his yellow pad. Once the Committee of Direction was satisfied with a proposed statement, it was passed on to the remaining seventy members of the commission for comment and criticism.[6]

---

[3]Richard Fagley, interview, 35; and John C. Bennett, interview, 4. Roswell Barnes, interview conducted by Philip A. Crowl, 11.

[4]Barnes, interview, 15.

[5]The Committee of Direction included such prestigious gentlemen as Dr. E. E. Aubrey of the University of Chicago Divinity School, Dr. John C. Bennett, and Dr. William E. Hocking of Harvard.

[6]The commission membership included Reinhold Niebuhr, John McNeill, Charles Clayton Morrison, John R. Mott, and Harry Emerson Fosdick. Pruessen mistakenly stated that the commission eventually had "several hundred members." In actuality, its membership never exceeded one hundred. He is evidently confusing participants at National Study Conferences with actual members of the commission.

In order to "clarify the mind" of the churches "regarding the moral, political and economic foundations of an enduring peace," and to "prepare the people" of the churches and nation "for assuming their appropriate responsibility for the establishment of such a peace," the commission viewed the publication of important educational materials as a primary part of its work.[7] The first such publication was a handbook entitled "A Just and Durable Peace." It contained a summary of major pronouncements made by religious bodies in recent years dealing with the issue of the peace.[8] The booklet also included a summary of secular proposals dealing with the prospect of a new world organization together with a syllabus of discussion questions. Over 450,000 copies were distributed.

The concerns of Dulles, and thus the commission, emerge clearly through retracing its publication record. Concern for needed reform in the international economic realm was first revealed by the commission in May 1941. At the time the "Memorandum" was issued, Dulles said,

> We do not believe that effective action is ever taken spasmodically. The Christians in this country will not exert an effective influence at critical moments unless through prior education and study they have background which enables them to appraise the significance and importance of some particular course of action.[9]

Developments in the secular arena often spurred some response on the part of the commission. The historic first meeting between President Roosevelt and Prime Minister Winston Churchill aboard the cruiser *Augusta* at Placentia Bay, Newfoundland provided the commission with its first such opportunity. Together, the American president and the British prime minister issued a vague joint declaration calling "for a better future world." About one month after the famous meeting on the battleship, the commission published Dulles's personal analysis of the Roosevelt-Churchill eight-point declaration (subsequently named the Atlantic Charter),

---

[7]*Annual Report* (1941) 94.

[8]Included was an accounting of the following: The Federal Council Biennial Meeting of 1940, the American Council of the World Alliance for International Friendship, the National Study Conference in Philadelphia, the Malvern Conference (7-10 January 1941) held in England under the auspices of the International Christian Fellowship and presided over by the archbishop of York, the Oxford Conference, and the Madras Conference.

[9]*Federal Council Bulletin* 24 (June 1941): 9.

which carried the title "Long Range Peace Objectives." It was warmly recommended to the churches for study and was accompanied by a guide containing questions raised by members of the commission concerning issues of the Atlantic Charter: economic sanctions, national sovereignty, and the future of a world organization.

The next major document to emerge from the Dulles Commission was initiated by a resolution from the Greater New York Federation of Churches dated 28 March 1941. Submitted to the Federal Council's Executive Committee, and referred to the commission, the resolution requested that a study be made by "the ablest possible individuals" that would set forth the "basic principles which the consensus of Christendom would feel should be the foundation of any peace emerging from this war." The principles, it read, should "be made as succinct as possible" and followed by the concerted effort "to make these principles, once established, familiar to the whole Christian community in the United States."[10] A tall order, the resulting statement took months to prepare. Formulating principles of this kind meant answering several prerequisite theological questions: "What are the implications of what Jesus said for finding the meaning of history?" "Does God control history?" "How and when does he intervene?"

Dulles felt very strongly that there was something definitive in the life and teaching of Christ to be applied to the practical affairs of humankind. On this basis, Dulles felt driven to make the transcendence of God and his moral law relevant to society as a whole. For Dulles, the only good theology was one that, through practical application, made a difference in the quality of life for humankind. He wanted the commission to make sense of belief in God and in his moral law so that its pertinence to peace questions could be clearly understood by all. Dulles and the rest of the commission set themselves to the completion of this task. The final product is a good example of Dulles's personal public theology.[11]

---

[10]*Annual Report* (1941) 122.

[11]On the general question of whether the whole of the commission's work accurately represented Dulles's own thinking, Cavert said, "I would hazard the guess that they [commission statements] weren't very far from expressing the main trend of Dulles's own thinking. . . . He really looked to some of the other people—the more theologically trained people—to formulate what you might call the specifically religious approach, but he was always watching not to let them get sentimental or superidealistic. He wanted them to have their feet on the ground" (Samuel McCrea Cavert, interview, 18-19).

The "Statement of Guiding Principles," issued in late February of 1942, was adopted by the Cleveland biennial meeting of the Federal Council in December.[12] The preamble to the "Guiding Principles" explains the logic behind their formulation.

> From [their] faith Christians derive the ethical principles upon which world order must be based. These principles, however seem to us to be among those which men of goodwill everywhere may be expected to recognize as part of the moral law. In this we rejoice. For peace will require the cooperation of men of all nations, races and creeds. We have therefore first set out (points 1 to 9) those guiding principles which, it seems to us, Christians and non-Christians alike can accept. We believe that a special responsibility rests upon the people of the United States. We accordingly (point 10) express our thoughts in that regard. Above all, we are impressed by the supreme responsibility which rests upon Christians. Moral law may point the way to peace, but Christ, we believe, showed that way with greatest clarity. We therefore, in conclusion (points 11 and 12) address ourselves to Christians.[13]

The guiding principles themselves were summarized in the *Federal Council Bulletin*. They clearly express the beliefs of the Reformed theological tradition.

> Moral law undergirds our world; disregard of the moral law brings affliction; revenge and retaliation bring no relief; we must find a way to bring into ordered harmony the interdependent life of the nations; this requires that economic resources be looked upon as a trust to promote the general welfare; also, because the world is living, and, therefore, changing, there must be ways of effecting peaceful change; colonial governments, too, must be administered in the interests of the colonial peoples; military establishments should be internationally controlled; there must

---

[12]This is contrary to Mulder's statement that the principles were issued for the first time with the six pillars in 1943 (John Mulder, "The Moral World of John Foster Dulles," *Journal of Presbyterian History* 49 [Summer 1971]: 170). The *Christian Century* commented on the "Guiding Principles" statement in the following manner: "We hope most of all that the substance and significance of this document may be borne in on those who head the government of the United States, for it speaks a word which they can ignore only at the nation's peril" ("The Churches and the Peace," *Christian Century* 59 [18 March 1942]: 342).

[13]*Biennial Report* (1942) 42.

be personal freedoms and liberties, without discrimination against nation, race or class; the power of the United States carries with it a special responsibility which we have neglected; a supreme responsibility rests upon the church of Christ; Christians should, as citizens, seek to translate their beliefs into realities; they must seek that the Kingdom of the world become the Kingdom of Christ.[14]

In the Executive Committee meeting of the Federal Council of 23 January 1943, Dulles stated that guiding principles four through nine should be given a new form, "changed from a 'credo' to policies which people can support."[15] Before the next Executive Committee meeting, 16 March, Dulles formulated what was originally titled "A Just and Durable Peace: Statement of Political Propositions." The title that became famous along with the statement was "The Six Pillars of Peace." Dulles's pillars gained rapid approval from his Committee of Direction, and he sent the statement to the other members of the commission along with a letter dated 12 March, which stated in part,

In the statement we describe six "pillars of peace" that are needed to support a just and durable world order and to the establishment of which this nation ought now to be committed. We have stated our propositions in simple terms which can effectively unite all those who favor organized international collaboration.[16]

On 16 March, the Executive Committee gave "hearty approval" to the six pillars and adopted the statement on behalf of the Federal Council.[17]

The six pillars comprised certain broad political conclusions that emerged out of the guiding principles. Dulles's plan, as he described it to President Roosevelt in a meeting with him one week after the release of

---

[14]The study "Conference on the Bases of Peace," *Federal Council Bulletin* 25 (April 1942): 9.

[15]*Annual Report* (1943) 97.

[16]Letter, JFD to all members of the commission, 12 March 1943, DP, Box 22.

[17]*Annual Report* (1943) 108. Richard Gould-Adams, on p. 42 in his *The Time of Power: A Reappraisal of John Foster Dulles* (New York: Appleton-Century-Crofts, 1962) incorrectly dates the six pillars as being issued in 1941 as a response to the Atlantic Charter. Gould-Adams is thinking of the "Long Range Peace Objectives." The six pillars were not written as a response to the Atlantic Charter. They appeared close to one and a half years after that document.

the statement, was to use church organizations to get the six points fully discussed by Christian laymen in the presence of their ministers.[18] Yet he emphasized in another context, "We do not pretend to speak with divine sanction; nor is there anything exclusively Christian about our proposals. We do not want them preached from our pulpits."[19]

The primary objective of the statement was "to provide thinking and action along realistic lines" by "outlining six areas within which national interdependence is demonstrated, and where, accordingly, international collaboration needs to be organized."[20] The substance of the six pillars called for continuing Allied collaboration after the war, and was to include as soon as possible the neutral and enemy nations; provision for international economic agreements; treaty structures that would be adaptable to changing conditions; assurances of autonomy for subject peoples; control of military establishments; and recognition "in principle" of the right to religious and intellectual liberty for peoples everywhere.[21]

Dulles's hope was that these six principles would force recognition that, in at least these six areas, the world had become factually interdependent and had demonstrated the need for political mechanisms that would insure cooperative action. In the cover letter accompanying the first mailing of the statement to all commission members, Dulles wrote that the "nation has now entered upon the critical period where public opinion must be crystallized in favor of organized international collaboration."[22] His largest fear was that the United States would once again walk to the trough of international cooperation but, at the last minute, refuse to drink. Therefore, he poured all of his energies during the next few years into attempting to sway public opinion toward the concept of American participation in some form of world organization.

---

[18]Memorandum written by JFD recording the events of his meeting with Roosevelt, 26 March 1943, DP, Box 22.

[19]"Dulles's Remarks," delivered at a luncheon of leading civic figures in New York City sponsored by John D. Rockefeller, 18 March 1943, 2, DP, Box 22.

[20]JFD, "Six Pillars of Peace," *Christianity and Crisis* 3 (31 May 1943): 5.

[21]When Roosevelt read the "in principle" part of the six pillars, he quipped that he could see that the Dulles group had given the statement a great deal of thought. (Memorandum, 26 March 1943, DP, Box 22.)

[22]Letter, JFD to the commission membership, 12 March 1943, DP, Box 22.

The "Six Pillars of Peace" was very widely distributed. As *Christianity and Crisis* reported, its proposals were "greeted by favorable editorial comments not only in this country but abroad." The London *Times* printed the statement on the front page with the commentary,

> They [the six pillars] are admirably comprehensive; they cover the economic as well as the political field; and, while avoiding all unnecessary detail, they constitute a definite programme, the adoption of which would be an immense step forward.[23]

Comment in the New York *Herald Tribune* was fairly representative of the rest of the American press opinion.

> These propositions are broad in concept; nevertheless they are definite enough, as the Commission says, "to force the initial and vital decision on the direction in which the nation will move." Can the American people seriously decide for less than the minimum ends as the Commission poses them[?][24]

Not only was the press coverage itself excellent, but prestigious figures in government like Sumner Welles, Thomas Dewey, and Senator Joseph Ball each heartily endorsed the six pillars by writing articles about them that were then published in many leading periodicals.[25]

A study guide of more than seventy pages, published by the commission in May, offered commentary on each of the six pillars. Advance orders from denominations alone totaled eighteen thousand copies. The guide was sent to every Protestant chaplain at home and abroad. Fourteen British church leaders, including the archbishops of Canterbury and York and the moderator of the Church of Scotland, accepted it as embodying the aims of British churchmen and issued "A Christian Basis for Reconstruction" that voiced their agreement. Once the six pillars made their way to Europe, they were microfilmed and flown to China.[26]

---

[23]Quoted in *Christianity and Crisis* 3 (17 May 1943): 3.

[24]Ibid.

[25]See, for example, *Christianity and Crisis* 3 (31 May 1943): 5-6; ibid. (28 June 1943): 6-8; and ibid. (12 July 1943): 6-7.

[26]JFD, "The Beginning of a World Order," 22 April 1945, DP, Box 27.

Dulles viewed the six pillars as one of the most constructive contributions the churches made to the formation of a new world order. He believed that the statement was one of those important factors that brought "the thinking of the nations into harmony" and helped to make possible both the signing of the United Nations Charter and its ratification by the Senate.[27] Though Dulles always tended to exaggerate the contribution of the six pillars to world organization, the overall positive effect the statement had should not be underestimated.

The real contribution of the document, and the reason it was described by Niebuhr as one of those "increasingly realistic" statements made by the commission,[28] lay in its ability to provide a middle road for divergent viewpoints. In an editorial published in *Christianity and Crisis,* Henry P. Van Dusen explained how this aspect of the statement was valuable.

> But its greater importance lies in the fact that, in our judgment, it furnishes the briefest, clearest and soundest agenda for post-war order which has yet been forthcoming from any source, within or outside the churches. . . . Thus it stakes a middle course between the two main schools of thought on the organization of peace—those who espouse a single over-all instrument of world order and those who favor a policy of "muddling through" by piecemeal solutions of separate problems. . . . The Commission's political propositions offer median ground with some hope of winning adherences from both parties.[29]

Though most reaction to the six pillars was extremely favorable, criticism did come from both secular and religious sources. From the secular side, Mortimer Adler perceived Dulles expressing too pessimistic a picture for his personal liking. Even though Dulles "included the notion of world government," writes Adler, it "is regarded as a remote objective to be approached through stages of progressively mitigated nationalism." Adler preferred an approach to world order like the one outlined in

---

[27]Ibid.

[28]Reinhold Niebuhr, "American Power and World Responsibility," *Christianity and Crisis* 3 (5 April 1943): 4.

[29]Henry P. Van Dusen, "The Six Pillars of Peace," *Christianity and Crisis* 3 (22 March 1943): 1.

Michael Straight's *Make This the Last War,*[30] which calls for full physical and economic unity of the world. Straight, he writes, "does not regard nationalism in all its forms as an insuperable obstacle to the institution of world government." Adler held what for Dulles was an unrealistic opinion, that world federation was not merely possible, but highly probable and could be attained within the twentieth century.[31]

Criticism from the religious side was voiced mostly by strident, and therefore usually disregarded, fundamentalists. Carl McIntire, the president of the fundamentalist American Council of Christian Churches, placed Dulles and his commission solidly in the pacifist camp and analyzed the statement from that perspective.

> Underlying these political propositions is the basic pacifist presupposition that all men are brothers and that such an ideal as suggested here could be practically worked out. . . .
> It has underestimated the nature of man and the motives of his heart.
> . . .
> All this brings out into the open the real communistic nature of the controlled world order desired. . . . In these six pillars where is the idea of punishment and retribution[?][32]

Where Adler felt Dulles's statement did not go far enough, McIntire felt the six pillars went too far. In reality, the statement also stood between these two positions. For these particular gentlemen, that was the weakness of the statement; for most other people, that constituted its greatest strength.

Expenses for the commission in 1943 were $54,675.10.[33] In no other year did the commission spend over $23,000; this expenditure is indicative of the importance placed on the "Six Pillars of Peace." A large portion of money was spent in publicizing and distributing the statement. There is further indication of the statement's importance: nearly every

---

[30](New York: Harcourt, Brace and Company, 1943).

[31]Mortimer J. Adler, *How to Think about War and Peace* (New York: Simon and Schuster, 1944) 16-17.

[32]Carl McIntire, *Twentieth Century Reformation* (Collingswood NJ: Christian Beacon Press, 1946) 121, 129, and 132.

[33]*Annual Report* (1943) 167.

statement issued afterwards by the commission, through the time of the signing of the United Nations Charter in the fall of 1945, is in some way related to the six-pillars statement.

Shortly after the statement was distributed, the commission began to publish a four-page, tabloid-sized paper, *Post War World,* intended to monitor developments in the proposed world organization and analyze them in light of the six pillars. Along with this small journal, the commission began to distribute statements by Dulles and other churchmen written as appraisals of the developing international situation as seen through these expressed principles. The first of these was Dulles's "Analysis of the Moscow Declarations." Later, the commission issued a statement over the signatures of a committee of churchmen dealing with a draft of the future peace settlements in Europe and Asia—particularly with special reference to Germany and Japan—that would be consistent with the six pillars. [34]

In January 1944, the commission published two more documents rounding out its emphasis on the six pillars. The first of those was a statement written by Dulles as a further explication of the six pillars entitled "World Organization—Curative and Creative: A Statement to Our Public Leaders and Our People." [35] The second document, entitled "A Guidebook for Action," was a manual of suggestions for the local church designed to help local church memberships appropriate the six pillars in an active sense.

The Public Acts

The printed words published by the commission were one way that it attempted to fulfill the directives established for it by the Executive Committee of the Federal Council. A second method the commission uti-

---

[34]John C. Bennett and Reinhold Niebuhr held the premier positions on this committee. The statement can be found in *Christianity and Crisis* 4 (26 June 1944): 6.

[35]Richard Fagley observed the following: "He really enjoyed looking forward to setting goals which were grounded in real possibilities, but pointed towards something more creative and curative. In fact, these were two of his favorite words—curative and creative—something that was healing and something that was forward looking, dynamic, constructive. These were two words we always associated with him" (Fagley, interview, 11).

lized to fulfill its charge involved the performance of particular actions in the public arena in order to attract more immediately the attention of both the media and the American people to its goals. These public acts usually involved the creation of a forum through which people would be drawn together to discuss and analyze the prospect of a new world order.

In a small way, this was achieved through setting aside special days for reflection upon, or prayer for, world order. An example of the former would be "World Order Day," 12 November 1944; on that particular Sunday, sermons on international reconstruction were preached from thousands of pulpits.[36] As an example of the latter, Dulles's group was influential in securing the action of Bishop Oxnam, president of the Federal Council, in calling for Sunday, 22 April 1945, and Wednesday, 25 April 1945, to be set aside "as occasions for special intercession" for the San Francisco United Nations Conference. A prayer specially written for the occasion was signed by moderators and presidents of thirty-four communions.

> Let us confess that we have been concerned too much with our own affairs, at times indifferent to the needs of others and unready to make sacrifices to prevent war and insure peace.[37]

The commission used a second and, in terms of practical results, more effective approach in order to keep the issue of America's role in the future world order before the church membership. It sponsored three study conferences centering upon particular aspects of the proposed peace. Of these, two were held for national church leaders and one was convened for international church leaders.

The first of these meetings, the "National Study Conference on the Churches and a Just and Durable Peace," was held in Delaware, Ohio at Ohio Wesleyan University on 3-5 March 1942. The conference was di-

---

[36]The Department of International Justice and Goodwill issued a six-page folder entitled "The Churches and World Order," which recommended the day "be observed in a spirit of utter obedience to Jesus Christ and with the one thought of rededicating our lives and our treasure to the winning of a peace universal in scope and redemptive in purpose" (*Biennial Report* [1940] 92).

[37]*Annual Report* (1945) 130-32. Dulles, in conjunction with the prayer Sunday, spoke before approximately eleven thousand people gathered in Oakland under the sponsorship of the Oakland Council of Churches.

vided into four sections for study: the (1) political, (2) economic, and (3) social aspects of a just and durable peace, and (4) the relation of the churches to a just and durable peace.[38] Three hundred seventy-seven delegates representing twenty-seven denominations assembled for the conference. The first official action of the conference was to give "general endorsement" to the recently issued "Guiding Principles" formulated by the Dulles Commission.

By almost any measure, the comments evaluating the success of this first study conference were, on the whole, very favorable. *Christianity and Crisis* concluded that "the Delaware assembly advanced farther and to more significant conclusions than any of them [the conference planners] had dared to hope."[39] Comment in the rival liberal Protestant journal, the *Christian Century,* credited Delaware as part of the reason that the church as it faced World War II was much more realistic than it was during World War I.[40] Overall, Dulles was pleased with the results of the conference. Even though Dulles was a firm believer in the necessity and importance of these meetings, he was, at the same time, a "little leery" of them. He was always afraid that there was too much of a tendency to push through "a whole lot of statements . . . by concerned churchmen [that] are not gone over as carefully as those specially prepared statements" of the commission.[41]

Conceivably, Dulles's cautious approach to conference statements emerged from his recent disappointment with the national conference, to which he was an invited guest and keynote speaker sponsored by the Commission on World Peace of the Methodist Church. The conference was a series of lectures and seminars dealing with the spiritual basis of democracy and treating discussion questions such as race, economics,

---

[38]See Francis J. McConnell et al., *A Basis for the Peace to Come,* Merrick-McDowell Lecture Series (New York: Abingdon-Cokesbury Press, 1942). This collection of the Merrick-McDowell Lectures, a series of lectures held annually at Ohio Wesleyan University, constitutes a collection of the major addresses delivered during this conference. Dulles's keynote address, "Toward World Order," is found on 31-57.

[39]*Christianity and Crisis* 2 (6 April 1942): 1.

[40]*Christian Century* 59 (18 March 1942): 342-43. See also Paul Hutchinson, "Proposed Bases for a Lasting Peace," ibid., 360-62. The complete text of the "Message" from the Delaware Conference is in *Christian Century* 59 (25 March 1942): 390-97.

[41]Fagley, interview, 30.

health, and labor. One of the seminar reports, to Dulles's dismay, put the emphasis on the pooling of armaments as a means of enforcing the peace, implying that the end sought was maintenance of the status quo. Dulles preferred that the emphasis be placed on orderly processes for peaceful change.

With all of his personal fears concerning ill-prepared statements, he seemed personally pleased with and supportive of the results of each one of the conferences sponsored by the commission. When he was critical of them, his criticisms were directed at the group's tendency to offer oversimplistic solutions to complex problems. A private letter written shortly after the Delaware conference illustrates this point.

> The defects of the findings are, I think, due to a tendency, to which we are all subject, to feel that lofty motives of themselves supply all that is needed to prescribe practical solutions. . . . This is perhaps particularly true in the very difficult field of economics. Certain objectives may have been stated without adequate considerations of how they could be practically achieved. In this respect, however, the conference was not unique. There seems to be so little truly scientific economic knowledge that almost every conference, under whatever auspices, which has sought to suggest a solution to our economic ills, has dealt largely in terms of surmise. . . . To my mind . . . the defects to which I refer are small blemishes upon which it would be a mistake to dwell, except as a stimulant to more solid effort. What is important is the spirit which runs through the findings. This I find to be wholly admirable.[42]

Dulles's imposing manner tended to control the proceedings at these conferences. Paul Hutchinson, editor of the *Christian Century,* cited Dulles as one of the individuals at Delaware who made the most direct contribution to the thinking of the delegates. Had it not been for the contribution of men like Dulles, Hutchinson wrote, things "might easily have gone on the rocks."[43] It is highly unlikely that much could have crept into the final reports of the commission conferences with which he would have disagreed. If it had, it is hard to imagine that he could have kept quiet about it for long. According to Henry P. Van Dusen, "There was never, as far as I recall, any minority judgment or any dissent during all the time

---

[42]Letter, JFD to Dr. William Barrow Pugh, 15 May 1942, DP, Box 21.

[43]Hutchinson, "Lasting Peace," 362.

that he was leading the thought of the churches. Of course . . . he was a very impressive person."[44]

The initial interest in holding an international conference probably resulted from Dulles's trip to wartorn England in the summer of 1942. The members of the commission requested that Dulles make the trip in order to keep in touch with foreign groups engaged in work similar to their own. He made the trip by clipper and paid his own way.[45] Henry Smith Leiper was in England shortly before Dulles's proposed trip was made. The commission asked him to sound out Archbishop William Temple and other British church leaders about their interest in meeting with Dulles. Leiper reported that the British leaders were most eager to meet with him.[46]

Upon his return from England, Dulles submitted to the Federal Council's Executive Committee a revised formulation of objectives for the commission, which included as one of its main points the suggestion that the commission should "collaborate closely with those who are seeking to promote [peace] in other lands."[47] The first real attempt at such collaboration followed one year later. The "International Roundtable of Christian Leaders" was convened by the commission, in cooperation with the Commission on Church and World Order of the United Church of Canada, on 8-11 July 1943, in Princeton, New Jersey. Sixty-eight

---

[44]Henry P. Van Dusen, interview, 38.

[45]His generosity in terms of the willing use of his own personal funds was almost as impressive to members of the commission as his vast donation of time and energy. (See Roswell Barnes, interview; Samuel McCrea Cavert, interview; and Henry Smith Leiper, interview.) Barnes records that "whenever he wrote articles for magazines or gave a speech and received honorariums he gave them to the commission if he thought he got the engagement because of his association with it" (Barnes, interview, 20). Dulles also made large personal contributions to the commission.

[46]Townsend Hoopes reports that the leading churchmen "showed no particular interest in even talking to him" (Hoopes, *The Devil and John Foster Dulles* [Boston: Little, Brown and Company, 1973] 52). Contrary to Hoopes's assessment, most of the evidence seems to indicate that the leading churchmen were genuinely interested in meeting with Dulles. As Barnes remembers the British sentiments concerning Dulles: "He was highly regarded—greatly respected—by the leaders of the churches in England at that time" (Barnes, interview, 10). It is true, however, that the British church leaders were not yet as enthusiastic about postwar issues as was Dulles. (See Walter W. Van Kirk, "Memorandum," July 1942, DP, Box 282.)

[47]*Biennial Report* (1942) 243.

churchmen, representing twelve countries, were in attendance.[48] The two delegates from Australia were flown in by a bomber placed at their disposal by General Douglas MacArthur. A large percentage of the delegates were laymen, including political scientists and government office holders. The conference defined its objective as intending

> to provide further information . . . on issues wherein the application of Christian principles ["Guiding Principles"] and of political propositions ["Six Pillars"] derived therefrom involves peculiar difficulties and complexities; to promote a better understanding of the views held by Christians in different countries; and to formulate, in so far as possible, a consensus of views on post-war reconstruction.[49]

John C. Bennett reported that the conference made a genuine attempt to be fair to peoples on both sides of the conflict and demonstrated "to an amazing extent the effectiveness of the perspective of the Christian faith in overcoming the pressures of national interest and the passions of war."[50] In a letter to Christians in lands on the other side of the conflict, the conference framed sentences reminiscent of St. Paul, "We long to come to you in person and to bring to you some material succor and to receive from you the fuller stimulus of your spiritual vigor."[51] The *Christian Century* reported that the conference added "yet another to the growing list of heartening expressions of the spirit of ecumenical Christianity in time of war."[52]

On its more primary concern, the establishment of mechanisms through which a constructive world order might be created, the conference issued ten recommendations. These recommendations were largely consistent with Dulles's six pillars. They especially emphasized the need

---

[48]*Annual Report* (1943) 63. See also "A Christian Message on World Order," *Christianity and Crisis* 3 (26 July 1943): 13. The report there indicates sixty-two delegates from fourteen countries.

[49]"A Christian Message," 13.

[50]John C. Bennett, "An International Christian Round Table," *Christianity and Crisis* 3 (26 July 1943): 1.

[51]Quoted in "Community Indestructible," *Christian Century* 60 (28 July 1943): 861. See also "A Message to the Many Christians Separated from Us by the Barriers of War Who Remain Steadfast in the Faith," DP, Box 291.

[52]Ibid.

for developing postwar machinery conducive to universal political and cultural collaboration among nations. Further, ever mindful of the great powers' susceptibility to exploit nations and peoples less powerful, the conference reminded the Allied countries of their responsibilities in the areas of relief and reconstruction. This concern was also consistent with liberal Protestantism's emphasis on ethical responsibilities in society during these years. To the citizens of the great powers, the delegates directed the reminder that they too must share responsibility for national policies in these areas.[53] The Dulles Commission circulated these recommendations among American churches—thereby contributing to the ever-growing awareness of church people that the United States would assume an active role in some kind of international order.

The third and final conference held under the auspices of the commission was precipitated by two meetings of the great powers on postwar planning. The first of these met at Bretton Woods, a resort area in the mountains of New Hampshire in July of 1944. There, representatives of forty-four nations agreed on a plan that was designed to stabilize international currencies, thus encouraging world trade. The delegates also established foundations for an International Bank for Reconstruction and Development. Its goal was to facilitate the rebuilding of wartorn areas. The second of these meetings took place the next month. American initiative brought British, Chinese, and American representatives to an estate known as Dumbarton Oaks just outside Washington in order to discuss the political makeup of the postwar system of collective security. The agreement reached there contained a tentative charter for a permanent international organization to be called the United Nations.

These Dumbarton Oaks proposals, along with the Bretton Woods agreement, served as the central themes for discussion at the National Study Conference held in Cleveland, 16-19 January 1945. The United States government, probably through Secretary of State Edward Stettinius (a fellow Presbyterian and friend of Dulles), officially requested Dulles's commission to deal with these proposals.[54] Therefore Dulles's

---

[53]The ten recommendations are listed in detail in "Princeton International Round Table," *Federal Council Bulletin* 26 (September 1943): 7.

[54]JFD, "America's Role in the Peace," *Christianity and Crisis* 4 (22 January 1945): 2. Also published under the title "Collaboration Must Be Practical," *Vital Speeches of the Day* 9 (1 February 1945): 246-49, and under the title "Ideals Are Not Enough," *International Conciliation* no. 409 (March 1945): 131-41.

group set up two study commissions in preparation for the Cleveland Conference. One of these dealt with studying the recent publications emerging from Bretton Woods and Dumbarton Oaks in light of the "Guiding Principles" and the "Six Pillars." Another study conducted by this first commission concerned the possible peace settlements with Germany and Japan. William E. Hocking of Harvard was appointed the chairman.

The second study commission was chaired by Walter Marshall Horton, professor of theology at Oberlin. Its task was to study those aspects of the Christian faith that were considered relative to the problem of peace; the primary intent was to try to understand the role the churches should play in the molding of public opinion and the methods by which that might be appropriately done. Both commissions were to provide all the appointed delegates to the Cleveland Conference with their findings one month in advance of the meeting. [55]

Four hundred eighty-one delegates representing thirty-four communions, eighteen religious bodies, and seventy city and state councils of churches met in Cleveland for the conference. Dulles, the chairman of the conference, opened the meeting with an address entitled "America's Role in the Peace." The address succeeded in setting a very realistic tone for the conference that followed. As the journal *Christianity and Crisis,* widely regarded for its realistic stance during this period, stated in an editorial note preceding the published text of Dulles's speech: "[It] charts a course for America which in a remarkable way avoids both the perils of perfection and the perils of expediency."[56] This assessment proved to be equally true for the overall results of the conference as well.

Dulles's work at Cleveland was an important contribution in that it helped to steer the thought of the Protestant church leaders in a more realistic direction. The conference, under Dulles's leadership, focused its attention on the relation between Christian purposes and practical politics. The main question under consideration was how the churches could properly maintain the tension between what Christian principles require and what can actually be achieved in the realm of national policy

---

[55]See "Plans for the Cleveland Conference," *Post War World* 1 (16 October 1944): 2.

[56]Ibid., 2.

without making the former concern irrelevant to the latter result. As the *Federal Council Bulletin* reported after the conference, "The churches must constantly seek to maintain a careful balance between prophecy on the one hand and the support of practical achievable results on the other."[57] The final "Message" of the conference stated the same concern in a slightly different manner.

> At all times Christians must keep the ultimate goals clearly in view but they have equal responsibility to mark out attainable steps toward these goals, and to support them. An idealism which will not accept the discipline of the achievable may lose its power for good and ultimately lend aid to forces with whose purpose it cannot agree.[58]

In effect, the "Message" stated that the Dumbarton Oaks proposals were not good enough to totally satisfy the churches, but they were good enough to support as "an important step in the direction of world cooperation." The results of the Cleveland Conference provide important evidence that the Protestant churches were not guided by a naive idealism; rather, here they were exhibiting a pragmatic understanding of realistic issues. Indeed, these were church leaders who, at Cleveland, were able to avoid the ever-present temptation to personify either of the two poles Reinhold Niebuhr defined as Christian moralism and Political Pharisaism.

> A final contribution to the Christian faith is its understanding of the relative, partial and partly corrupt character of all human standards of justice. We must seek justice according to our best human insights; but all these insights contain elements of positive corruption. . . . The Christian moralists will have nothing to do with such a peace because of the taint of sin which will be upon it. But the Political Pharisees (and all political morality tends toward Pharisaeism [*sic*]) will call it a righteous and just peace and will accentuate the injustices in it because they will have no contrite recognition of the corruption which their own egotism has introduced into it.[59]

---

[57]*Federal Council Bulletin* 28 (February 1945): 3.

[58]"Cleveland Conference on a Just and Durable Peace," ibid., 6.

[59]Reinhold Niebuhr, "The Christian Perspective on the World Crisis," *Christianity and Crisis* 4 (1 May 1944): 5.

The *Christian Century,* in its report on the Cleveland Conference, inaccurately stated that the conference supported the Dumbarton Oaks proposals only on the condition that the nine amendments recommended by the conference were adopted.[60] John C. Bennett of *Christianity and Crisis* chided the *Century* for its mistake in reporting, which, in his view, "caused serious misunderstanding of the Cleveland Conference." The actual wording of the conference proposal is as follows:

> Accordingly, we recommend that the churches support the Dumbarton Oaks Proposals as an important step in the direction of world cooperation, but because we do not approve of them in their entirety as they now stand we urge the following measures for their improvement.[61]

The problem was one of interpretation of the phrase following the "but." In the view of a minority of pacifists and the editors of the *Christian Century,* that "but" meant a conditional acceptance based on the inclusion of the amendments. However, in the view of the majority of the delegates at the conference, the "Message" urged support of the actual achievements of Dumbarton Oaks while, at the same time, suggesting measures that would help to bring the proposals more in line with Christian principles.[62] As J. Milton Yinger, a well-known sociologist of religion, noted in 1945, Dulles "called for unconditional support of the Dumbarton Oaks plan, while striving for its improvement."[63]

The nine measures suggested by the conference and directed toward the improvement of the Dumbarton Oaks agreement urged that the charter for a world organization provide for: (1) a general reaffirmation of the Atlantic Charter's purposes; (2) increased development of international laws; (3) the revocation of any nation's right to vote when its own case is being judged; (4) a liberalized amendment procedure; (5) a special agency on the colonial situation; (6) a special commission on human rights;

---

[60]"It Was Not Unconditional," *Christian Century* 62 (7 February 1945): 166-67. The complete "Message" of the conference is found ibid., 174-77, 191.

[61]*Christianity and Crisis* 5 (5 March 1945): 2.

[62]See John Paul Jones, "Advance from Cleveland," *Social Progress* 35 (March 1945): 2-4, 29-30.

[63]J. Milton Yinger, *Religion in the Struggle for Power: A Study in the Sociology of Religion* (New York: Russell and Russell, Inc., 1961) 172. This book was originally published by Duke University Press in 1946.

(7) eventual universal membership; (8) promptly initiating limitation and reduction of national armaments; and (9) more clearly protecting and defending smaller nations from the possible arbitrary power of the great nations.[64]

The debate concerning these amendments, and whether or not the support of the conference for the Dumbarton Oaks proposals was unconditional, continued in the religious press well after the conference was over. Objections on the part of some of the pacifist delegates, most notably John Haynes Holmes and A. J. Muste, were cited in the pages of the *Presbyterian Tribune*. For the most part, their objections fell on deaf ears. Most of the members of the Federal Council recognized, along with Bennett, that "to allow their [the pacifists'] criticism to encourage defeat of treaty ratification in the Senate [would] repeat tragic history."[65]

Peer Judgment

The success of the Commission to Study a Just and Durable Peace in fulfilling the original directives assigned to it by the Federal Council is impressive. Much of the credit for this accomplishment belongs to John Foster Dulles. As Bennett asserts, "It was a Dulles Commission." This is not to say that he was inflexible or closed to meaningful dialogue that allowed for the contribution of other members.[66] He proved through his leadership, his dedication to the task, and his incredible breadth of knowledge concerning international affairs that the Federal Council had chosen wisely. Dulles, because of "the realism in his own approach to international affairs," effectively led the churches toward a responsible position on the subject of a future world order.[67]

---

[64]"Christian Standards and Current International Developments," pt. 2 of "A Message to the Churches," from the Cleveland Conference of 1945, *International Conciliation* no. 409 (March 1945): 142-49.

[65]John C. Bennett, "Editorial Notes," *Christianity and Crisis* 5 (5 March 1945): 2.

[66]Van Dusen, interview, 11; Cavert, interview, 17. Bennett remembers that Dulles "didn't polarize things as much in regard to the war as he did later with regards to communism" (Bennett, interview, 4; see also 11).

[67]Van Dusen, interview, 54.

Dulles's understanding of the "complexity of international affairs" led the church to the middle position of calling for a new international order "with effective but limited powers."[68] He was one of the first Americans of this time to call for such an organization and, through the work of the commission, one of the most influential in promulgating the idea. Frederick Nolde, a fellow churchman known for his consistent realism in political matters, commented that, concerning world order, "what Dulles was after at the time was revolutionary."[69] John C. Bennett described Dulles's contribution to the concept of a realistic limited world organization:

> I've always said that I thought that it's very interesting that the American churches never went in heavily for world government, because of the influence of Reinhold Niebuhr and John Foster Dulles. Niebuhr providing, perhaps, the broader rationale, but Dulles also having this intuitive sense of the way things developed, that they didn't develop by fiat . . . it was a rather empirical movement toward world order that rejected short-cuts, like world state—and, of course, he [Dulles] rejected all pacifist short cuts. . . . And the establishment of the United Nations itself, was a major goal. But I think the improvement of it and the perfecting of this kind of world order was also hoped for—not, as I say, in terms of some kind of panacea. The panacea had been pretty well discounted, as I say, by Dulles's influence and by Niebuhr's.[70]

Dulles's contribution to the life of the church during these years was a very important one. As Henry Smith Leiper assessed it, "There was

---

[68]Mulder, "The Moral World," 176. Here Mulder very astutely understands the importance of Dulles's contribution in this area.

[69]Frederick Nolde, interview, 9. For secular recognition of Dulles's commission and its contribution, see the following: Robert Divine, *Second Chance: The Triumph of Internationalism in America during World War II* (New York: Atheneum, 1967) 252ff.; and idem, *Foreign Policy and the United States Presidential Elections, 1940-48* (New York: New Viewpoints, 1974) 91-92; Cordell Hull, *The Memoirs of Cordell Hull* (New York: Macmillan Company, 1948) 1625-26; "Truman and Dulles Exchange Letters," *Post War World* 3 (15 December 1945): 2: "If today we Americans have a clearer understanding of our place in world community—as I believe we have—it is due, in no small part, to the churches' advanced position in international thinking taken by the Federal Council" (Letter, President Truman to JFD, 6 November 1945).

[70]Bennett, interview, 4-5, 11; see also Roswell Barnes, interview conducted by Philip A. Crowl, 21.

no other factor that was as important, in this particular aspect of the church, nor as effective, as Dulles—and very few that even stood beside him in this connection." Bennett concurred when he said, "There aren't too many of these lay public figures to be lionized . . . John Foster Dulles was one of them." People who would not listen to churchmen on this issue, listened to Dulles. "That was the thing," said Leiper, "that I think was outstanding."[71]

The commission members, for the most part, all felt that particular events in the political sphere were directly traceable to the influence of the commission. The successes of both the Fulbright-Connally resolutions in Congress calling for American leadership in the formation of a postwar organization, and the issuance of the Moscow Declaration pledging the great powers to commit themselves to "a general international organization," represent two such instances most often cited, as "in a measure at least, the reflection of the body of opinion which had been developed in the churches."[72] Whether or not Dulles's commission was truly as influential in the secular mind as the members, including Dulles, have always claimed, the one fact that cannot be disputed is that the commission helped to unify solidly the opinion of the Protestant churches during these years in favor of world order.[73] This accomplishment in itself could have contributed very critical support for the activities of the political leaders in the public sphere, perhaps even *the* support that made the difference between success and failure.

In a book published during these years investigating religion's ability "to control the relations of men to each other according to its precepts," sociologist J. Milton Yinger discussed Dulles's commission in a section entitled "Contemporary Religious 'Prophecy.'" He believed that Dulles's commission made a significant contribution to "the breaking up of tradition." Describing Dulles and churchmen like him as "very able strategists" who "were deploying their power in the most effective way

---

[71]Henry Smith Leiper, interview, 45; Bennett, interview, 8.

[72]Luman J. Shafer, "American Approaches to World Order," *The International Review of Missions* 33 (April 1944): 177.

[73]An article that traces the effect of the commission's work on the Presbyterian Church is Dennis L. Tarr, "The Presbyterian Church and the Founding of the United Nations," *Journal of Presbyterian History* 53 (Spring 1975): 3-32.

possible," Yinger concluded, from his contemporary perspective, that they could help to

> so prepare public opinion that it will be easier to break down traditional barriers; they can give the new order an ethical justification; and they can keep the churches in a position where they can reduce the harshness of a given society even if they cannot determine it completely. Thus religious prophecy, however caused, is today a factor in the field of interaction in which new economic and political forms are being worked out. [74]

Thus, even in the minds of secular sociologists, Dulles's commission was regarded as prophetic in message and intent.

One of the often-raised questions concerning Dulles's participation in the work of the churches during these years is whether or not he was using the churches to gain in political stature. Journalist Marquis Childs described as "shrewd" Dulles's involvement with the churches. [75] Childs seems to represent a minority opinion. Most of the churchmen had nothing but the deepest respect for Dulles. In describing him, they used such phrases as "sincerely committed"; "a Christian with deep convictions"; "he really had a sense of Christian vocation"; "his religious heritage more than any other single factor . . . was operative"; and "he was taking [his work] very seriously." Bennett sums it up well.

> They [the churchmen] were proud of him. He was a big figure who had— I think, quite in a disinterested way—come to identify himself with the churches, and I think he made this for a time perhaps his major interest. [76]

There were, however, churchmen on both the far right and the far left ends of the spectrum who were unhappy with Dulles. Either they were anxious for him "to get people more warmed up—to go on crusades" or they were pacifists who "were a bit critical of him for what they would have called compromising, or being too much concerned with the immediate practicalities." Even here, though, according to Roswell Barnes,

---

[74]Yinger, *Religion in the Struggle for Power,* 175; see also 15, 161-74.

[75]Marquis Childs, interview, 2.

[76]John Mackay, interview, 34; Leiper, interview, 22; Cavert, interview, 8; Fagley, interview, 30; Barnes, interview, 11; and Bennett, interview, 7.

those who were "close enough to know him" liked him and appreciated the level of his commitment. [77]

Dulles's work with the churches, by almost any standard, must be considered a highly successful one. While there is no evidence to indicate that Dulles worked in these circles with the intention of gaining in public stature as an expert in international relations, there is no doubt that this was the end result of his diligent work with the churches. During these years, Dulles gained a significant reputation as an international analyst and he became a prime candidate for a position of leadership in the secular arena.

---

[77]Barnes, interview, 39, 40; Cavert, interview, 20.

5

"What Is":
Diagnosing the Problem
of International Relations

John Calvin was convinced that God was working out his purposes in history. Thus, Presbyterians, true to their Calvinist heritage, have taken the world seriously. They have defined their task in history as one of bringing about the creation of a new humanity in Christ. As John Mackay writes, Presbyterians view the true life of humankind as consisting "in struggling with the help of God to create an order of existence which shall be of God, for God, and like God." Further, that life "should be adjusted to God and his eternal purpose in Christ."[1] Most Presbyterians have tried to remember that this task will never be completed in history; the struggle begins and will never be completely resolved in the historical setting of humankind. Occasionally, a lapse in memory has resulted in this or that

[1]John Mackay, *The Presbyterian Way of Life* (Englewood Cliffs NJ: Prentice-Hall, Inc., 1960) 168-69.

social structure being hailed as the Kingdom in process. Usually when this has happened, some theologian sounds the call back to finitude.

As Niebuhr, a Calvinist himself, has written, "Every individual is a Moses who perishes outside the promised land."[2] Niebuhr's statement reflected his belief that humankind, like Moses, "has glimpsed the promised land from afar, and . . . has made some progress toward it on this earth, but . . . will not enter into it in history."[3] In Niebuhr's view, the task of the Christian involved the criticism of present events in light of the perspective gained through the Christian vision of the Kingdom of God. This task is therefore essentially prophetic. The prophet "who would speak to his own age, if he is to be a prophet of the Lord, . . . must have some perspective which lifts him above the prejudices of his time."[4] Niebuhr believed that such a perspective only comes through a proper understanding of the dialectic between "transcendence and creatureliness, between eternity and time, between God and world."[5] Thus, for Niebuhr, the transcendent God impinges on history yet can never be considered as "identical with any portion of it."[6] The goal of humankind in history is to use human spiritual freedom to be open to the future and to attempt to transform it into a closer approximation of the Kingdom. At the same time, though, no social order can ever be viewed as representative of the Kingdom. Niebuhr believed that "the Kingdom of God can become present only insofar as it is viewed as continually transcendent."[7] Thus the prophetic nature of the church's task is unending.

These convictions of Calvin and Niebuhr form the heart of Dulles's prophetic realism during these years. This policy was exemplified by

---

[2]Reinhold Niebuhr, *The Nature and Destiny of Man*, 2 vols. (New York: Charles Scribner's Sons, 1943) 2:308.

[3]Robert E. Fitch, "Reinhold Niebuhr's Philosophy of History," in *Reinhold Niebuhr: His Religious, Social, and Political Thought*, ed. Charles W. Kegley and Robert W. Bretall (New York: The Macmillan Company, 1961) 294.

[4]Ibid., 305.

[5]Langdon Gilkey, "Reinhold Niebuhr's Theology of History," in *The Legacy of Reinhold Niebuhr*, ed. Nathan A. Scott, Jr. (Chicago: The University of Chicago Press, 1975) 40.

[6]Ibid., 43.

[7]Ibid., 48.

Dulles's reaction to the Dumbarton Oaks plan: he urged acceptance of realistic steps toward his goal even though they fell far short of what a prophetic understanding of the Kingdom might demand. His prophetic Protestantism served as the standard by which he measured present events and developments. Yet this is not the same as saying that he expected historical attainments which would be equivalent to his vision of the ideal. He did believe, however, that it was important to point to present deficiencies in order to make progress toward the ideal. During his years of leadership in the Federal Council, Dulles worked to educate public opinion concerning these deficiencies. This education, he felt, might make the public more willing to take the steps necessary to correct them.

The Moral Law

During the years 1937-1945, Dulles devoted his capacity as a thinker to the task of defining a norm for international morality. Indeed, the problem of international morality represented a lifelong concern for Dulles. Yet the moralism he espoused in these years "was not the kind of hardened moralism that many . . . felt later on when he was dividing the free world from the slave world and so on."[8] Rather, it was a moralism that served as an ideal type embodied in what Dulles called the moral law. This particular brand of moralism, as Dulles expressed it, had no concrete representative among the world of nations. Every nation falls short of recognizing and incorporating into its international policy the concept of "the universal brotherhood of man," which is the heart of the moral law.[9]

The Dulles Commission dealt with the moral law most explicitly in its "Statement of Guiding Principles." The first two principles are concerned directly with this subject.

> We believe that moral law, no less than physical law, undergirds our world. There is a moral order which is fundamental and eternal, and which is relevant to the corporate life of men and the ordering of society.

---

[8]John C. Bennett, interview, 11. Earlier in the interview, Bennett stated the following: "And I want to keep saying that the same churchmen who had accepted him would have been very critical of the hardening tendencies that came later" (7).

[9]JFD, "As Seen by a Layman," *Religion in Life* 7 (Winter 1938): 41.

We believe that the sickness and suffering which afflict our present society are proof of indifference to as well as direct violation of the moral law. All share in responsibility for the present evils. There is none who does not need forgiveness. A mood of genuine penitence is therefore demanded of us—individuals and nations alike.[10]

The preamble to this document reveals the ultimate source of the moral law.

As members of the Christian church, we seek to view all problems of world order in the light of the truth concerning God, man and God's purpose for the world made known in Jesus Christ. We believe that the eternal God revealed in Christ is the Ruler of men and of nations and that His purpose in history will be realized. For us, he is the source of the moral law and the power to make it effective.[11]

Since the moral law originated with God and its aim is the universal "brotherhood of man," invoking it served the purpose of revealing the difference between the "what is" and the "what ought to be" of international policy. Dulles emphasized the moral law in order to bring individual citizens and national leaders to the realization that the universal "brotherhood of man" eventually ought to replace the concept of national sovereignty as the motivating force behind all international decision making. Such a realization is necessary expressly because it corresponds with reality. "Of course," he confidently asserted, "the greatest of all fundamentals is the Golden Rule." This fundamental concept "influences many [particularly the membership of the Christian church], and should influence all."[12]

Throughout this early period of his life, Dulles expressed an international ethic that is quite similar to H. R. Niebuhr's description of *cathekontic* ethics, the ethics of the "fitting response." Niebuhr writes that such an ethic should find itself led by experiences to the

---

[10]JFD, "Statement of Guiding Principles," *Biennial Report* (1942) 42-45. See also "Introductory Statement," in *A Just and Durable Peace: Statement of Political Propositions* (New York: Commission on a Just and Durable Peace [hereafter CJDP], 1943).

[11]Luman J. Shafer, "American Approaches to World Order," *The International Review of Missions* 33 (April 1944): 176.

[12]JFD, "Article Prepared for *New York Times Sunday Magazine*," 7 August 1945, DP, Box 26.

notion of universal responsibility, that is, of a life of responses to action which is always qualified by our interpretation of the actions as taking place in a *universe,* and by the further understanding that there will be a response to our actions by representatives of universal community, or by the generalized other who is universal, or by an impartial spectator who regards our actions from a universal point of view, whose impartiality is that of loyalty to the universal cause.[13]

The fact that the leadership and population of each nation view their particular ideas as right, or universally applicable, constitutes the major obstacle to realizing a world of nations that will heed the moral law as the norm for international policy making. Throughout this period of his association with the churches, Dulles concentrated on (1) defining this problem; and (2) offering a solution based on the dictates of the moral law.[14] His first major written work, *War, Peace and Change,* resulted from devotion to these issues. Although he utilized a plodding lawyerlike writing style,[15] the book received good reviews, especially among the leadership in the churches. It represented well the concerns of Oxford.[16] The editorial staff of *Christianity and Crisis,* made up of men like Reinhold Niebuhr and John C. Bennett, regarded the work as "an excellent analysis of the basic principles which must underlie a new world order."[17]

Even though the moral law for Dulles was synonymous with a concern for the welfare of humankind, he recognized the fact that each nation had its own way of interpreting what that concern meant. Every

---

[13]H. Richard Niebuhr, *The Responsible Self: An Essay in Christian Moral Philosophy* (New York: Harper and Row, 1963) 88. Emphasis is that of Niebuhr.

[14]The next chapter will deal with Dulles's proposed solution.

[15]Isabel Paterson, in her review of the book, described it as follows: "His style of writing is such that the human eye rebounds from it like a tennis ball." (Isabel Paterson, review of *War, Peace and Change* [New York: Harper and Brothers, 1939] by John Foster Dulles in *New York Herald Tribune,* 7 January 1939.)

[16]Platig suggests that *War, Peace and Change* is more representative of the conference at Paris than the one at Oxford. I, however, believe that the opposite is true. My reason for this will become clear in the following pages. E. Raymond Platig, "John Foster Dulles: A Study of His Political and Moral Thought Prior to 1953 with Special Emphasis on International Relations" (dissertation, The University of Chicago, 1957) 72.

[17]*Christianity and Crisis* 2 (23 February 1942): 7.

nation bases its international policy upon its own expressed or unexpressed ideals. In his Merrick-McDowell Lecture, delivered in March of 1942 at Ohio Wesleyan University, Dulles emphasized that "there are lacking any such common mores throughout this world as are the necessary condition to common rules being understood and deemed reasonable."[18] More simply, he said on another occasion, no "adequate and world-accepted definitions of right and wrong exist." Such definitions might begin to develop, he continued, "but only if national groups learn to work together in peace."[19] For a new international morality to become a reality, every nation, through peaceful collaboration with other nations, would have to be willing to compromise on its own ideals. Dulles knew this would not be an easy task; he wanted to prepare Americans so they would not delay the collaboration process. "We must not be dogmatic," he told the messengers gathered at the 1945 Cleveland National Study Conference, "our particular ideals and sense of vital interest are not the only ones in the world."[20]

On the one hand, then, Dulles asserted a universal moral law. The heart of the moral law, which all nations should heed, consisted of the recognition of humankind's interdependence and thus reflected ultimate concern for the general welfare of the human race. On the other hand, and equally important, Dulles urged all individuals, including those in political power, to realize that no single nation possessed ideals synonymous with the dictates of the moral law. Nor were any "universal moral judgments about national conduct" easily discernible.[21] Every nation expressed its own ideals through its foreign policy, as foreign policy generally emerges out of national self-interest considerations; therefore, conflict between ideals is inevitable.

Dulles often emphasized that the nature of the politician's job required both a quest for power and a concern for the national interest.

---

[18]JFD, "Toward World Order," in Francis J. McConnell et al., *A Basis for the Peace to Come,* Merrick-McDowell Lecture Series (New York: Abingdon-Cokesbury Press, 1942) 46.

[19]JFD, "The Churches and a Just and Durable Peace," *Biennial Report* (1944) 28. This speech was delivered before the 1944 biennial meeting of the Federal Council of Churches. See also *World Affairs* 57 (March 1944): 34-37.

[20]JFD, "America's Role in the Peace," *Christianity and Crisis* 4 (22 January 1945): 5.

[21]JFD, "A Just and Durable Peace," 28.

Dedication to the universal welfare of humankind strikes most politicians as an intrusion from the outside. At most, it can only be a secondary concern. "The political leaders of each nation," wrote Dulles, "have, in law, a duty only to their own people. The welfare of others in no wise restricts what they may do."[22] However, the task of the individual citizen is different from that of the political leader. The American people—especially the Christian audiences he addressed—should, according to Dulles, try to press universal concerns on their political leaders. Thus, out of their mandate to serve the expressed needs of the people, political leaders might occasionally transcend normal behavior by including other than merely national concerns in their policy decisions.

In *War, Peace and Change*, published just one year before the fall of France, Dulles considered these aspects of national and international human affairs. The structure of the book is true to Dulles's desire to contrast the "what is" with the "what ought to be." His speeches, and the commission's statements during the years 1937-1945, were entirely consistent with the ideas expressed in *War, Peace and Change*. The focus was on presenting the problem ("what is") and proposing the solution ("what ought to be"). Presenting this contrast occupied Dulles for most of his life, though his definition of the problem measurably changed after 1945.[23]

The Problem:
Understanding "What Is"

Human Nature. John Mulder commented that Dulles's "speeches to church groups and his statements as chairman of the Commission rarely contained references to sin."[24] He points out that "Dulles never seemed

---

[22]JFD, "Christianity in This Hour," 13, 21 April 1941, DP, Box 20; and JFD, "The Churches' Role in Developing the Bases of a Just and Durable Peace," 16, 28 May 1941, DP, Box 20. See also JFD, *War, Peace and Change*, 117-18, where he explains that there are "valid reasons" for such a mandate: "It is a sound principle of international practice which bids each nation avoid interference with the internal affairs of another."

[23]Thus his view of "what ought to be" was changed as well. See pt. 3.

[24]John Mulder, "The Moral World of John Foster Dulles," *Journal of Presbyterian History* 49 (Summer 1971): 180.

to comprehend Niebuhr's insistence on the ambiguity involved in all ethical decisions, the dimension of finitude and fallibility in all human institutions, and the degree of self-interest, self-preservation, and self-
righteousness implicit in every exercise of power."[25] When this statement is used to describe the Dulles who emerged after 1945, its truth is
verifiable. However, when used in the context of his work with the
churches, as Mulder used it, the description proves somewhat inaccu-
rate. One of the most consistent themes expressed by Dulles throughout this period warned American Christians that "any human order is
bound to be finite and fraught with evil."[26]

Though Dulles rarely used the word "sin," he was highly cognizant
of its existence in the context of international problems. He aptly described the heart of the problem when he wrote that "man is by nature
selfish."

> Whenever life assumes a form which involves consciousness there is an
> awareness of needs and a desire to satisfy them. Selfishness in this sense
> is a basic human instinct. . . . The fact that human beings, all selfish, are
> in contact with each other inevitably brings dissatisfaction.[27]

Human selfishness, Dulles elaborated, is combined with a tendency
toward "gregariousness." One's needs cannot be satisfied in isolation.
Since the desire to satisfy selfish needs is a driving force in human nature, the desire for association with others who can satisfy those needs
is overwhelming.[28] Therefore, communities are formed. Human beings
begin to meet the needs of their neighbors—not out of a spirit of self-
sacrifice, but rather out of the expectation that their own personal needs

---

[25]Ibid., 181. See also Townsend Hoopes, *The Devil and John Foster Dulles* (Boston:
Little, Brown and Company, 1973) 35.

[26]JFD, "Christianity: Solvent of World Conflict," *Social Progress* 33 (January 1943):
5. See also the widely circulated statement that was presented to the Atlantic City biennial meeting of the Federal Council, where Dulles admonished Christians never to fail "to
remember that all human institutions are finite and prone to error." ("The American
Churches and the International Situation," 3, 19 December 1940, DP, Box 19.) Still another example of his awareness concerning this issue may be found in JFD, "A Christian
World Hope," *The Presbyterian Tribune* 60 (November 1944): 3.

[27]JFD, *War, Peace and Change,* 52, 6-7.

[28]Ibid., 6-7.

will be met in return. Due to our human nature, "we are prone to give to others under circumstances where some return, even if it be only gratitude, can be experienced." Human nature is such that self-satisfaction through giving comes only by satisfying those we love, know, or at least like. One must be able, through personal contact, to see the gratification that results from personal action. That is why, wrote Dulles, "discontent beyond our ken is apt to be a matter of indifference."[29]

As the borders of one's community begin to solidify, one begins to see it as the *only* moral community. Thus, one group's dissatisfaction leads to a wish to acquire at another group's expense. Such forced acquisition is justified by the members of the acquiring community through reference to their perceived "righteous" standing. The selfishness of humanity comes through ever more dangerously as the selfishness and self-righteousness of the community.[30] In this way, the national deification process begins.

Nationalism. To examine Dulles's repeated warnings during these years that nationalism was a cause of almost insurmountable tension between nations makes one realize the extent of the transformation in his thought before he assumed the office of secretary of state. In *War, Peace and Change,* Dulles defined nationalism as "that form of patriotism which personifies the nation as a living being endowed with heroic qualities, who lives bravely and dangerously in a world of inferior, and even villainous, other nation personalities."[31] Why is the need to deify the state so enticing? Dulles believed that the explanation "lies in the failure of the churches to provide mankind with a loftier means of satisfying its spiritual cravings."[32] Human beings, according to Dulles, demand a creed through which they can achieve spiritual exaltation. Sounding like Freud, he expressed the following presupposition concerning human nature.

Aware of his own finite character, and his inadequacies, man seeks self-

---

[29]Ibid., 17.

[30]The ideas expressed in this regard are quite similar to those of Reinhold Niebuhr, *Moral Man and Immoral Society* (New York: Charles Scribner's Sons, 1932).

[31]JFD, *War, Peace and Change,* 57-58.

[32]JFD, "The Churches' Contribution toward a Warless World," *Religion in Life* 9 (Winter 1940): 38.

exaltation by identification with some external cause or Being which appears more noble and more enduring than is he himself.[33]

Dulles differed from Freud in that he viewed this longing for self-exaltation as proof that human beings need to maintain a vital connection with God in order to become whole. Thus the search for identification with some higher entity should logically end in a relationship with God. However, "religious leaders have seemed unable to make vital and gripping the concept of God as revealed by Christ." Because of the decline of "vital" religion, "the false gods of nationalism have been imagined to fill the spiritual need which most men feel."[34] The state becomes "an incorporeal being endowed with perpetuity and possessed of qualities which seem noble and heroic."[35]

Not only did religious leadership encourage deification of the nation through failure to direct the spiritual cravings of the human race to God, but religious leaders, according to Dulles, were equally guilty of a far more serious charge: they identified righteousness with one or another national cause. "In many churches," Dulles told his listeners in 1939 at the United Christian Convention in Hartford, Connecticut, "the national flag and national anthem today replace the Christian symbols." He continued,

> This seems the easy way. Thereby an anemic church draws vitality from the coursing blood of nationalism. But this not merely aggravates the problem we are seeking to solve. It also exposes a dependence of the churches upon the human rather than the divine. Political leaders are not slow to draw the obvious inference. The church becomes to them a human institution upon which they can stomp whenever it serves their purpose. This today is occurring in not a few of the so-called "Christian" countries.[36]

As Dulles expressed it, the drift toward "rendering unto Caesar that which is God's" was extremely disconcerting, even potentially explosive. Devotion to an ideal, coupled with willingness to sacrifice, is among

---

[33]JFD, *War, Peace and Change,* 6.

[34]JFD, "The Churches' Contribution," 38. See also JFD, *War, Peace and Change,* 64.

[35]JFD, *War, Peace and Change,* 114-15.

[36]JFD, "The Churches' Contribution," 39. See also JFD, "As Seen by a Layman," 37.

the finest of human traits; however, warned Dulles, when the ideal itself is unworthy of such devotion, the sacrificial action should be considered dangerous.[37] Dulles urged the churches to educate themselves regarding the dangers of nationalism. "Too often," he cautioned,

> spiritual and secular motives become unconsciously mixed, and it requires unusual practical experience to detect the pitfalls which the worldly constantly prepare to secure for themselves the appearance of church benediction.[38]

The churches must "teach humbleness rather than [the] self-righteousness which creates false moral cleavages."[39]

At the 1945 Cleveland National Studies Conference, Dulles scolded the churches for their part in inspiring the leadership of the United States, since World War I, to "stand aloof, and utter lofty pronouncements which pander to their sense of moral superiority."[40] Just as Dulles chastised religious leadership for uncritically blessing national goals, he expressed equal dissatisfaction with political leadership for spiritualizing national-interest considerations. Throughout 1940 and 1941, Dulles consistently warned Christians to avoid the temptation of falling under the influence of political leaders who "seek to advance the national self-interest by identifying it with righteousness."[41] The "extraordinary parallelism between moral judgments and national self-interest" leads to an international policy that is offensive to other nations and only serves to endanger the peace.[42] Ironically, in the years to come, Dulles, as secretary of state, would have leading churchmen accuse him of defending his policies by cloaking them in moral pretense.[43]

---

[37]JFD, *War, Peace and Change*, 117.

[38]JFD, "As Seen by a Layman," 43.

[39]JFD, "Summary of Address Entitled 'The United States and the World of Nations,'" 3, 27 February 1940, DP, Box 19.

[40]JFD, "Ideals Are Not Enough," *International Conciliation* 409 (March 1945): 134-35.

[41]JFD, Statement, 8 April 1940, DP, Box 19.

[42]JFD, "United States and World of Nations," 14.

[43]See, for example, Reinhold Niebuhr, "The Moral World of John Foster Dulles," *The New Republic* 139 (1 December 1958): 8.

Even though his later expressions indicate other beliefs, while with the churches Dulles emphasized that the linking of moral judgments with national self-interest resulted only in popular misunderstanding of the aspirations of peoples in other lands. He often reiterated that political leaders recognize that it is within the national interest for citizens to be united into a cohesive whole. They view internal dissension as devastating both to the promise of their future as political leaders and to the strength of the country itself as viewed by other nations.

> Thus group authorities find it convenient always to keep alive among the group members a feeling that their nation is in danger from one or another of the nation-villains with which it is surrounded.[44]

This "feeling" serves "to enlarge and perpetuate" the power of the existing political leadership as well as to unify the masses. However, Dulles pointed out, "through dependence upon such artificial stimulation of internal (national) harmony, we engender international disharmony."[45]

When one or more other nations are cast in the role of "villains," the national groups are much more susceptible to misunderstandings. Perceptions of one another become based totally upon imagined attributes rather than factual traits.

> One's own hero, always in the right, is in constant peril from such other nations. In the face of intrigue and peril the personified nation-hero comports himself with courage, forbearance, and wisdom. Never a bully, he sponsors the cause of righteousness and of the oppressed; never bellicose, he has, nevertheless, a high sense of dignity and of personal honor which others affront at their peril.[46]

Whenever conflicts between nations arise, they "are attributable, not so much to the desires imputed to one's own state as to the desires imputed to other states. The latter are of such a character as to be calculated to provoke even a saint-like person."[47]

---

[44]JFD, *War, Peace and Change,* 63.

[45]Ibid., 34-35.

[46]Ibid., 58-59.

[47]Ibid., 108.

Another example of misplaced moral judgment that Dulles condemned during these years is the policy of nonrecognition by one state
of a de facto situation in another state. Moral judgment of this type, Dulles
announced, was "of dubious value." In 1939 he wrote,

> There are too few nations which have so controlled their own conduct
> that their officially expressed moral indignation rings true to others. Un-
> der these circumstances a policy of "non-recognition" of the fruits of
> aggression serves as an irritant rather than a pacificator.

Nonrecognition of a de facto situation, Dulles concluded, is an absurd policy.

> For any nation to close its eyes to such changes, and to treat them as
> non-existent, means the election of such nation to live in a world as un-
> related to reality as that of Alice in Wonderland. [48]

Dulles believed that the excessive claims of nationalism after World
War I were responsible for destroying the effectiveness of the League
of Nations. In April 1941, in a speech describing the aftermath of the First
World War, Dulles said, "The machinery for peace had been provided.
But there was lacking the popular understanding to make it work."[49] Nationalism makes it impossible to arrive at anything other than a perverted
understanding of the world: this was one of Dulles's favorite maxims. At
Oxford, he had asserted that proponents of nationalism "cannot risk the
disillusionment which comes from free international intercourse and its
teaching that no nation has a monopoly of the virtues or of the vices."[50]

Nationalism causes a "boundary consciousness" that inhibits international cooperation. Each sovereign country caught up in nationalism
begins to restrict immigration, imports, exports, and alien ownership of
land. This boundary consciousness leads to a further insulation of the na-

---

[48]Ibid., 88, 87. See also "Political and Economic Conditions in Costa Rica," 22 May
1917, 9-11, DP, Box 1; and his belief that the Soviet Union should be recognized by the
United States: JFD to Esther E. Lape, 16 March 1933, DP, Box 12, and JFD to James
McDonald, 15 November 1926, DP, Box 8.

[49]JFD, "The Aftermath of World War," *International Conciliation* no. 369 (April 1941):
269.

[50]JFD, "The Problem of Peace in a Dynamic World," *Religion in Life* 6 (Spring 1937):
206.

tion and increases the feeling of self-righteousness. As this attitude of superiority grows stronger, the moral justification for projection of the home culture over others is altogether too easy to find. Thus the danger of one nation attempting to universalize its national faith becomes a reality.[51]

Once the concept of the nation-hero is developed, it is often called into action. Whenever some cause "which he has sponsored (democracy, fascism, communism, or, in former days, some form of religion) appears to be jeopardized," the personified nation-hero rises up and asserts himself. The result, stated Dulles emphatically, is usually totalitarian war.

> Of the many possible variations [of the nation-hero] there are certain types which particularly conduce to war. One is the crusading hero, who champions the cause of justice and succors the oppressed. Another is the ambitious, hard-working and deserving youth, who is repressed and prevented from realizing his potentialities by the greed, indifference or falsely assumed superiority of those who surround him. . . . Seldom, if ever, do we find the nation-hero endowed with unselfish and sacrificial qualities. The characteristics imputed are essentially those of the natural, primitive, man untouched by the influences we have called "ethical." . . . At times, to be sure, the nation-hero is deemed to feel sentiments of chivalry—but principally when to act on those sentiments will involve an increase of prestige by bringing the weak or oppressed under his influence and away from that of another nation personality.[52]

Dulles was firmly convinced that democracies were just as capable of surrendering to the wiles of nationalism as were the authoritarian states, perhaps even more so.

> Democracies always face great peril because the evil qualities I have mentioned seem, peculiarly, to have a mass appeal. Human beings in the mass find it pleasant to deify their corporate group; they like to be told that they are pre-eminently endowed with virtues; they get a pleasur-

---

[51]See particularly JFD, "The Problem of Peace." On this point Dulles and Hans Morgenthau are in agreement. See Hans J. Morgenthau, *Politics among Nations: The Struggle for Power and Peace* (New York: Alfred A. Knopf, 1948); see particularly 191-96.

[52]JFD, *War, Peace and Change,* 65-69. See also JFD, "Radio Talk," 20 May 1937, 1, DP, Box 289. As Morgenthau describes this conflict between opposing faiths: "Little do they know that they meet under an empty sky from which the gods have departed" (*Politics among Nations,* 196).

able thrill by being stirred to passionate hate; and they often choose for themselves political leaders who pander [to] those trends.[53]

Thus Dulles warned Americans that the possibility for international peace is at its lowest point when the stage of action is occupied by leaders

> who extol patriotism as the noblest emotion, and who seek national unity by fomenting hatred and fear of other people and who proudly boast that they are not as other men. . . . The "devil" theory of causation has always been popular. Thus we used to explain floods and other violent outbreaks of nature. We still thereby seek to explain the explosions of human energy. This is simple; it saves us from mental exertion and relieves us of all causal responsibility. But it is not an explanation which can satisfy those who really think.[54]

When members of a democracy choose leaders who depend upon manipulating the emotions of the electorate in order to guarantee their status as leaders, conflict with other nations becomes inevitable.

Emotionalism and War. When Foster Dulles spoke, he did so with conviction and with earnestness. However, "He was very suspicious of any appeal to emotion and insisted on a reasonable approach."[55] An anecdote related by Elliot Bell reveals this aspect of Dulles's character with interesting clarity.

> You will remember that in the early stages following Pearl Harbor, there was an enormous revulsion here against the Japanese, and we thought of the Bataan death march and the terrible episodes in the concentration camps, and so on. About that time I was talking to Foster and something impelled me to say that what the Japanese had done was unforgivable. Foster just sat . . . and opened and closed his mouth with a noise . . . and said, "Jesus Christ tells us that nothing is unforgivable." . . . It wasn't that he didn't feel as indignant about what the Japanese had done as I felt; but he was reminding me that as far as Jesus—and he was a very devout

---

[53]JFD, "The Churches and World Order," in *The Spiritual Legacy of John Foster Dulles,* ed. Henry P. Van Dusen (Philadelphia: The Westminster Press, 1960) 28.

[54]JFD, "Christianity in This Hour," 10. See also JFD, "The Churches' Role," 9.

[55]Roswell Barnes, interview conducted by Philip A. Crowl, 15.

Christian—was concerned, we had been admonished against precisely such careless statements and such rash emotions as I had expressed.[56]

Mass emotion developed to a pitch of abnormality along national lines inevitably leads to war. Dulles reiterated the truth of this statement throughout the duration of his association with the churches. Emotion negates the will to practice reasoned unselfishness. The moral law will never be realized when emotion is uncontrolled. "Evil and misfortune" are natural concomitants of the "blindness and stupidity" that assuredly arises "when emotion becomes the directive of human action."[57] When under the influence of emotion, political leaders are rarely capable of understanding the ramifications of their actions.

The stimulation that comes from hatred and vengefulness is like the stimulation produced by drugs and alcohol. There is created, to be sure, a sense of fervor. But that sense is false. . . . They [emotions] confuse the thinking, blur the vision and burn out the souls of those who rely upon them.[58]

The concept of the nation-hero is built on the foundation of emotion. The possibility of war is imminent under these circumstances.

International warfare, in the present state of society, is largely due to the perversions of the imagination, to the artificial stimulus of emotion and to the dedication of the masses, under emotional influence, to an ideology which is in large part fictitious.[59]

---

[56]Elliot V. Bell, interview conducted by Richard D. Challener in 1964, 8.

[57]JFD, Foreword to *Reparation at the Paris Peace Conference from the Standpoint of the American Delegation,* by Philip Mason Burnett (New York: Columbia University Press, 1940) 1:xiv.

[58]JFD, "The American People Need Now to Be Imbued with a Righteous Faith," in *A Righteous Faith for a Just and Durable Peace,* ed. with an intro. by John F. Dulles (New York: CJDP, 1942) 12. The same theme is expounded in similar words in JFD, "Opening Address" (delivered at the National Study Conference in Delaware, Ohio), 3 March 1942, DP, Box 21; and in JFD, Statement, 28 April 1942, DP, Box 21.

[59]JFD, *War, Peace and Change,* 134. See also *Six Pillars of Peace: A Study Guide Based on "A Statement of Political Propositions,"* ed. with an intro. by John F. Dulles (New York: CJDP, 1943) 72; and "The Problem of Peace," 192.

Modern warfare, warned Dulles, is totalitarian. The lives and resources of entire populations are involved. "Old conceptions regarding
blockades, contraband, fortified zones and the rights of civilians and neu-
trals are no longer tenable."[60] Obviously, then, the emotional excesses
that could lead to war became more dangerous than ever before.

Dulles's stance with regard to American involvement in World War
II becomes more clearly understandable when his repulsion for emotional nationalism is taken into account. His position during the prewar
years has largely been misunderstood because this factor has been ignored by his critics. Townsend Hoopes claims that Dulles "preached his
opposition to the war by ignoring its reality."[61] Carl McIntire called him
a pacifist.[62] Neither view quite does justice to the truth.

In *War, Peace and Change,* Dulles clearly argued that whenever a
clash between popularly deified nations occurs, it "is due to causes to
which both peoples have contributed and for which both must accept responsibility (though perhaps in varying degrees)."[63] In early January of
1940, Henry P. Van Dusen circulated a statement among leading churches
which, while admitting common guilt for the ultimate causes of the conflicts in both Europe and Asia, emphasized that a "basic distinction between civilizations in which justice and freedom are still realities" and
"those in which they have been displaced by ruthless tyranny" must be
made.[64] Dulles signed the statement. Nazism represented nationalism at
its worst; Hitler stood for everything Dulles opposed. Germany's personified and deified state had already committed atrocities in Austria,
Czechoslovakia, and elsewhere. Now France was being threatened. From
early in his youth, dating from the years he traveled to Europe with his
father, Dulles had reserved a special place in his heart for things French.

---

[60]JFD, *War, Peace and Change,* 3.

[61]Hoopes, *The Devil,* 52.

[62]Carl McIntire, *Twentieth Century Reformation* (Collingswood NJ: Christian Beacon
Press, 1944) 121.

[63]JFD, *War, Peace and Change,* 67.

[64]JFD, "The American Churches and the International Situation," 22 January 1940,
DP, Box 19. The statement bears the signatures of Reinhold Niebuhr, Charles Gilkey,
Henry Sloane Coffin, and John R. Mott among others. This statement should not be con-
fused with the Dulles document of the same name.

He knew that Germany's actions constituted a great evil, an evil that could not safely be ignored. Of course he signed the statement.

However, shortly after the statement was released, Dulles came to regret signing it. The statement was, in his opinion, being misread and misused. A letter written 18 March 1940 to Van Dusen explained why he felt this way.

> The press, here and abroad, has rather generally isolated certain sentences from their context to give the impression that the signers felt that the present war involved a great moral issue, with right wholly on the side of the Allies and wrong wholly on the side of Germany. I do not think the statement as a whole, if carefully read, warrants this view. Certainly, if I had thought so I would not have signed it. But I do think that, if you plan to make further use of it, care should be taken to avoid the appearance of coincidence between moral judgement and self-interest which is all too prevalent and which is unconscious hypocrisy.
>
> As one of the satisfied powers it is very much to our self-interest to see the Allies suppress a revolt against the established order. This revolt, like most revolts, has among its leaders dangerous and unscrupulous men and is attended by much evil. This evil we can denounce, but only, in my opinion, if we equally denounce the evils and selfishness of a system which makes inevitable such revolts.
>
> While I think the statement we signed, taken as a whole, does this, I regret the partial use made of it which played directly into the hands of those who are constantly seeking to identify morality and self-interest.[65]

As this letter once again makes clear, Foster Dulles abhorred the effects of nationalism. Throughout the years of the war, he spent considerable blocks of his time trying to prevent Americans from falling into its excesses. He genuinely feared that American reaction to Nazism would foster a nationalism just as dangerous as the one in Germany. This was a potentiality he worked feverishly to prevent.

Nazism represented an evil. Yet it was not the only evil that needed correcting. Other evils could be found much closer to home. For example, the satisfied peoples of the world, in attempting to guarantee the status quo, were ignoring the dynamic needs of much of the world's

---

[65]JFD to H. P. Van Dusen, 18 March 1940, DP, Box 19.

population.[66] In Dulles's opinion, many of the roots of the present conflict were to be found here. Americans, as well as other victors of the First World War, were at least partially responsible for the evil that resulted from this deed. To ignore that fact, Dulles was convinced, would only lead to a hypocritical self-righteousness that would further endanger the possibility of ever achieving a just and durable peace.

A few months later, Niebuhr, Van Dusen, Coffin, Brown, and others asked Dulles to sign a statement urging that the United States increase commitment to the Allies by promising further moral and material resources short of military involvement. He responded by saying that actual involvement was about the only thing left. What was the point of pushing political officials to promise something that they could not deliver? He expressed these sentiments to Henry Sloane Coffin.

> Therefore, I do not see, concretely, what are the new measures of practical assistance to be rendered as "the best hope of avoiding military involvement." I do not think that this objective is served by talking big when we can neither help our friends nor hurt our enemies. This is merely to damage our prestige and invite trouble. . . . During the years when it was possible to think calmly of these matters, I resolved that I would constantly strive not to identify national self-interest with righteousness. It seems to me that the proposed statement cannot be reconciled with that resolution. . . . I know that you and the other signatories are far more devout Christians than I. I cannot and do not presume to tell you that you are wrong. But, unhappily, I cannot follow your leadership along a path which is definitely in conflict with my own profound convictions.[67]

In this case, Dulles expressed the very real concern—one which even the realist Niebuhr seemed to miss—that the statement would only serve to raise false hopes by giving the impression that the United States could still deliver more and stay out of the war. William Adams Brown, upon reading Dulles's letter to Coffin, wrote to him explaining his reason for

---

[66]Dulles was very concerned about developing, and then maintaining, the proper balance between static and dynamic countries so that peaceful change could occur. This is explained at greater length in the next chapter.

[67]JFD to H. S. Coffin, 20 May 1940, DP, Box 19. See also JFD to W. Van Kirk, 13 June 1940, DP, Box 19.

signing the statement. This letter serves to confirm Dulles's assessment of the statement.

> I find myself in sympathy with much that you say. . . . Had the American churches spoken with a clear voice on the moral issues of the war, I should have preferred to be silent in view of the complication of the international situation but only a few days ago Dr. Buttrick, President of the Federal Council, Dr. Fosdick and other leading American churchmen signed a pacifist statement which I cannot but regard as seriously misrepresenting the position of the American churches. . . . I realize that the course we advocate is not substantially different from that which the country is now following, and my motive in signing was not the belief that our statement would make any particular difference in the action taken but in the hope that it might bring courage and moral support to our colleagues in the churches abroad. [68]

Dulles saw no point in trying to raise the hopes of colleagues abroad when they were sure to be false hopes. The United States could do nothing more significant to help the Allied cause short of entering the war. To imply otherwise would be a dangerous thing to do. False hopes are not worthwhile hopes.

One other aspect of this statement bothered Dulles. The desire to encourage the European church leadership was in itself a noble one. Yet the cost of fulfilling that desire would be far too high if, at the same time, the methods utilized encouraged a rising nationalism at home. As Dulles assessed it, the statement being circulated by the American church leadership was guilty of just such a charge.

Shortly after the historic Atlantic Charter was issued, Dulles worked to demonstrate that false hopes created by the political leadership were just as damaging as those created by the religious leadership. He reprimanded the Allied political leadership for their "attempt to weaken Germany's resistance by seeming to promise what may not be performed." [69] In his "Long Range Peace Objectives," he accused the Allies, including the United States, of fomenting "violence and unrest within German oc-

---

[68] W. A. Brown to JFD, 24 May 1940, DP, Box 19.

[69] JFD to Professor J. T. McNeill of the University of Chicago Divinity School, 1 October 1941, DP, Box 20. Here Dulles is explaining to McNeill why he wrote certain parts of his essay, "Long Range Peace Objectives," in the form he did.

cupied territory" by "holding out great hopes of personal freedoms and material plenty if only men will rebel against Germany's new 'order.' " He warned that it would fall upon the United States "to repress much of the violent unrest and unreasonable hope which we will have excited." As a partial solution to the problems caused by this action, he suggested that the Allies commit themselves immediately to the task of storing large stocks of medicine, food, and clothing aside to provide for these peoples at the close of the war.[70]

Dulles's opposition to American involvement in the war was primarily based on his fear of the excessive nationalism that would probably precipitate it. He was sincerely afraid that American involvement would be forced by the mass emotions of the people. In a letter written to United States Representative Ralph A. Gamble more than a month before Pearl Harbor, he expressed his reservations about such a forced entry into the war.

> Under such conditions I think the most dangerous thing for the country is to have the foreign policy governed by the mass emotions of millions of people who cannot possibly form any intelligent judgement.
>
> I do not believe that the foreign policy at these times should be made a popular political football, whether by the isolationists or reservationists. I believe that the President should be put in the position where through bi-partisan effort he can command a backing in Congress sufficiently strong so that it is unnecessary to whip up popular emotions in order to over-ride Congress, and which emotions, when they become strong, make the executive their prisoner.
>
> I think it is dangerous for the country for Republicans to be trying to make political capital either through obstructive tactics or, as indicated by Willkie's last effort, by trying to push the President faster and further than he deems it wise to go.[71]

Dulles, as the above letter partially indicates, was not necessarily opposed to American involvement in the war so long as the country did not rely upon popularly whipped-up emotions to sustain and drive the war effort. Further support for the fact that Dulles feared emotional nationalism more than the possibility of American entry into the war is provided

---

[70]See JFD, "Long Range Peace Objectives," 18 September 1941, DP, Box 20.

[71]JFD to Representative Gamble, 27 October 1941, DP, Box 20.

by his letter to Under Secretary of State Sumner Welles in July of 1941. Writing about the need to unify Americans in order to successfully launch a responsible war effort, Dulles offered an alternative to emotionalism.

> There must, I think, be some affirmative goal, something which holds out the practical promise of better conditions for the future. For this they [the American people] will be prepared to unite for sacrifice. What I say is particularly important in relation to Christian groups and the youth. [72]

The "affirmative goal," as Dulles often expressed it, should be the formation of a flexible world organization in which the United States would play an active role. As early as 1939 in an address delivered before the Economic Club, Dulles expressed the condition that would justify American involvement in the European war:

> I would not oppose affirmative action [involvement in the war] if our policy were based upon a genuine understanding of the causes of the present crisis and was intelligently designed to achieve a world order whereby recurrent crises might hereafter be avoided. [73]

American leadership, as Dulles viewed it, was a long way from developing such an understanding of events. Therefore, a policy of nonintervention made the most sense at the time.

After Pearl Harbor, Dulles played a very important role in getting the churches to concentrate on the problem of developing this postwar order. A dangerous cleavage had developed in the ranks of the churches due to the feuding between pacifists and interventionists. The fact that Dulles had not aligned himself with either side, and had criticized them both equally from a more moderate position than either espoused, enabled him to rally support from both sides for the cause of establishing a just and durable peace. He steered the churches clear of a division over the war itself by concentrating on the problem of developing some kind of new world order; in this respect, Dulles believed, the churches must exert a united influence. A divided church membership during the war would weaken the chances of a just peace after the war ended.

---

[72] JFD to Under Secretary Welles, 24 July 1941, DP, Box 20.

[73] JFD, "Our Foreign Policy," 1, 22 March 1939, DP, Box 18.

The unity statement of December 1940, which was commissioned by the Department of International Justice and Goodwill of the Federal Council and written by Dulles, proved that he could articulate the common concerns of both the pacifist and the interventionist.[74] Largely due to his leadership, the Commission on a Just and Durable Peace, consisting of interventionists like Reinhold Niebuhr and John C. Bennett and pacifists like Harry Emerson Fosdick and Walter Van Kirk, was able to remain unified and work efficiently on planning "what steps had to be taken after the war to prevent it from happening again."[75] This was no small achievement.

The theme that Dulles consistently sounded with regard to the commission's efforts in planning the peace was that "victory-itself is not the end." Rather, it "is the means to an end, namely the organizing of a better world." To whip up popular emotion by emphasizing the need to crush the enemy and thereby become victorious could only be counterproductive; achievement of the proper end, that of a better world, "requires a national purpose forged by hearts and minds that are comprehending and free from the evil emotions which Christ condemned."[76] Americans must not practice the evils they denounce in their enemies. "We must not in this matter play the role of the Gaderene swine."[77] Trust must not be placed "in peace efforts that primarily rely upon emotion." The best avenue to peace is paved by the commitment *not to be emotional.*"[78]

Dulles often reiterated that "the spirit of internationalism was still-born at Versailles" precisely because of emotional excesses.[79] This sad fact helped to bring on World War II.

It is impossible to analyze the last twenty-five years without realizing the futility of individual human action, however brave and sacrificial, if it forms

---

[74]JFD, "The American Churches and the International Situation," 19 December 1940, DP, Box 19.

[75]Richard Fagley, interview, 20.

[76]See JFD, "Opening Address," 1. See also JFD, Statement, 28 April 1942, 1.

[77]JFD, "A Just and Durable Peace," 24.

[78]JFD, *War, Peace and Change,* 74 (emphasis Dulles).

[79]JFD, "The Aftermath," 270.

part of a national policy which is dominated by blind passion and narrow selfishness. [80]

As World War II was drawing to a close, Dulles sought to educate the American people concerning the wisdom of avoiding a peace based upon emotional hostility. His work was interrupted by an American war action that could be construed as the epitome of "blind passion" and "narrow selfishness."

The first atomic bomb was dropped on Hiroshima on 6 August 1945, immediately killing some 80,000 people and turning to rubble approximately 4.4 square miles of the city. The day after the bomb was dropped on Hiroshima, Foster Dulles—expressing once again his concern "that there has been in this war too little moral restraint"[81]—and Richard Fagley drafted a statement designed to express official church reaction and wired it to Bishop Bromley Oxnam, president of the Federal Council of Churches, for his signature. The statement urged that

> as soon as practicable control of this cosmic power be placed under international supervision at [the] service of peace and human welfare. Atomic energy must serve [the] whole family of nations, or mankind will perish. [82]

On 9 August, the day the second bomb was dropped, an official statement was issued by the Federal Council bearing the signatures of Oxnam and Dulles. It urged suspension of the air attack program in order "to give the Japanese people adequate opportunity to react to the new situation through leaders who will accept the surrender terms offered them." The statement continued:

> If we, a professedly Christian nation, feel morally free to use atomic energy in that way, men elsewhere will accept that verdict. Atomic weapons will be looked upon as a normal part of the arsenal of war and the stage will be set for the sudden and final destruction of mankind. [83]

---

[80]JFD, "Christianity in This Hour," 7. See also JFD, "Summary of Remarks," 1 (delivered by JFD at a meeting of the National Peace Conference held in New York City), 17 March 1941, DP, Box 20.

[81]JFD to S. M. Cavert, 14 August 1945, DP, Box 26.

[82]Telegram, JFD and R. Fagley to B. Oxnam, 7 August 1945, DP, Box 26.

[83]JFD, Statement, 9 August 1945, DP, Box 26.

Truman responded to the action of the Federal Council in his character-istically frank manner: "When you have to deal with a beast [Japan] you have to treat him as a beast."[84]

Dulles often boasted that the quick response of the churches had some influence on the fact that no further bombs were dropped on Japan before the country surrendered on 14 August. He later joked about this boast when Secretary of War Stimson's memoirs revealed that the United States only had two bombs. His indiscriminate boasting, however, does not obscure the fact that he was among the first major public figures in America to push for international control of this terrible new source of energy. Later, in November of 1945, on the occasion of Henry P. Van Dusen's inauguration as president of Union Theological Seminary, Dulles once again stated his beliefs concerning the need for international control of atomic energy.

> Out in Tennessee there is a plant which turns out bombs. Here we have a plant which turns out ministers of the Gospel. The two seem re-mote and unrelated. Actually, the issue of our time, perhaps the issue of all human time, is which of the two outputs will prevail. . . .
>
> We should make it clear that we are prepared to subject our atomic knowledge to the dictates of the same world opinion that we would in-voke in favor of other postwar settlements. We have set up a General Assembly to be the "town meeting of the world." Let us invite, and heed, its judgment on what we should do.[85]

Foster Dulles's reaction to the question of the morality of the atomic bomb was consistent with his general position concerning armaments as it was spelled out in *War, Peace and Change* some six years earlier.

> It is, however, unsafe to place our hope of peace upon the terrifying in-fluences of vast armament. The consequences of being wrong are too appalling. Furthermore, the achievement of such armament in itself re-quires the highly emotional state which is capable of precipitating a to-talitarian war.[86]

---

[84]President Truman to S. M. Cavert, 11 August 1945, DP, Box 26.

[85]JFD, "The Atomic Bomb and the Moral Law," 1 and 6-7, 15 November 1945, DP, Box 27.

[86]JFD, *War, Peace and Change*, 90.

Again, his belief at this time regarding the ineffectiveness of a military establishment as a road to peace amply illustrates the extent of his later transformation: as secretary of state he would develop a philosophy that laid the foundation for modern-day theories of deterrence. Yet it is clear that during these years he believed that solutions leading to peace relied on other factors.

6

"What Ought To Be":
Suggesting a Solution
for the Problem

Foster Dulles attempted during the years 1937–1945 to do more than simply point out the obstacles to international peace. Certainly the problems as he presented them seemed immense. Yet Dulles believed that, with proper education and direction, nations could begin to overcome them. Therefore, he was anything but timid in offering his version of the proper solution to the world's troubles. His Presbyterian nature demanded of him at least an attempt to bring some order out of the chaos of international relations.

In order for any solution to be effective, Dulles maintained, it must further the potentiality of bringing world nations together in a forum that would not be so new or unfamiliar that the international political leadership would be unprepared to participate in it. Rather, the new international order must be one that made the attainment of political solutions possible. It must, above all, be an order based upon existing political realities. Otherwise, the nations of the world would not be willing to accept it.

Equally as important to Dulles was the concept of a world organization that would not try to perpetuate the status quo. "That," Dulles said, "would be stultifying." The "bridge from the immediate situation to the Christian ideal" is "the possibility of change." Therefore, part of a realistic assessment of world affairs must necessarily promote the need for orderly processes of change.[1]

Before a new international organization can be judged successful, it must be one that recognizes the "what is" of international relations while, at the same time, possessing mechanisms that will enable it to move toward the "what ought to be." Dulles proposed two strategic avenues, the ethical and the political, which he believed would bring about the felicitous completion of the task at hand. A closer look at these twin components of his suggested solution will reveal more fully the realistic and prophetic thrust of the Dulles philosophy as it was expressed during these years.

The Ethical Solution

The ethical solution was defined by Dulles as including "those efforts which are primarily directed to states of mind." The objective involved was to "mould the human spirit so that desires will either be so diluted in intensity or so metamorphosed in character that conflicts of desire will be minimized."[2] Following through on this objective would ultimately produce that "new international morality"[3] which would serve as the foundation for cooperation among nations. Dulles was committed to the belief that in order for international law to be effective, it "must be based on a common ethos—that is, a common foundation of moral convictions."[4] Laws based on the mores of a particular region could not be use-

---

[1]JFD, "Appraisal of United States Foreign Policy," 5 February 1945, 9, DP, Box 27.

[2]JFD, *War, Peace and Change* (New York: Harper and Brothers, 1939) 9.

[3]JFD, "The Churches and the Charter of the United Nations," *Annual Report* (1945) 152.

[4]J. H. Oldham, ed., *The Oxford Conference: Official Report* (New York: Willett, Clark and Company, 1937) 158. See also JFD, *War, Peace and Change,* 13.

fully applied by leadership in areas where such mores were not commonly shared.

For Dulles, as earlier indicated, the main stumbling block to the establishment of a common international morality was the deification of one's own state accompanied by the simplistic casting of other nations as cruel or callously selfish villains. Since "all peoples . . . act in ways which are reprehensible," the utilization of a "nation villain concept is preponderantly fictitious." Many of the apparent conflicts of desire between nations could be eliminated if only the populations involved could learn to conceive of each other "in the light of . . . factual background."[5] The "differences of language, custom, and culture will persist." Yet, when nations are able to "think of other peoples as not superior or inferior, but different," perhaps people will "learn to respect and appreciate this difference." Out of the resulting "solid basis of mutual respect and tolerance, a common ground of understanding [could] be built up."[6] Actions once viewed as arising from an enemy's hatred could, in this setting, be viewed for what they are: expressions of concern for security in a complex and pluralistic world.

Once "the simple expedient of saying the foreign people is [sic] 'possessed of a devil' " is removed, "the sense of dependence on one's own state as a necessary agency for combating the selfishness and arbitrariness of others" could be diminished. Whenever national leadership feels that some form of vocal protest to another nation's policies is necessary, they "need never assume the indictment of an entire people or nation." Only rarely are there occasions "when those who condemn should not couple their condemnation with repentance, in word and deed, for the causative part played by their own nation." It would help if recorded history were written to reflect the truth of this perspective. Perhaps then the populace as a whole would more fully appreciate the folly involved in the deification of any given state.[7]

---

[5]JFD, *War, Peace and Change*, 110-11.

[6]JFD, ed., *Six Pillars of Peace: A Study Guide Based on "A Statement of Political Propositions"* (New York: Commission to Study the Bases of a Just and Durable Peace, 1943) 77.

[7]JFD, *War, Peace and Change*, 113.

A nation rarely finds leadership "which dares to treat national emergencies other than with the dynamics of cheap emotion." Even when such leadership does emerge, it "is alone inadequate" in meeting the challenge of establishing a sound world order. It must be backed "by a steady weight of public opinion."[8] How could that public opinion be formed? Dulles believed that religion was the best vehicle "for the projection of the ethical solution beyond national lines." Religions seek "to create a new state of mind, such that certain desires are suppressed or supplanted by new desires which are non-conflicting or which may even call for the giving of satisfaction to others."[9] The deification of the state, "which has developed so dangerously," could be checked

> by some form of spiritual revival which will alter and broaden the concept of what is worthy of devotion and sacrifice. . . . The concept of a duty to fellow-man, without regard to propinquity, or to race, creed or nationality, is so pure as to lack ready appeal. Even so, there are many who could derive satisfaction out of association together to promote the welfare of the human race. This is, indeed . . . the objective of Christianity. . . . There is ample evidence that religious concerns remain potentially inspiring and able to create a spiritual unity which overrides national boundaries.[10]

Dulles saw to it that the Christian church attempted to fulfill its appointed role in checking the tendency to deify the state. He embarked on a personal campaign to bring about the "spiritual revival" that he viewed as a necessary prerequisite to the demise of nationalism. One of his more important contributions in this regard was overseeing the publication of an anthology entitled *A Righteous Faith for a Just and Durable Peace*. Articles were written by such notable churchmen as William E. Hocking, Henry P. Van Dusen, Luther A. Weigle, John A. Mackay, John C. Ben-

---

[8]JFD, *The Christian Forces and a Stable Peace* (New York: Committee on Public Affairs, National Board, Young Men's Christian Association of the United States, 1941) 4. See also JFD, "The American People Need Now to Be Imbued with a Righteous Faith," in *A Righteous Faith for a Just and Durable Peace,* ed. JFD (New York: The Commission to Study the Bases of a Just and Durable Peace, 1942) 8; and JFD, "Statement," 8 April 1940, DP, Box 19.

[9]JFD, *War, Peace and Change,* 19, 12.

[10]Ibid., 118-19.

nett, and Harry Emerson Fosdick. The book was written as part of the commission's effort "to assure a faith that will be righteous, and that, because it is righteous, can be shared by other peoples and lead to a just and durable peace."[11] Dulles authored the lead article entitled "The American People Need Now to Be Imbued with a Righteous Faith."

John Mulder and Townsend Hoopes claim that this particular essay illustrates that Dulles himself had succumbed to the pitfalls he had cautioned churchmen about in 1937 when he had observed that

> too often spiritual and secular motives become unconsciously mixed, and it requires unusual practical experience to detect the pitfalls which the worldly constantly prepare to secure for themselves the appearance of church benediction.[12]

These two authors interpret Dulles's plea for a "righteous faith" as an identification of the moral law with United States policy. By making this claim, the authors are guilty of interpreting the earlier years of Dulles's life in light of the later years.[13] Since a breach occurred between the earlier Dulles and the later Dulles, the above interpretation leads to a distortion of the essay's intention.

From a somewhat different perspective, Ronald W. Pruessen, in his recently published biography of Dulles, also misinterprets this important article. He believes that it presents solid evidence that Dulles, after American involvement in the war, had "succumbed to the emotionalism of his countrymen." "Dulles's righteous faith," he writes, "lent itself to something like millennialism in 1942 and 1943." Pruessen attributes to Dulles "the waxing of vigorous nationalist energies during World War II," which caused "much of the subtlety and sophistication of vision" that he had possessed "to be lost."[14]

---

[11]JFD, introduction to *A Righteous Faith*, 4.

[12]JFD, "As Seen by a Layman," *Religion in Life* 7 (Winter 1938): 43.

[13]John M. Mulder, "The Moral World of John Foster Dulles," *The Journal of Presbyterian History* 49 (Summer 1971): 170; Townsend Hoopes, *The Devil and John Foster Dulles* (Boston: Little, Brown and Company, 1973) 55.

[14]Ronald W. Pruessen, *John Foster Dulles: The Road to Power* (New York: The Free Press, 1982) 200-201, 508.

This description of Dulles's zeal is not quite accurate. Yes, his language is characterized by a sense of urgency; one might even call it emotional. However, it was an entirely different degree of emotion than that being expressed by many "of his countrymen." As Dulles explained it,

> This paper forms part of an effort by the Churches to assure peace which will be just and durable. Many question the timing of our effort. They urge that our thoughts should be of nothing beyond military victory and our emotions only those which, they conceive, best feed the flames of war.

These emotions were precisely what Dulles hoped his efforts would help to diminish. "Such emotions," Dulles asserted, "are false stimulants which weaken men by burning out their moral fibre."[15]

In Pruessen's view, Dulles represents the fervent millennialist waving "verbal banners, to try to rouse marchers for the great crusade that would bring a bright, peaceful future."[16] He implies here, in much the same way as Hoopes and Mulder do elsewhere, that Dulles was guilty of a nationalistic emotionalism that interpreted the war effort as a "great crusade" with right on one side and wrong on the other. Dulles's own words provide a fitting response to Pruessen's assessment of his state of mind. They were penned as an answer to a similar charge levelled by Loren C. McKinney, a history professor at the University of North Carolina, shortly after this essay was published in *Life* magazine.

> I think you misapprehend the import of my article perhaps because you assume that Christians generally are imbued with self-righteousness and that, therefore, since mine is a Christian article, it must be colored by the same taint. Actually, if you were familiar with my writings you would know that self-righteousness is one of the things against which I feel most strongly and which I most constantly attack. I specify in the *Life* article that "self-conceit" was one of the things against which Christ principally inveighed.[17]

Pruessen's point seems to be that Dulles's involvement with the churches began and hastened the demise of his flexibility and openness

---

[15]JFD, "The American People," 5.

[16]Pruessen, *The Road to Power,* 201.

[17]Letter, JFD to Loren C. McKinney, 1 February 1943, DP, Box 22.

concerning change: "Though his formal Protestant ties dwindled after 1946, it is well known that highflying rhetoric regarding divine approval did not."[18] The implication is that Dulles's self-righteous nationalism—as it was to emerge most strongly during the period immediately preceding his tenure as secretary of state—was evident in, and even due to, his association with the Protestant churches. In other words, Dulles's prior commitment to American self-interest became joined with a moralizing rhetoric as a result of his work with the Federal Council of Churches.

Thus Mulder, Hoopes, and Pruessen all underline that Dulles makes an emotional plea in this essay for the development of a national faith, "a faith so profound that we, too, will feel that we have a mission to spread it through the world.[19] All three use this quotation as evidence that Dulles had fallen prey to the temptation to link the moral law with actual United States policy. However, when this sentence is placed back into its original context, its meaning becomes clear. The faith Dulles hoped to "spread" throughout the world was, as he termed it, a "righteous faith." As his concept of a righteous faith is developed in this article and throughout the remainder of his writings during this period, it is evident that he is not referring to the need for faith in the righteousness of American foreign policy.[20]

Rather than attempting to revive and universalize an already existing national faith, Dulles's emotional plea was directed toward instilling in Americans a "new" national faith based on the moral law. "What we need," Dulles explained, "is a national purpose which conforms to great human needs, a purpose that is responsive to the insistent demand of suffering humanity."[21] Thus righteous faith is that which would teach "the subordinate role of immediate material objectives" and "comprehend the essential unity and equal worthiness of all human beings." In order for a faith

---

[18]Pruessen, *The Road to Power,* 506.

[19]JFD, "The American People," 7.

[20]See JFD, "The Churches' Contribution toward a Warless World," *Religion in Life* 9 (Winter 1940): 39; JFD, "The American People," 8; and JFD, "Christianity: Solvent of World Conflict," *Social Progress* 33 (January 1943): 3, where he explicitly denounces such a faith.

[21]JFD, "Opening Address" (delivered at the National Study Conference in Delaware, Ohio), 3 March 1942, DP, Box 21.

to be characterized as righteous, it must be a faith that is free from the "false sense of fervor" that comes from "hatred and vengefulness."[22] Such a faith "is incompatible with national selfishness and isolation."[23] It would be different from the evil faiths of nationalism in that it would be free from seeing "the defects in others and only the virtues in yourself."[24]

The desire to foster a sense of this righteous faith among the American people occupied Dulles throughout these years. In speech after speech, article after article, the same message comes through. America needs a constructive purpose "which is contagious and inspiring" so the country can abandon the defensive support of the "status quo of a world system which has become vitally defective and which is inevitably productive of just such convulsions as the present world war." One particular passage appearing repeatedly in Dulles's writings with only a slight change in phrasing defines the righteous faith in the following manner, which is reminiscent of prophetic Protestantism:

> We require a vision which will see true despite the distortions of war propaganda. We require a purpose which will hold resolute, without dependence on the cheap emotions of hate and fear. We require the courage to hear the criticisms which in time of war are the probable lot of those who remain calm and concentrated on long range objectives. We require a sense of values conceived in terms of the general welfare rather than that of our particular nation, race, or class. We require group action sufficiently powerful to influence political leaders. These are qualities which we can find above all in the followers of Christ.[25]

He who fulfills these requirements "will become a person of righteous and creative faith." If this begins to happen "in sufficient numbers,

---

[22]JFD, *War, Peace and Change*, 94-96. See also JFD, "The American People," 8.

[23]Cover letter for the statement "A Just and Durable Peace: Statement of Political Propositions," JFD to all members of the commission, 12 March 1943, DP, Box 22.

[24]Statement of JFD in "C.B.S.: The Peoples Platform," 19 December 1942, DP, Box 21.

[25]JFD, "Christianity in This Hour," 21-22, 21 April 1941, DP, Box 20; JFD, "The American People," 9-10; JFD, *The Christian Forces,* 9; JFD, "The American Vision," in *The Spiritual Legacy of John Foster Dulles,* ed. Henry P. Van Dusen (Philadelphia: The Westminster Press, 1960) 59-61; JFD, "Opening Address," 3; JFD, Statement, 2, 28 April 1942, DP, Box 21; JFD, "A Righteous Faith," *Life* 13 (28 December 1942): 50-51.

then and only then" will the nation assume "a creative role in world affairs."[26] The nation would perhaps then become

> responsive to the insistent demand of suffering humanity that a way be found to save them [sic] and their children and their children's children from the misery, the starvation of body and soul, the violent death, which economic disorder and recurrent war now wreak upon man.[27]

It is only natural that Americans, "since they are healthy, wealthy, and fed," should "lead the way as an example for the rest of the United Nations to follow."[28]

Christians in the United States should provide the example for Americans by showing how to implement the ethical solution. One of the most important ways for Christians to aid in reaching this goal was for them, "in a spirit of humility, [to] avoid even the appearance of thanking God that we are not as other men."[29] Christians "must not seek to equate the Kingdom of God with any particular structure of society."[30] The proper understanding of Christian duty

> requires that we vitalize belief in a God who is the Father of us all, a God so universal that belief in Him cannot be reconciled with deification of Nation. . . . There can be no salvation until we have set right the fundamentals. The urgent task of the Church is to restore God as the object of human veneration and to recreate in man a sense of duty to fellow man. National governments must be seen to be what they are—pieces of po-

---

[26]JFD, "The American Vision," 62.

[27]JFD, "Opening Address," 5.

[28]JFD, "Article Prepared for *New York Times Sunday Magazine*," 8.

[29]JFD, *Long Range Peace Objectives: Including an Analysis of the Roosevelt-Churchill Eight Point Declaration* (New York: The Commission to Study the Bases of a Just and Durable Peace, 1941) 2.

[30]JFD, Statement, 18 October 1940, DP, Box 19. See also JFD, "Christianity: Solvent of World Conflict," 5. This passage and others like it are particularly reflective of Dulles's adherence to a typology similar to the one put forth by Reinhold Niebuhr. As Langdon Gilkey has expressed, Niebuhr believed that "the Kingdom is a judgment and a lure for all historical achievement; its essential role and meaning in history is precisely in that transcendence and would be lost the moment it was regarded as directly ingredient in history" ("Reinhold Niebuhr's Theology of History," in *The Legacy of Reinhold Niebuhr,* ed. Nathan A. Scott, Jr. [Chicago: The University of Chicago Press, 1975] 59).

litical mechanism which involve no sanctity and which must be constantly remolded and adapted to meet the needs of a world which is a living, and, therefore, a changing organism.[31]

Two understandings of the mission of America have often been in tension in American history. One of these emphasizes the concept of *manifest destiny,* which interprets the mission of America in terms of the active expansion of American principles. Such American expansion is viewed as ordained by God, thus putting Americans under the obligation to fulfill that destiny and continually safeguard American principles throughout the world. This particular understanding of the American mission has been inherently imperialistic. Dulles, at this point in his life, argued against this notion since it represented nationalism in its most developed state.

The other understanding of American mission emphasizes *example,* as demonstrated by the Puritan leader John Winthrop's admonition that "we must consider that we shall be as a city upon a hill, the eyes of all people are upon us." This concept of the American mission—also embraced by those who have viewed America as a "light to the nations"—admonishes Americans to keep their own house in order. Historically, this view has supported American isolationism. Dulles, though hardly isolationist, argued that this is a proper understanding of the American mission. True to the covenant theology of John Winthrop, Dulles emphasized the duty of all Americans to encourage peace by living up to their covenant with the universal God through caring for the needs of suffering humanity at large. Dulles avoided the traditional isolationist stigma associated with this view of American mission by calling upon Americans to become sacrificially involved in serving the needs of the international community. By this plea, he hoped that others would be won over to such action by the force of the American example.

Dulles believed that one of the duties of the informed Christian leader was "to seek to appraise any projected major foreign policy in light of the probable long-term reaction to it of Christian people." This belief was based upon his premise "that this nation [America] will not pursue consistently any major foreign policy which Christian people of this country

---

[31]JFD, "The Churches' Contribution," 39-40. See also JFD, "The American People," 8-9.

preponderantly find incompatible with their moral judgment."[32] The churches, therefore, in order to live up to the responsibility this entails, must be prophetic and vocal in appraising United States foreign policy; the ethical solution is dependent upon it. Only in this manner can the necessary spiritual attitude for realizing the universal "brotherhood of man" be firmly implanted in the hearts and minds of human beings. The future "well being of posterity depends upon statesmen now being able to build upon minds which are tolerant and serene and upon sympathies which are generous and broad."[33]

Dulles often reminded his listeners that the task of the Christian church in this endeavor was not an easy one. The way of nationalism was firmly entrenched in the history of the world. What is worse, Christianity had helped to foster it.[34] Nevertheless, if recognition of a flexible body of international law were ever to become a reality, progress must be made toward defining the ethical dimensions of the overall solution.

> I know that it is difficult to enlist sacrifice except by invoking the ideology of combat and hate. But I also know that mankind is paying a fearful price for its worship of false gods and that never before did the world so need a vital belief in a universal God. That need is the measure of our opportunity and it must equally be the measure of our works and of our faith.[35]

The Political Solution

Whereas the ethical solution seeks to alter human desires so that they are no longer in conflict, the political solution recognizes the presence of conflicting human desires and seeks to work with them through collaboration in order to achieve a satisfactory result. Because desires always remain, the ethical solution cannot be the sole means of resolution. Both approaches, ethical and political, must be utilized.

---

[32]JFD, "Confidential Draft on American Foreign Policy," 7 December 1943, DP, Box 22.

[33]JFD, Statement, 18 October 1940.

[34]JFD, "The Churches' Contribution," 37.

[35]Ibid., 40.

The usefulness of the political solution comes in channeling human conduct that is impelled by these conflicting desires into nonviolent outlets. Procedures must be established "to determine what acts are permissible to gratify desires and what acts must be suppressed."[36] This requires a flexible international law that is responsive to the various peoples of the world as their needs develop. Achieving permanence in international law, then, is not the primary consideration.

> In international affairs—as indeed elsewhere—we should seek to abolish any sense of finality. "Never" and "forever" are words which should be eliminated from the vocabulary of statesmen.[37]

In the vocabulary of Foster Dulles, one of his most beloved phrases was "peaceful change." Peace, if it is to be lasting,

> must also take account of the fact that life is essentially dynamic, that change is inevitable, and that transformations are bound to occur violently unless they are provided ways of peaceful change.[38]

His thinking concerning the concept of peaceful change was inspired originally by the French philosopher and Nobel Prize winner, Henri Bergson. Echoing the illustrious French philosopher under whom he once studied, Dulles came to view all reality as being in a constant state of flux.[39] Even though many have interpreted Dulles's actions as secretary of state as indicative of an inflexible and static philosophy, change, for Dulles, was the law of life. It remained so throughout his long public career; however, as the years passed he became increasingly desirous of attaining a firmer control over selecting and allowing only those changes that most suited the needs and security of the free world. This is only natural in that he eventually, after 1945, began to equate the aims and the policies of the free world, particularly those of the United States, with the universal welfare of humanity.[40]

---

[36]JFD, *War, Peace and Change,* 12.

[37]Ibid., 156.

[38]JFD, "Peaceful Change," *International Conciliation* no. 369 (April 1941): 493.

[39]One can find the basis for much of what Dulles wrote concerning change in Henri Bergson, *Creative Evolution,* trans. Arthur Mitchell (New York: Henry Holt and Company, 1911).

[40]See chs. 8-10 for further information concerning this transition in his thought.

The best place to begin in understanding Dulles's view of change is with his definition of the word itself. "Change," Dulles wrote in 1939, "is the result of the dynamic prevailing over the static."[41] As is often the case, one definition leads to the need for further definition. Use of the term *dynamic* refers

> to those who desire the structure of their society to be changed or their group enlarged in order to give greater scope to their energy or to adventurous disposition or in the hope of thereby improving, relatively or absolutely, their material or social status.

Static, on the other hand, refers

> to those who are sufficiently satisfied with what they have—in the way of possessions and opportunities—to not want any important change in the structure of the society in which they live.

While he was associated with the churches, Dulles consistently expressed his conviction that the static forces of the world needed to give some satisfaction to the dynamic forces of the world. In other words, the satisfied nations would need to learn to live with a certain degree of insecurity.[42] "Change," he asserted,

> is the one thing which cannot be permanently prevented and the effort to perpetuate that which has become artificial will inevitably break the person or nation committed thereto.[43]

The commission's Guiding Principle "Number Six" expressed the same idea in yet another way: "Nor must it be forgotten that refusal to assent to needed change may be as immoral as the attempt by violent means to force such a change."[44]

Dulles acted on the assumption that "the demand for change at its inception is generally moderate and largely justifiable."[45] This caused him

---

[41]JFD, *War, Peace and Change,* 138.

[42]Ibid., 30-33.

[43]Letter, JFD to Thomas M. Debevoise, 30 April 1940, DP, Box 19.

[44]JFD, "Statement of Guiding Principles," 44. See also JFD, "The American Churches and the International Situation," 19 December 1940, DP, Box 19.

[45]JFD, *War, Peace and Change,* 144.

to exhibit a sincere concern for the rights of the inhabitants of what is now referred to as the Third World. He was one of the few public leaders calling attention to the poverty and economic distress of that area. From the experiences of the French and Russian revolutions, international leaders should have learned

> the imperative necessity of political devices which assure equality of opportunity and which constantly are at work to prevent conditions becoming rigid and fixed to the advantage of one class and to the detriment of another.[46]

Dulles held that this pertained to the economic conditions of nations as well. He demonstrated through his persistent expression of these concerns that, at this time, he "was most open toward the revolutionary world"—much more so "than the later developments would indicate."[47]

Foster Dulles insisted that the political leadership of the satisfied nations recognize the legitimacy of the dynamic impulse and become willing to accept the change that accompanies it. Willingness to adapt international agreements to the realities of change is a prerequisite for lasting peace. One of the realities demanding change is that in several parts of the world the population is larger than the natural resources readily accessible for that population. This unfortunate circumstance was due largely to the fact that "the natural bounties which God has provided for the benefit of mankind are not apportioned in accordance with the national boundaries which man has drawn."[48]

Repeatedly, Dulles expressed his belief that the victors in World War I were largely responsible for the advent of World War II. The leaders of England, France, and the United States

> had a power, in respect of such matters as trade, control of raw materials, markets, and money which vitally affected the peoples of Japan, It-

---

[46]JFD, "The Churches' Contribution," 32.

[47]Bennett, interview, 14. For particular expression of this openness as it affects economic relations between nations, one might begin with JFD, *War, Peace and Change*, 22, 29-33, 39-44, 95-96, and 135. This aspect of Dulles's thought will be treated further in the next chapter.

[48]JFD, "The Problem of Peace in a Dynamic World," *Religion in Life* 6 (Spring 1937): 192.

aly and Germany. They exercised that power without responsibility for the welfare of these other people.[49]

The nations dominating the League of Nations "conceived the League primarily as an instrumentality for perpetuating the status quo."[50] Therefore, to the governments of the dissatisfied peoples, the league "assumed the character of a strait jacket."[51]

The victors in the First World War misused the League of Nations. For this reason, Dulles was unwilling to place majority blame for World War II upon the Japanese, German, and Italian peoples. According to Townsend Hoopes and Leonard Mosley, such unwillingness is proof that he did not fully understand the gravity of the international situation.[52] Dulles, for his part, could not see the good in simply chopping away the sickest branches (Germany, Italy, and Japan) of a diseased and contagious tree while leaving the roots and trunk (an international system committed to the maintenance of the status quo) intact. He recognized that the national faiths of these countries "were shot through with evil"[53] but, in his opinion, so was the system. It, too, had to be changed.

The major fault, as Dulles saw it, lay with the system. World War II might have been avoided if access to the natural wealth of the world had been made more readily available to the dynamic nations and if the peace had been less vindictive and more conciliatory. Most people want to live in peace. However,

there are always, in every country and at every time, those who are ea-

---

[49]JFD, "The Churches' Contribution," 33.

[50]JFD, *War, Peace and Change,* 81. See also JFD to Sumner Welles, 24 July 1941, DP, Box 20.

[51]JFD, "The Aftermath of the World War," *International Conciliation* no. 369 (April 1941): 268. Dulles here calls for action that is fundamentally congruent with H. Richard Niebuhr's definition of what is necessary for the fulfillment of a responsible Christian ethic: "The responsible self is driven as it were by the movement of the social process to respond and be accountable in nothing less than a universal community" (*The Responsible Self* [New York: Harper and Row, 1964] 88).

[52]See Leonard Mosley, *Dulles: A Biography of Eleanor, Allen and John Foster Dulles and Their Family Network* (New York: The Dial Press/James Wade, 1978) 95-99; Hoopes, *The Devil,* 52.

[53]JFD, "The American People," 9.

ger to lead the masses in ways of violence. They can be rendered innoc-
uous only by preventing the many from feeling that they are subject to
power which is exercised without regard for their welfare and which con-
demns them to inequalities and indignities.[54]

An international system must be implemented so the essential needs of
the dynamic peoples could be met. Flexibility is essential. A world system "is doomed if it identifies peace and morality with a mere maintenance of the status quo."[55]

The ultimate goal of the political solution, and thus the task of political
leadership, is that of "striking a fair balance between static and dynamic,
to prevent the growth of violent tendencies on the part of great numbers."[56] In order for this goal to become a reality, a flexible "body of international law adequate to settle or dissipate the political, economic and
ideological strains" among nations needs to be developed. Because no
such recognized law exists, nations resort to force for the settling of disputes, such as the United States did in acquiring the Panama Canal.[57] Such
action is then legitimized and made secure through the signing of a treaty.

Dulles contended that the problem with existing international law was
its incorporation in treaties. When formulating a treaty, each nation seeks
to enshrine its own particular interests. Indeed, the motivating factors
behind the art of treaty making are the concern for security, for permanence, and for maintenance of the status quo. Treaties are not designed
to create a condition of elasticity and they are not changeable except
through force or the threat of force.

> Peaceful and non-disturbing evolution could occur in the world as a whole
> if we had fewer treaties, and if those we had were less permanent and
> more conducive to the development of a flexible body of international

---

[54]JFD, "The Churches' Contribution," 35. See also JFD, "Christianity in This Hour,"
7; and JFD, "The Problem of Peace," 205.

[55]JFD, "Peaceful Change," *International Conciliation*, no. 369 (April 1941): 493.

[56]JFD, *War, Peace and Change*, 32.

[57]JFD, "The Beginning of a World Order," 11, 9, 22 April 1945, DP, Box 27. See also
JFD, "Has the U.S. the Right to Exclude from the Use of the Canal Any Class of Foreign
Vessels?" delivered at the Seventh Annual Meeting of the American Society of Inter-
national Law in Washington, 25 April 1913, 4-5 and 7, DP, Box 289.

practices which might ultimately become so grounded in the mores of the world community as to attain the status of law.[58]

International cooperation must precede the development of a flexible body of international law. Thus the formation of some kind of international organization is an integral part of the political solution. Even though "there may be little that they [international authorities] can promptly achieve and there will be doubt as to the sincerity and practicability of the effort represented thereby," an international organization is essential to lasting peace. In the beginning the organization would, of necessity, be limited in its authority.

> It would be utopian, to attempt to establish any body having authority to dictate changes in the national domains. No nation would consent to delegate to others such powers over its own life. But experimentation in ways which would commit no nation could now be usefully attempted. If the experiment succeeded, then its implications would be farreaching.[59]

Dulles hoped that one of the first achievements to emerge from attempted international cooperation would be a lessening of the boundary consciousness that lay beneath excessive nationalism. "The people of the world can come to know each other better and trust each other more."[60] This would not come easily. The nations

> are like frontiersmen or tribal chieftains who have always lived independently, relying upon their own skill and their own weapons to survive. Some disaster brings them to feel that there is a better way of living. So as a first step, they gather around a campfire or a meeting hall. They are wary of each other. If they were searched, many lethal weapons would be found concealed about their persons. But they have at least come together to talk about matters of common interest. That is the first step toward civic order.[61]

---

[58]JFD, *War, Peace and Change,* 158; also see 40-48.

[59]Ibid., 151.

[60]JFD, "Draft," 14, 26 January 1944, DP, Box 23. See also JFD, *War, Peace and Change,* 123.

[61]JFD, "The Beginning of a World Order," 4.

In order to learn to trust one another, nations would first need to be willing to cut "safety valves . . . through the barriers of boundaries."[62] These apertures could be created through the maturing of "international practices which will to some extent open up opportunity throughout the world."[63] Dulles proposed development in four areas. First, he suggested reestablishing "national monetary units in some reasonably stable relationship to each other" in order to make it easier for nations to exchange goods and services. Second, measures should be taken to facilitate access to the raw materials of the world so that nations with need can obtain them. The important thing to remember here, however, is that trade must be balanced. Therefore, satisfied nations must be willing to import products from nations needing raw materials. Third, Dulles recommended that restrictions concerning the movement of people across national lines should be lightened. As people travel more freely among nations, they are better able to appreciate the customs and traditions of others. Finally, Dulles suggested that the duration of treaties should be limited in order to allow adjustment in light of the underlying changes in international conditions. Perhaps, if political steps such as these were attempted, the tendency toward nationalism could be dealt a severe blow. Obviously, nations would continue to use their resources in their own national interest; however, impressions, techniques, and manners could be changed for the better.[64]

In order to "reconcile" peacefully the "different interests and different ideals" of their nations, international political leaders must realize that negotiation "is not a process of coercion but of reason."[65] Dulles de-emphasized the use of force as a solvent to world problems. He openly disagreed with Secretary of the Navy Frank Knox and others who believed that peace consisted in having with England the power to coerce the rest of the world. In the first place, such an alliance "would be bound to the maintenance of the status quo."[66] To the poorer nations, "a federation of

---

[62]JFD, "The Problem of Peace," 197.

[63]JFD, *War, Peace and Change,* 133.

[64]Ibid., 128-31; and JFD, "The Problem of Peace," 200-203.

[65]JFD, "Our Vital Peace Decision," *Vital Speeches of the Day* 12 (15 October 1945): 7.

[66]JFD, "Long Range Peace Objectives," 4.

the so-called democracies would . . . appear as the banding together of the well-to-do." There could be "nothing more hopeless, more sure to fail."[67] In the second place, such a policy would be totally unrealistic since

a police force cannot serve and is not designed to serve as a substitute for the creation of a healthy balance between dynamic and static forces. A police force is effective only in conjunction with the attaining, otherwise, of such a balance. It can deal effectively only with marginal and usually abnormal elements which do not accept a form of society which is acceptable to the great mass as providing for a peaceful reconciliation of their normal desires.[68]

A world policeman of the sort that Secretary Knox proposed would only "create great antagonisms throughout the rest of the world."[69] Dulles was totally opposed to playing such a role.

As Dulles saw it, once negotiations among the nations of the world were undertaken in earnest, force would become less and less a factor in international relations. If an "elastic form of society is provided," dynamic energies will "peacefully diffuse themselves." When violence occurs, it will be "due to abnormalities which, under normal conditions," are of "insignificant proportions." As a result, the necessary restraints would be "well within the range of possibility."[70]

According to Dulles, reasoned negotiation was the key to the political solution. National leaders throughout the world must put their "heads together." Each nation's leadership must be willing to compromise, to "try to see the best, not the worst, in each other." Thereby, perhaps everyone could experience firsthand "the many fine qualities possessed by other peoples." "If we want peace," concluded Dulles, "then we must intensify and universalize" the negotiation process.[71] In this context, every nation's ideals and goals would be subject to the checks and balances of an

---

[67]Letter, JFD to Under Secretary of State Sumner Welles, 24 July 1941, DP, Box 20.

[68]JFD, *War, Peace and Change,* 96. See also letter, JFD to James P. Warburg, 8 October 1941, DP, Box 20.

[69]Letter, JFD to Reverend Bradford S. Abernethy, 15 October 1941, DP, Box 20.

[70]JFD, "The Problem of Peace," 194.

[71]JFD, "The Political Cost of Peace," *International Journal of Religious Education* 20 (October 1943): 3.

international organization that, as a result, might contribute in a more meaningful way to finding fairer solutions to the world's problems. This concern was uppermost in Dulles's mind as he prepared to attend the United Nations Organization Conference in San Francisco.

7

Moving from Problem
toward Solution:
The United Nations Charter

During the first week of February 1945, Churchill, Stalin, and Roosevelt met at Yalta. One of the least controversial agreements to emerge from that meeting involved the decision to call a conference of nations together in order to draft a charter for a new league of nations. A few months later, on 25 April 1945, 282 delegates from nations around the world gathered in the elegant San Francisco Opera House. They met in the collective hope that the end result of their meeting might be the establishment of a permanent basis for postwar security. The location of their meeting place symbolized America's arrival to center stage in the theater of world politics. Aging Europe had passed the mantle of power on to her precocious offspring.

As Townsend Hoopes and Ronald Pruessen have pointed out, Foster Dulles was able to secure an appointment as a legal adviser to the American delegation of the San Francisco United Nations Conference largely through the intervention of Bernard Baruch and Senator Arthur H. Vandenberg.[1] Dulles was excited about the opportunity to go to San Francisco. The idea of forming an international organization was, for him, a lifetime goal. His vocal presence at Versailles in 1919 is testimony to that fact. Even before then, as early as 1917, he considered the "creation of a world of new international relationships" of "utmost importance."[2] His commitment to such an organization was the natural outgrowth of religious and international influences that had early on contributed to the formation of his world view.

Now that he would be present in San Francisco, Dulles felt he could do his part to see that the mistakes of Versailles were not repeated. Victory in World War II must be used to establish the proper world order.[3] He often quoted the *Federalist Papers* to communicate the urgency he felt regarding this matter.

> It seems to have been reserved to the people of this country, by their conduct and example, to decide whether societies of men are really capable or not of establishing good government from reflection and choice, or whether they are forever destined to depend for their political constitutions on accident and force. The crisis at which we are arrived may be regarded as the era in which that decision is to be made, and a wrong election of the part we shall act may deserve to be considered as the general misfortune of mankind.[4]

In order to avoid potential criticism of his official appointment to the American United Nations delegation, Dulles immediately resigned from his responsibilities with the Federal Council of Churches. The statement including his official acceptance of his role as general adviser made it clear

---

[1]Townsend Hoopes, *The Devil and John Foster Dulles* (Boston: Little, Brown and Company, 1973) 58; see also Ronald W. Pruessen, *John Foster Dulles: The Road to Power* (New York: The Free Press, 1982) 236-37; see also *The Private Papers of Senator Vandenberg,* ed. Arthur H. Vandenberg, Jr. (Boston: Houghton Mifflin Company, 1952) 87, 124, and 159, where the origins of the growing friendship between Dulles and the senator are duly noted.

[2]JFD, "Draft on War," 3, August 1917, DP, Box 1.

[3]JFD, "Opening Address" (delivered at the National Study Conference in Delaware, Ohio), 1, 3 March 1942, DP, Box 21; and JFD, "Address," 1, 28 April 1942, DP, Box 21.

[4]See, for example, JFD, "The Churches and a Just and Durable Peace," *The Biennial Report of the Federal Council of Churches of Christ in America* (1944) 3.

that, from his viewpoint, "no question of religious representation is involved. I am, and always have been, strongly opposed to representation of the churches at any peace conference."[5]

Even though he disassociated himself from the churches, he retained all the ideological baggage he had accumulated during the last several years concerning his church-associated views of what the international organization should achieve. He hoped to see an international organization dedicated to bringing the nations together in an atmosphere where tough negotiation and compromise might become a reality between national sovereignties hoping to get what they perceived as necessary for their security and economic interests. On this point Dulles's position is illustrative of the heart of realism.

As Kenneth W. Thompson defines realism, "[It] assumes that international politics, like all politics, is compromise, give-and-take, and reconciliation. The watchword of diplomacy is accommodation; a political settlement is the most to be hoped for among rival states."[6] Throughout the war years, Dulles and his commission consistently expressed the necessity of accommodation in international matters. "It must be made clear," the commission wrote, "that collaboration implies not merely the spirit of compromise but equally the right, on the part of every nation, to persist in its efforts to realize its ideals."[7]

Dulles hoped that the solutions resulting from the compromise among nations would form the foundation of a flexible body of international law that could be referred to in future negotiations and adapted to developing situations in a world where change was the only certain law.[8] Out of col-

---

[5]JFD, "Acceptance of Appointment as General Adviser to the U.S. Delegation, San Francisco Conference," 5 April 1945, DP, Box 292.

[6]Kenneth W. Thompson, *Ethics, Functionalism, and Power in International Politics: the Crisis in Values* (Baton Rouge: Louisiana State University Press, 1979) 20.

[7]JFD, "Christian Standards and Current International Developments," 144; see also JFD, "America's Role in the Peace," *Christianity and Crisis* 4 (22 January 1945): 5.

[8]As I have mentioned, Dulles realized that the nations of the world had no common recognition of anything like what he defined as the moral law. Differing customs acted as a limitation upon any such legislation. (See JFD, "The Beginning of a World Order," 11, 22 April 1945, DP, Box 27; JFD, "Comments on the Fifth Statement. Pattern for Peace; 5. International Institutions to Maintain Peace with Justice Must Be Organized," *World Affairs* 107 [March 1944]: 35; JFD, "Toward World Order," in *A Basis for the Peace to Come,* ed. Francis J. McConnell [New York: Abingdon-Cokesbury Press, 1942] 46; JFD, "A Just and Durable Peace," 28; and JFD, "World Organization: Curative and Creative," *Biennial Report* [1944] 136.)

laboration among nations "there can come a common judgment" concerning what constitutes "decent national conduct," as well as the necessary belief that "the general welfare should take precedence" over any other consideration. [9]

At this time, however, I should reiterate that Dulles did not envision an automatic curtailment of national sovereignty to result from the process of collaboration. "The American people," he said, "and in general all national groups, will for the time being retain control over their own destinies." [10] Only over time, as national groups realized the expediency of such collaboration, would they learn to "share with others decisive authority over their destiny." [11] Dulles, therefore, entertained no illusions concerning the right of individual nations to safeguard their own interests. In other words, Dulles tempered his prophetic Protestantism, which hoped for a world order reflecting the general welfare of all citizens of the world, with a political realism that recognized the particular concerns of the separate nations of the world. It was from this perspective that Dulles hoped to influence the proceedings of the United Nations Conference in San Francisco.

The Major Crises
in San Francisco

The work of the American delegation to San Francisco was seriously complicated as various crises developed concerning certain issues. In all of these major disagreements, Foster Dulles contributed to the final formulation of the American position. Obviously, these crises are much more complex than the following summaries might indicate. Nevertheless, by briefly examining each major crisis, the contribution of Dulles to the conference will come into sharper focus.

---

[9]JFD, "A Just and Durable Peace," 28-29.

[10]JFD, "Draft," 11, 26 January 1944, DP, Box 23.

[11]*Christianity and Crisis* 4 (7 February 1944): 8; see also JFD, *War, Peace and Change* (New York: Harper and Brothers, 1939) 151; and JFD, "Memo to Professor Clyde Eagleton," 27 May 1941, DP, Box 20.

Regionalism. As nearly every general diplomatic history covering the formation of the United Nations Charter indicates, one of the major logjams in San Francisco arose over the question of regionalism.[12] Some of the big powers wanted the Charter to reflect special recognition of regional arrangements. No argument was raised over including the series of security treaties negotiated by the Soviet Union with various countries pertaining to Germany. However, the trouble arose when Senator Vandenberg required special consideration of the Monroe Doctrine, particularly as it related to the Pan American nations. He wanted to protect the security system derived at the Chapultepec Conference in March of 1945.[13]

Dulles argued, against Vandenberg and the other supporters of inclusion for the regional security pacts, that the issue was really unimportant. More than likely, the Monroe Doctrine could be taken for granted without explicit reference to it being contained in the Charter. Seeking its inclusion would only encourage similar regional arguments from the other great powers—with the net result of quartering off sections of the world where the United States would have no voice.

By the time of the United Nations Conference, Dulles had recognized the unavoidable fact that the Soviet Union would have a free hand in Eastern Europe. He approved of language which guaranteed that right. However, he did not wish to open the door to future arrangements of that kind. Realistically, he argued that the price for universal recognition of the Pan American system might cost the United States too much. Not only could such a provision cause problems in both Europe and China, it could also subvert the international character of the world organization.[14]

---

[12]See, for example, Alexander De Conde, *A History of American Foreign Policy* (New York: Charles Scribner's Sons, 1963) 635-36; Thomas A. Bailey, *A Diplomatic History of the American People*, 4th ed., enl., with a foreword by Dixon Ryan Fox (New York: Appleton-Century-Crofts, Inc., 1950) 847; and Thomas G. Paterson, J. Garry Clifford, and Kenneth J. Hogan, *American Foreign Policy: A History Since 1900*, vol. 2, 2d ed., enl. (Lexington: D. C. Heath and Co., 1983) 408.

[13]For some of what follows, I depend upon Pruessen's excellent discussion of the practical aspects of Dulles's participation concerning these issues, though I disagree with his conclusions (Pruessen, *The Road to Power*; see esp. 239-52).

[14]Ibid., 245.

Dulles's efforts to convince his countrymen on this issue were unsuccessful. Threatening that the Senate might not pass the Charter without some explicit protection of Pan American concerns, Vandenberg persuaded the American delegation to push for the appropriate language. Dulles provided his legal expertise to help form the draft that eventually became Article 51, in which general agreement was reached that regional action in response to outside armed attacks was acceptable. [15]

Colonialism. Another crisis developed at the conference over the fate of backward or dependent peoples. On this issue, the Soviet Union, since it did not possess any overseas colonies, took a liberal line. Dulles, once again, assumed a position which resembled that of the Soviet Union more than that of his own colleagues. As early as May of 1943, he posed the question, "What will be the attitude toward some international repercussions of our administration of Puerto Rico? Will we accept for ourselves what we have urged upon others?"[16] Consistently over the years, he had argued that some kind of mandate system had to be established "where the territory is to be administered in trust, first for the well-being and advancement of the local populations, and then for the benefit and equal opportunity of the whole world."[17]

In San Francisco, Dulles reiterated these basic concerns. He was not bothered by the possibility that the new world organization would be required to check on the conditions in Puerto Rico, Hawaii, or other American possessions.[18] Again, Vandenberg, in league with various military advisers interested in the strategic Pacific islands acquired during the war,

---

[15]Ibid., 246.

[16]JFD, *Six Pillars of Peace: A Study Guide Based on "A Statement of Political Propositions,"* ed. with an intro. by John Foster Dulles (New York: Commission to Study the Bases of a Just and Durable Peace, 1943) 55.

[17]JFD, "The Problem of Peace in a Dynamic World," *Religion in Life* 6 (Spring 1937): 200; see also JFD, *War, Peace and Change,* 131; JFD, "Statement of Guiding Principles," *Biennial Report* (1942) 44; JFD, *Long Range Peace Objectives: Including an Analysis of the Roosevelt-Churchill Eight Point Declaration* (New York: The Commission to Study the Bases of a Just and Durable Peace, 1941) 13; and JFD, *Six Pillars of Peace,* 57.

[18]Pruessen, *The Road to Power,* 251; see also *Foreign Relations of the United States: Diplomatic Paper, 1945, General: The United Nations,* 1 (Washington: Government Printing Office, 1967) 320.

convinced the general delegation that the international organization should be limited in some respects concerning this issue. A compromise was reached that created the Trusteeship Council. Its function was to supervise the former colonies of defeated powers. Previously held colonies of the Allied powers remained unaffected. However, Dulles helped to secure commitment that promised eventual independence to all colonial areas. Decisions concerning strategic areas, such as those represented by the Pacific islands, fell under the jurisdiction of the Security Council— an area where the United States could exercise its veto power.

The Sovereignty of Nations. The question of domestic jurisdiction was another difficult issue causing serious debate. Foster Dulles had very definite commitments on this point as well. For years he had argued that the interdependence of the world needed to be recognized by all nations.[19]

As a result, he did not envision an authority with the power to "dictate changes in the national domains."[20] Rather, he hoped for an elemental beginning whereby nations would begin to recognize the "principle that power entails [the] responsibility" to consider the welfare of all those peoples affected by that power.[21]

In order to most forcefully present his argument, Dulles divided it into two sections. First, he believed it politically expedient to accept the principle that power must be accompanied by responsibility. "It is practical wisdom," he asserted, "to recognize that attempts at arbitrary restraint and the monopolization of natural advantages in the long run defeat themselves and are self destructive."[22]

---

[19]See, for example, JFD, "Statement of Guiding Principles," 43-45; JFD, "Long Range Peace Objectives," 15-17; JFD, "Toward World Order," 50-56; JFD, "Speech," delivered in Madison Avenue Presbyterian Church, 13, 20 October 1941, DP, Box 290; JFD to Lionel Curtis, 17 July 1940, DP, Box 19.

[20]JFD, *War, Peace and Change*, 158; see also 40-48. Further discussion of the issue is found in JFD, "A Just and Durable Peace," 9.

[21]JFD, "The Churches' Role in Developing the Bases of a Just and Durable Peace," 15, 28 May 1941, DP, Box 20; see also JFD, *The Christian Forces and a Stable Peace* (New York: Committee on Public Affairs, National Board, Young Men's Christian Association, 1941) 6-7; JFD, "Statement of Guiding Principles," 43; JFD, "Peaceful Change," *International Conciliation* 369 (April 1941): 494-95; JFD to Eugene Staley, 3 January 1940, DP, Box 19; JFD to Gordon A. Sisco, 29 April 1941, DP, Box 20.

[22]JFD, "Peaceful Change," 497.

The fact that this position constitutes enlightened self-interest becomes clearer, according to Dulles, when one realizes that the hoarding of natural resources naturally results in "areas of disaffection which give men of violence the opportunity to make themselves more formidable."[23] World War II had its origins in just such an environment. Dulles believed that the failure of the World Economic Conference convened in 1933 in London brought on still more severe international conditions than had previously existed. The conference failed, said Dulles, because the "nations of the world and, conspicuously, the United States, were not prepared to cooperate in planning for the benefit of all." Such selfishness paved the way for the rise of Hitler.[24]

The second section of Dulles's argument was his belief that recognition of the interdependence of nations would be a major step toward the development of a flexible international law that would more closely resemble the moral law. Universal rights of humankind would be emphasized by such a step. Nations would recognize that their actions are judged by something beyond their own individual sovereignties. Dangerous perceptions of "nation-heroes" and "nation-villains" would be dealt a fatal blow. Willingness to make economic resources available to the needy on a basis that they can afford would bring an enlightened understanding of one another among peoples who differ. In turn, this would result in the lowering of "artificial barriers" and freer movement of the world's populations.[25]

In San Francisco Dulles attempted to persuade his fellow delegates of the importance of recognizing this principle. As Pruessen records the events,

> During an early delegation review . . . Dulles waded into the discussion with all the assurance of his long experience. He said he had "objected

---

[23]JFD, "The Churches' Contribution toward a Warless World," *Religion in Life* 9 (Winter 1940): 33; see also JFD, "The Problem of Peace," 195; JFD, "The Aftermath of the World War," *International Conciliation* no. 369 (April 1941): 266-67; JFD to Grenville Clark, 7 March 1940, DP, Box 19; and JFD to Hamilton Fish Armstrong, 18 March 1940, DP, Box 19.

[24]JFD, *Six Pillars,* 21; see also JFD, "The Aftermath," 270; and JFD, "The Churches' Contribution," 37.

[25]JFD, "The Aftermath," 266-67; see also JFD, "The Problem of Peace," 197-203; and JFD, *War, Peace and Change,* 128-33.

to the paragraph at the time of his discussions with Secretary Hull in the fall of 1944. It was . . . a contradiction in terms to say that a matter which threatened the peace of the world was solely a matter of 'domestic jurisdiction.' How could that be? . . . The Security Council should have authority to consider any matter which threatened the peace of the world."[26]

Yet, once again, Vandenberg and Connolly raised objections to Dulles's viewpoint. The Senate would never accept any dilution of the nation's sovereignty in these matters. If such an action were attempted, the Senate would not approve the Charter. Dulles was forced, due to his belief that the formation of a world organization was an absolute necessity, to acquiesce once again. His overall objective was to get a charter accepted by Americans. Thus the international organization's authority on the domestic jurisdiction question had to remain limited in scope.

Veto Power. The final crisis, and in the view of many observers the most serious, involved the question of veto powers in the Security Council among the great nations. The Soviets insisted upon the right of any one of the Security Council members to veto any substantial decision in the Council, even the motion to permit debate to take place. In order to support their position, they cited assurances made in the Yalta Conference.

Americans held a more liberal understanding of the Yalta agreements. They recognized that the powers had agreed that unanimous consent was required in order for an investigation of problems or a recommendation of solutions to take place. Thus veto power was recognized in these two areas. However, discussion of problems was a different matter: no one power should be able to prohibit that from taking place. It would be equivalent to gagging the smaller powers.

During the discussion Dulles was absolutely inflexible. He had long argued that ideally the Security Council should have unlimited rights in all three areas.[27] Publicly, in San Francisco, he urged the "delegation to go 'on record' as being supportive of the principle of a more open ap-

[26]Pruessen, *The Road to Power,* 249.

[27]JFD, "From Yalta to San Francisco," 9, 17 March 1945, DP, Box 27; JFD, "Letter to Editor of the *New York Times,*" 3, 6 March 1945, DP, Box 27; and "Comments on Current Discussions of International Order," *Christian Century* 61 (4 October 1944): 1148.

proach than that embodied in the Yalta formula."[28] Yet a realistic assessment of the present state of the world required less than the ideal. As he stated in his working memorandum,

> It is natural that the nations which would have to bear by far the greater part of the burden of maintaining or restoring peace and security should want at all stages to preserve as between themselves a unanimity without which effective action is difficult if not impossible.[29]

Realities aside, however, Dulles believed the issue of discussion should not be subject to a veto. A reasonable beginning to a world organization would be impossible if it were decided otherwise. On this point, the entire American delegation concurred.

The stalemate was finally broken when President Truman contacted Harry L. Hopkins, the presidential negotiator in Moscow, to approach the Kremlin and plead the issue before Stalin. The aged and extremely ill Hopkins negotiated a reversal of the Soviet position on the veto.[30] He died less than seven months after this achievement.

Shortly after the Charter passed the Senate, Dulles reflected upon the general question of the Security Council nations' right to veto. The veto power, he said, certainly "hobbled" the Security Council. In fact, it might even "make it a rather impotent body." However, it resulted from "the inevitable consequence of the fact that no one of the great powers trusted the others sufficiently to hand over to them the control of its destiny."

Distrust and fear among nations limited the potential development of a more liberalized Charter in all its aspects. "Those realities," said Dulles, "make inevitable a world organization which lacks the political powers commonly relied upon to preserve the peace. That is too bad. But the task of statesmanship is to relate theory to reality."[31] The fifty nations

---

[28]Pruessen, *The Road to Power*, 247.

[29]Quoted ibid., 247.

[30]Daniel Yergin, *Shattered Peace: The Origins of Cold War and the National Security State* (Boston: Houghton Mifflin Co., 1977) 103.

[31]JFD, "The Atomic Bomb and the Moral Law," 3, 15 November 1945, DP, Box 27; see also JFD, "The Churches and the Charter of the United Nations," *Annual Report* (1945) 151-52.

represented in San Francisco, according to Dulles, had taken an initial step toward alleviating the distrust in the world. Always careful to emphasize "the political inadequacies of the Charter," Dulles nevertheless felt that the "first phase" in obtaining durable peace was realized. [32]

Most of the praise Dulles had for the Charter resulted from his belief that his long-advocated principle of "peaceful change" was institutionalized. The "dynamic forces" of the world now had a forum in which to express their needs and desires. Their peoples could "work for the kind of change that will make the world better." [33] Thus the San Francisco Conference had helped to extend realization of the moral law. Such an extension, Dulles believed, would not "be without results." "The most important protection we can get," he concluded, "comes, not from where we are, but from the way in which we are moving." [34] These words barely had time to be heard when historical events broke down the protective barriers Dulles felt the Charter had established.

Assessing Dulles's Role in San Francisco

Because Dulles worked diligently and conscientiously to defend the American position while a member of the American delegation in San Francisco, some historians have questioned his commitment to the ethical principles he promoted during his association with the Federal Council of Churches. [35] I believe, however, that Dulles's actions in San

---

[32]JFD, "Statement," 21 August 1945, DP, Box 26.

[33]JFD, "Article for the *New York Times Sunday Magazine*," 3, 7 August 1945, DP, Box 27.

[34]JFD, "The Atomic Bomb and the Moral Law," 8.

[35]See particularly Pruessen's *The Road to Power* where the author states that the political role played by Dulles in San Francisco had a virtually "Machiavellian stripe to it that one sees little evidence of in the church settings he moved through at the same time." Thus, according to Pruessen, Dulles "was quite capable of devising strategy that was beneath the ethical standards taken for granted by his church associates." On the whole, Pruessen's assessment of Dulles's role in San Francisco is evident in his statement that "as a member of the United States delegation, both the tone of his [Dulles's] words and

Francisco were fully consistent with the position so clearly outlined by his church commission. This consistency can be demonstrated in two ways: first, through examining Dulles's commitment to a realistic understanding of accommodation among nations—a commitment that was clearly evident in all his commission's pronouncements on world order and that also guided much of his activity in San Francisco; and second, through taking a closer look at the nature of the role he was asked to fulfill at the United Nations Conference.

Meaningful Accommodation. Throughout the years previous to the United Nations Conference, Dulles and the other members of the commission realistically emphasized that the process of meaningful international cooperation would not be immediate. Members of the church commission, men like Reinhold Niebuhr, John C. Bennett, Roswell Barnes, Henry P. Van Dusen, and William E. Hocking, possessed a very clear idea of the practical sacrifices involved in reaching their goal of significant international interaction among nations. One of the primary tasks of the commission specifically included the attempt to educate the church people in America concerning this very point. The United Nations Charter, if it were to become a reality, would involve a willingness on the part of the American people to accept less than an ideal beginning.

During his years with the churches, Dulles repeatedly asserted that "any 'joint' statement loses its vitality through the necessity of composing different viewpoints."[36] The pragmatic character of collaboration, he wrote, demands that American Christians accept "practical situations which fall short of our ideals." Christians "must not be dogmatic."[37]

> It seems to me that unless it be conceded that Christians in their capacity as citizens have the duty to choose what seems the lesser of two evils, then they are made impotent through seeking to be perfectionists. . . .

---

the thrust of his advice would almost surely have caused some surprise among his colleagues at the Commission on a Just and Durable Peace." "It seems clear," concludes Pruessen, "that this was a situation in which Dulles demonstrated his ability to drift away from the ethical standards he could so eloquently discuss" (see 255-57). I disagree with this interpretation. The following pages offer a different assessment of Dulles's role in San Francisco. For a broader look at Pruessen's interpretation, see *The Road to Power,* 239-58.

[36]JFD, "Long Range Peace Objectives," 1.

[37]JFD, "America's Role in the Peace," 4-5.

While one never should compromise one's belief, it is often necessary to compromise one's action. By using one's influence to achieve the lesser of two evils, one still does not admit that the lesser evil is on that account not evil at all.

In order to clarify his point, Dulles made a further distinction between the actions of the churches as a whole and the action of the individual Christian citizen. Churches "do not have the dilemma of having to act or else be impotent in relation to world affairs." The main concern of the churches is to "teach beliefs and beliefs as such should not be compromised." Individual Christian citizens, on the other hand, have "a duty of action." Each must "act not in the hope or even the possibility of achieving perfection, but in the hope of achieving progress toward perfection which still, however, will be partly evil."[38] On the basis of this reasoning, Dulles argued that "participation in organized collaboration should not be rejected merely because it will seem to make us parties to initial evils." On this particular point he believed education to be essential.[39]

One of the motivations behind Dulles's efforts to educate the public concerning the character of collaboration was his belief that government officials feared public reprisals from Americans who would be dissatisfied with the results of collaboration.

Under such conditions, government is not disposed to work in such mire as much of the world is today. It is afraid of the criticism which will be heaped upon it when it comes back with some of the mire adhering to its hands and feet.[40]

Thus on the one hand, he urged Americans to be accepting of "the mire." On the other hand, he urged the government to collaborate, especially with the Soviet Union. "No one can contemplate with satisfaction the fate

---

[38]JFD to Katharine H. Parker, 1 February 1943, DP, Box 22.

[39]JFD, "Christian Strategy," 7 December 1943, DP, Box 22; see also JFD, "Appraisal of United States Foreign Policy," 5 February 1945, 10-11, DP, Box 27; JFD, "The Atomic Bomb and the Moral Law," 3; JFD, "A Christian World Hope," *The Presbyterian Tribune* 60 (November 1944): 3; JFD, "Address," 5 December 1943, DP, Box 22; JFD, "World Organization: Curative and Creative," 135; JFD, "From Yalta to San Francisco," 3.

[40]JFD, "America's Role in the Peace," 3.

of the small nations if the great powers start girding themselves for possible war against each other."[41] Dulles's actions in San Francisco are indicative of his willingness to both work in the "mire" of international accommodation and to accept the criticism which inevitably results from that approach.

The criticism of Frederick Libby, of the National Council for the Prevention of War, serves as an example of this particular kind of criticism. Regarding Dulles's actions in San Francisco, Libby offered the following remarks: "I find myself in general agreement . . . when you are speaking as the chairman of the Commission on a Just and Durable Peace," Libby wrote. "It is when your client is our State Department that I find divergence between our positions." Dulles responded to his criticism by saying,

> I am not aware of having departed, in an official capacity, from what I have advocated as Chairman of the Commission on a Just and Durable Peace. On the contrary, at San Francisco . . . I stood strongly for the principles which the Commission had advocated and to a considerable extent these principles became the official American position. Of course, one who has official responsibility must conduct himself somewhat differently from one who, as a private citizen, stands on the sidelines giving advice. I'm sure you realize that.[42]

In keeping with his emphasis on accommodation and compromise, Dulles initially applauded Roosevelt's efforts at Yalta. At that particular time, Dulles felt that cooperation with the Soviet Union was essential to peace. The distrust between the two countries had to be alleviated in order for peace to gain a firm footing in the world. In answer to those who claimed that we could not trust the Soviets, Dulles realistically asserted that

> on their side, [they] have little reason to trust us. We opposed their revolution. We gave military aid to the counter-revolutionaries. For many years we sought to prevent their having economic and diplomatic intercourse with the rest of the world. Our public leaders attacked them right

---

[41]JFD, "From Yalta to San Francisco," 3.

[42]Frederick Libby to JFD, 20 December 1945; JFD to Libby, 24 December 1945, DP, Box 27; also quoted in Pruessen, *The Road to Power,* 257, in support of his position.

up to the moment when Germany's attack made us perforce comrades in arms.[43]

At the time of Yalta—as reported by *U.S. News and World Report*— Dulles urged his countrymen to understand the "security" needs of the Soviet Union and to place events in Eastern Europe in the context of the "historical ambitions of the Russian nation."[44] In other words, he attempted to disassociate the political situation in Eastern Europe from the developing public belief in the existence of an international Communist plot. The foreign policy of the Soviet Union must not be viewed as an extension of its domestic policy; rather, in order to be properly understood, it should be placed in the context of the traditional concerns and ambitions of the Russian people. As early as 1943 Dulles was concerned about public attitudes, particularly among the membership of the Christian churches, with regard to postwar settlements in Eastern Europe. To Secretary of State Welles he wrote:

I foresee that among the greatest difficulties that we face in achieving an organized structure of international cooperation will be those involved in reconciling the views of the U.S.S.R. with the national aspirations of peoples such as those of Finland, Latvia, Lithuania, Esthonia, Poland, etc. There is danger that the church people of this country, who entertain a great sympathy for these peoples, and who have a considerable prejudice against the atheistic tendencies of the U.S.S.R., may feel that we should reject a collaboration which might seem to them to involve sacrificing moral principles to expediency. While I certainly do not feel we should abandon the ideals of the Atlantic Charter, I place organized cooperation between Britain, Russia, and the United States as a prime essential to durable peace. Without this the ultimate fate of the people in question will, I think, be much worse than if their future can be dealt with within a framework which Russia can feel assures continuing peace and minimizes the necessity for her action being dictated wholly by strategic considerations. It seems to me that if this is true then some reasonable compromise may have to be accepted as part of a realistic treatment of the situation.[45]

---

[43]JFD, "Appraisal of United States Foreign Policy," 8.

[44]*U.S. News and World Report* 26 (21 January 1945): 32.

[45]JFD to Sumner Welles, 6 May 1943, DP, Box 22.

For this reason, the Yalta Conference, as Dulles assessed it, opened "a new era." Cooperation between the great powers had begun and that beginning, imperfect as it might be, was to be applauded. "Our responsibility is not to guarantee what posterity might do," he said. Rather, "our responsibility is to give posterity a chance."[46]

Evidence supporting the conclusion that Dulles was extremely successful in educating the churches on this matter is quite impressive. Both *Christianity and Crisis* and *Christian Century* published the Dulles Commission's document, which stated that "any world organization is bound to be imperfect and that the future will have to mold it."[47] The Executive Committee of the twenty-five-million-member Federal Council of Churches adopted a similar statement written by the Dulles Commission and, stating that it reflected the opinion of its constituency, issued it as a news release.[48] As Reinhold Niebuhr, a member of the commission, commented,

> The hazards to success are so great that we must be prepared to accept anything which keeps the future open; but we must also be prepared to contend for everything which represents a basic requirement for justice.
> . . . A profound Christian faith knows something of the recalcitrance of sin on every level of moral and social achievement, and is, therefore, not involved in the alternate moods of illusion and disillusionment which harass the world of idealists and secularists. It knows something of the similarity between our sin and the guilt of others; and will therefore not be pitiless if ideal possibilities are frustrated by the selfishness of others.[49]

---

[46]JFD, "From Yalta to San Francisco," 3-4.

[47]"Comments on Current Discussions of International Order," *Christianity and Crisis* 4 (16 October 1944): 6; and "Dulles Commission Meets: Federal Council Body Issues Comments on Postwar Plan for Peace," *Christian Century* 61 (4 October 1944): 1148.

[48]"Commission on a Just and Durable Peace Issues Practical Statement of Position," *Christianity and Crisis* 4 (7 February 1944): 7-8. See also principle number 11 in JFD, "Statement of Guiding Principles," *Biennial Report* (1942) 45; another statement adopted by the Executive Council was obviously influenced by Dulles on this point, for it was adopted right after he delivered his address entitled "The Churches and a Just and Durable Peace." See "The Churches and the Dumbarton Oaks Proposals," *Biennial Report* (1944) 185.

[49]Reinhold Niebuhr, "Plans for World Reorganization," *Christianity and Crisis* 2 (19 October 1942): 6.

In light of the consistency demonstrated in the writings of Dulles, his commission, and church leaders like Reinhold Niebuhr, it seems that Dulles's actions in San Francisco were entirely congruent with earlier expressions. The context established above seems to indicate that Dulles's performance in San Francisco corresponded to the principles established by his commission. Dulles's actions at the United Nations Conference merely demonstrated that he was a realist. He argued his positions and, when the majority of the American delegation lined up on the opposite side—either because they feared nonacceptance of the Charter in the Senate or because they wanted to protect American interests—Dulles backed down. His major objective, and thus the major objective of his commission, was to see an international organization formed that was "as perfect as is consonant" with the "vigorous survival" of political institutions "in the existing environment." He felt the United Nations had, with few exceptions, successfully completed that very difficult task.[50]

The Nature of Dulles's Role in San Francisco. Any attempt to judge Dulles's active participation in San Francisco against his previous ethical expressions should take into account the role Dulles was assigned in the American delegation. The nature of any particular role can sometimes limit the ethical expressions of the person who fills that role. Dulles's role in San Francisco was explicitly that of a legal adviser. In no way can he be considered as powerful a contributor to or determiner of the American position as were men like Senator Vandenberg, Senator Connally, and Edward Stettinius.[51]

Specifically, Dulles was appointed to the delegation in order to perform the function of a "guard dog."[52] Once the American delegation decided on a position, Dulles was expected, as legal adviser, to make sure that the delegation expressed the position as envisioned and protected it from external tampering. Thus it could be only natural, in this setting,

---

[50]JFD, "The Atomic Bomb and the Moral Law," 3.

[51]Pruessen, *The Road to Power,* 253.

[52]Pruessen uses this term in a negative way in order to describe Dulles's participation in the United Nations Conference. I am using it in a positive sense, in that this was precisely the role Dulles was hired to perform at the conference; as a "guard dog," Dulles was limited in the type of contribution he was expected to make to the conference.

that the style of Dulles's rhetoric changed. He was expected to defend "in the traditional resonances of the global political arena"[53] whatever the American delegation decided on any given issue.

Indeed, one might even contend that Dulles stepped out of his appointed role when, during the initial discussion on some issues, he argued against the leadership of the American delegation in favor of positions resembling those espoused by his church commission over the last several years. That was not necessarily his task. Perhaps the fact that he did so is evidence of just how strongly he felt that those ideas deserved a hearing. At the very least, one can assert that Dulles's actions in San Francisco, though not explicitly indicative of his position as a churchman, were not contradictory to his stance as a loyal and ecumenically minded Presbyterian.

---

[53]This is another of Pruessen's phrases describing Dulles's conduct in San Francisco.

From Prophet of Realism
to Priest of Nationalism:
The Years of Transformation,
1945-1952

Toward Noncooperation, 1945-1946

Analyzing Dulles's activities carefully, as one would analyze pieces of a jigsaw puzzle, is a necessity if any meaningful understanding of the man is to be accomplished. At this point, an examination of the pieces fitting together to form the frame of his prophetic-realist position seems in order. Once this position is summarized, I will move on to explain how events occurring after 1945 led to a transformation of it.

The complex prophetic realism of John Foster Dulles, which lay behind his quest for international reform while an active participant in the Federal Council of Churches, can be broken down into at least three basic realistic observations. Each of these observations served as the foundation upon which Dulles constructed and expressed a corresponding prophetic dimension in order to remind hearers who were self-righteous and complacent that they had not "arrived" yet. The three realistic observations, along with their respective prophetic dimensions, really form an integrated whole. Each depends upon and clarifies the others; no one of them stands alone. Together, they form the philosophical framework for Dulles's commitment to cooperation among nations in international relations.

The first component of Dulles's realism arose from his recognition that nations, in their foreign affairs, act out of concern for their own national interests. Every good government is expected to protect what it perceives as the best interests of the nation it is appointed to serve. Most nations are not anxious to recognize obligations beyond their own interests. Political leaders are mainly concerned with pursuing those that seem to safeguard the particular interests of the country they serve.[1]

The prophetic expression accompanying this first realistic observation advised political leaders and their constituencies to avoid the attempt to cloak pragmatic and essentially selfish actions with moral pretense.[2] Since all foreign policies naturally arise out of selfish concerns, moral pretenses are unnecessary, even dangerous. They can only lead to an unhealthy self-righteousness that inevitably results in feelings of hostility and distrust among other nations affected by such policies. Such feelings, in turn, result in foreign actions and attitudes that pose a new threat to the national interest.[3] Dulles expressed, in this regard, a belief very similar to the Niebuhrian concept of the dualism in humankind. Good *and* evil are present in every person, and much more present in every nation. Therefore, self-righteousness is synonymous with hypocrisy.[4] The world is populated by people who are both good and evil, not by people who are good and people who are evil. The latter dichotomy is false. During the war years, Dulles emphasized that peace involved more than merely defeating one's enemies. The unfortunate

---

[1]See JFD, "Christianity in This Hour," 13, 21 April 1941, DP, Box 20; JFD, "The Churches' Role in Developing the Bases of a Just and Durable Peace," 16, 28 May 1941, DP, Box 20; and JFD, *War, Peace and Change* (New York: Harper and Brothers, 1939) 117-18.

[2]See, for example, "Article for the *New York Times Sunday Magazine*," 7 August 1945, DP, Box 26; JFD to F. Earnest Johnson, 16 April 1941, DP, Box 20; JFD, "United States and the World of Nations," 14, 27 February 1940, DP, Box 19; JFD to Henry S. Coffin, 20 May 1940, DP, Box 19.

[3]JFD, "United States and World of Nations," 14.

[4]JFD to Henry P. Van Dusen, 18 March 1940, DP, Box 19.

conditions, out of which people tending toward evil emerge, needed strong emphasis. Merely eradicating the people who are victimized by destructive conditions could not be viewed as a final solution.

Dulles consistently reminded Americans of the need for humility. He warned of the dangers inherent in the crusading tendency to declare oneself or one's country righteous in order thereby to gain power over others.[5] Such a policy was doomed to failure. Not only was it based on a false presupposition (that any country could be righteous), but, in the case of America, it was generally coupled with the equally erroneous attempt to identify peace and morality with the status quo.[6]

In order for peaceful change to occur, Dulles argued, a "fair balance needed to be struck between dynamic and static powers." When either set of powers becomes bent on universalizing its own system of morality and belief, the tragic dimension of existence emerges victorious. Thus concepts of "nation-hero" and "nation-villain" were to be avoided at all costs.

Occasionally, generally perceived moral principles happen to coincide with the national interests. On such occasions policies emerge from what Dulles referred to as "enlightened self-interest."[7] These rare occurrences should be recognized as the highest attainment for a nation's policies. However, such recognition should be given with full understanding that national interest, not moral commitment, was the determining factor in formulating the particular policy in question.

Though the role of the political leadership in any given country is dictated by a dedication to national-interest considerations, Dulles equally emphasized the prophetic need for a country's general population to press universal concerns upon its government. Such an expression might force government leaders more actively to seek policies where national-interest considerations will coincide with internationalist concerns. Policies born from such a coincidence serve to increase trust among nations and

---

[5]JFD, *War, Peace and Change*, 65-69.

[6]JFD, "Peaceful Change," *International Conciliation* 369 (April 1941): 493.

[7]See JFD, *Six Pillars of Peace: A Study Guide Based on "A Statement of Political Propositions*," ed. with an intro. by John Foster Dulles (New York: Commission to Study the Bases of a Just and Durable Peace, 1943) 30; and JFD to Hamilton Fish Armstrong, 18 March 1940, DP, Box 19.

improve the potential for future concurrence between national interest and moral principle.[8]

The fact that leaders from each nation act out of concern for particular national interests naturally leads to the conclusion that no one nation's policies are synonymous with the moral law. This realization constitutes Dulles's second realistic observation. During his tenure with the churches, Dulles maintained that national policies were rarely either right or wrong. International relations were much too complex to be grasped by such a simple approach. No nation is ever entirely righteous or pure in its policies since national-interest considerations are inherently selfish.

Based on this observation, Dulles repeatedly emphasized his prophetic belief that each nation's foreign policy ultimately should be judged by something outside itself. For Dulles, the moral law was the ultimate judge standing over and above each nation's policies. Rooted in God, its concern was universalistic. Every individual nation must be held accountable for activities that affect the world community. Thus, each nation's policies must be subjected to realistic, objective standards.

This involved granting that, national interests aside, no nation possessed the inherent right to act with impunity. Nations periodically need to be reminded of the universality and interdependence of humankind. During the late 1930s and early 1940s, Dulles struck just such a prophetic note.

Dulles's third realistic observation naturally follows from the first two. Since nations are motivated by national interests, and since no one nation can completely embody the moral law in its policies, it follows that the interests of one nation will quite often conflict with the interests of other nations. Dulles, therefore, consistently advanced the notion of the interdependence of nations. He stressed the need for balancing the competing interests of nations. No nation embodies absolute truth; therefore, international relations should foster temporary coalitions among nations and encourage each nation to choose between the lesser of two evils in particular situations.

---

[8]See, for example, JFD, "As Seen by a Layman," *Religion in Life* 7 (Winter 1938): 18-22; JFD, "The Problem of Peace in a Dynamic World," *Religion in Life* 6 (Spring 1937): 207; and JFD, "The Churches' Contribution toward a Warless World," *Religion in Life* 9 (Winter 1940): 31; JFD, "Christianity in This Hour," 21-22.

For Dulles, the United Nations was not intended to be a world government with the power to enforce one system of values at the expense
of other systems of values; rather, he hoped it would provide the forum
wherein competing value systems could negotiate differences, each acting as a check or balance against the others. Peace for the world depends
upon such a check and balance system, argued Dulles, simply because
national political leaders are primarily concerned with the extension of
power, either for themselves or for their nations. Thus due to the selfish
nature of existence, Dulles fervently pressed for the development of the
United Nations. Out of hard-fought compromise and accommodation
among nations, there might arise a sense of trust and a system of values
that nations could begin to hold in common.[9]

Based on this realistic understanding of the complex world of nations
and their competing value systems, Dulles again emphasized a prophetic
corollary: Christians, he said, must be willing to accept practical situations that fall short of their ideals. He feared that the power of Christian
idealism might thwart American acceptance of a meaningful role in a new
world organization. Thus, as particularly exemplified by the Cleveland
National Study Conference, Dulles and his commission actively worked
to counteract such idealism.[10]

These three couplets of realistic observation and prophetic expression provided the theological grist from which Dulles ground out his world
view from 1937 to 1945. His experience in international affairs and the
respect he earned as a thinker among the religious leaders of the Federal
Council of Churches enabled him to make a significant impact on the political thinking of the churches during those eight years.

Anyone who lived through the Eisenhower presidency, and who paid
any attention to the conduct of foreign affairs during the seven years John
Foster Dulles headed the State Department, might legitimately wonder,
given the picture painted of the man thus far, what happened to the realist? The John Foster Dulles who was secretary of state is best remembered for his moralistic and self-righteous conduct of foreign affairs. The
realism of these earlier years was seemingly absent.

---

[9]See JFD, "Our Vital Peace Decision," *Vital Speeches of the Day* 12 (15 October 1945):
7.

[10]See the discussion on 78-82.

Likewise, the prophetic dimension of his speech, which reminded America that God judges as well as shapes a nation, gave way to a more priestly style. The early Dulles's transcendent God was replaced by God "the friendly neighbor" who was on the side of Americans in the struggle between good (democracy) and evil (Communism). In the words of a contemporary observer, A. Roy Eckardt, penned in late 1954, "the God of judgment [had] died."[11] What caused his demise?

The Many Crises
of a Postwar World

Immediately after World War II, Americans were experiencing unprecedented affluence and international prestige. Then, suddenly, Americans were faced with the Cold War. Former allies had become enemies. Such changes require interpreters. Dulles, increasingly involved as a leader in civil affairs, became one of the major spokesmen interpreting the new events for an alarmed and worried public. In the process of fulfilling that role, Dulles's personal philosophy began to undergo a transformation.

In order to understand the changes wrought in Dulles's approach to international problems, one must place him in the context of the events that helped bring on the Cold War. After the 1945 San Francisco Conference, Dulles became a firsthand observer of and prominent participant in the formation of American foreign policy. He served as a delegate to every regular session of the United Nations Assembly from 1946 to 1950, with the exception of 1949, the year he spent four months as a senator from New York State. He also attended four of the Foreign Minister Councils: London in 1945, Moscow and London in 1947, and Paris in 1949. His most extensive contribution to American foreign policy resulted from his appointment as an ambassador-at-large in 1950 when he successfully negotiated the Japanese Peace Treaty. These experiences caused him gradually to transform his political philosophy.

---

[11]A. Roy Eckardt, "The New Look in American Piety," *Christian Century* 71 (17 November 1954): 1396.

At the end of World War II, Dulles recognized the "abnormal mental state" characterizing much of the world's population.[12] "Half of the population of the world—one billion people—face today the task of rebuilding economic, social and political order. All of their established institutions have been swept away."[13] No simple solution awaited the problems of the world. Of those who held an unrealistic view of the United Nations' potential to deal with those problems, Dulles reminded them that "no single act [such as the formation of the United Nations] could put an end to the age-old practice of fighting."[14]

For those who idealistically believed the wartime alliance between the United States and the Soviet Union would continue indefinitely, Dulles expressed his sincere belief that the unity which the Allies experienced during the war would quickly evaporate unless new perils were found to replace the common threat to peace that Germany had recently posed. "If a gambler were making bets on the basis of past performance," he quipped, "he would probably give odds of 10 to 1 that within five years the reality of unity would have departed from the United Nations."[15] As things turned out, it would have been a good bet.

As difficult as the situation was in 1945, Dulles still believed collaboration was possible. The emerging goals of the Soviet Union represented only one small aspect of the potential crisis facing the international scene. "Human nature on the whole," Dulles warned, "is still very imperfect and, in practice, fellowship on a large scale only comes when some opponent makes that fellowship seen as a matter of expediency."[16] He urged the members of the United Nations to view the widespread economic maladjustments, psychological perversions, and epidemic diseases rampant in the world as just such a common opponent.[17]

---

[12]JFD, "Appraisal of United States Foreign Policy," 1, 5 February 1945, DP, Box 27.

[13]JFD, "New Year's Statement," 1, 22 January 1944, DP, Box 23.

[14]JFD, "Article," 1; see also JFD, "From Yalta to San Francisco," 8, 17 March 1945, DP, Box 27; and JFD, "The Beginning of a World Order," 4, 22 April 1945, DP, Box 27.

[15]JFD, "Article," 3.

[16]Ibid., 5.

[17]Ibid.; see also JFD, "The United Nations," 3, 21 August 1945, DP, Box 26.

In February Dulles asserted that "in whatever direction we look, we face hard problems."[18] Conditions in Europe that helped to promote war in the first place were still in place. Social and economic problems also plagued Latin America and elsewhere. Further, new feelings of nationalism were emerging in Asia. In assessing these problems, Dulles also mentioned the need for improved relations with the Soviet Union. Yet problems in that area were seen as merely one aspect of the entire picture. There is no hint here, as there was explicit reference in later years, that the Communist party in Moscow was responsible for all the other problems on the world scene.

In recent years Dulles had clearly expressed his opinion that the Soviet Union was simply acting much like the United States had acted in the past.

> "Aggression" is a subtle thing. Does it include economic aggression?
> Some nations are in a position by economic pressures to coerce others.
> We have not infrequently done this over the past. And does it include
> political interference in another country which brings about revolution-
> ary change of government from which a foreign nation is a beneficiary,
> as, for example, Texas, Panama and, perhaps now, Poland?[19]

Acting in its own interest, the Soviet Union could ignore international law. As Dulles wrote to Henry Luce, international law is no law at all "because among other things, no nation is, or feels bound to conform to any course of action other than its own interest." "International law," he continued quoting Dr. Philip Jessup, "can be twisted to suit any national interest." Every nation twists it and it is "not accurate" to claim the United States is the exception.[20]

The portrait of world affairs painted by Dulles as late as 1945 suggests that he was aware of the magnitude of the postwar difficulties as well as the complexity of causes that brought them about. He urged governmental leaders to adopt and proclaim long-range goals that would re-

---

[18]JFD, "Appraisal of United States Foreign Policy," 2.

[19]JFD to Marquis Childs, 29 February 1944, quoted in Ronald W. Pruessen, *John Foster Dulles: The Road to Power* (New York: The Free Press, 1982) 273.

[20]JFD to Henry Luce, 29 September 1943, quoted in Pruessen, *The Road to Power*, 273.

flect the highest ideals of American policies. However, he reminded them that accommodation would be necessary. In the diplomatic arena, the government must be prepared to compromise on its ideals in order to make any progress in their accomplishment. Therefore, Dulles pressed the electorate to judge the government, not according to ideal expectations, but on the basis of whether or not it achieves practical results. [21]

A little more than five years after he had expressed the need for collaboration, he chastised himself and other governmental leaders for the naiveté that characterized such an attitude. Fortunately, in his view, American leadership quickly wised up. This he described as a move "toward realism." This is a surprisingly ironic turn of events. By mid-year 1950, Dulles viewed the realism of his 1945 perspective as naiveté. Further, what he had formerly denounced as idealism, he was now describing as realism.

According to Dulles, this move from "naiveté" toward "realism" took place in four phases between the years 1945 and 1950. The first phase Dulles termed the phase of "cooperation." This phase, as Dulles reflected upon it, constituted a drastic miscalculation that resulted in "large Soviet postwar expansion in both central Europe and Asia." The second phase, which began with the London Foreign Ministers Conference in 1945, was a slight improvement over the first. He called it the phase of "non-cooperation." This second phase signaled the end of "appeasement" toward the Soviets. The third phase of American policy, that of "prevention," was "marked by the realization that there was an irreconcilable conflict between the ambitions of Soviet Communism and the interests and welfare of the United States." It emerged out of the two 1947 Foreign Minister Council Meetings. The final phase in the evolution process stemmed from the North Korean attack on South Korea. Writing shortly after the attack, he termed this phase the phase of "opposition." [22]

Dulles's categories are helpful in tracing his personal transformation from prophet of realism to priest of nationalism. He was instrumental in guiding American foreign policy through each succeeding phase. The

---

[21]JFD, "Appraisal of United States Foreign Policy," 9.

[22]JFD, "U.S. Military Action in Korea," *Department of State Bulletin* 23 (17 July 1950): 88-91.

sweep of historical events led him to more elaborate nationalist expressions. In these, he attempted to interpret the challenges facing the nation and to construct policies that would lead toward the eventual resolution of those challenges. In that process of transforming American foreign policy, Dulles himself was transformed. His newfound realism was, in fact, simply a personification of his one-time arch-enemy, "self-righteous nationalism."

Disillusionment in London

In June of 1945, in response to President Truman's request for recommendations concerning how the peace settlement might best be enacted, the State Department suggested that a Council of Foreign Ministers be established. A general peace conference along the lines of Versailles seemed out of the question to the department because of the inherently awkward and cumbersome qualities of such a large gathering. Thus a Council of Foreign Ministers composed of the permanent members of the Security Council seemed a reasonable alternative. Limiting the council to those members would keep each major power "from trying to add nations sympathetic to their views."[23] At Potsdam the delegates created the Council of Foreign Ministers and scheduled its first meeting for September in London.

James F. Byrnes had been secretary of state for only two months when the *Queen Elizabeth* set sail for London on 5 September 1945. Conscious of the need for Republican cooperation in making the peace, he invited Dulles to join the delegation. On board the ship, the two "met with the State Department advising staff twice a day to plan the position of the United States on all the issues before the Council."[24]

Byrnes believed the London Foreign Ministers Conference could, within less than two weeks, conclude the essential features of five peace treaties: Italy, Hungary, Rumania, Bulgaria, and Finland. With the power of the atomic bomb and the promise of U.S. economic aid, Byrnes ex-

---

[23]Patricia Dawson Ward, *The Threat of Peace: James F. Byrnes and the Council of Foreign Ministers, 1945–1946* (Kent: Kent State University Press, 1979) 10.

[24]James F. Byrnes, *Speaking Frankly* (New York: Harper and Brothers Publishers, 1947) 92.

pected little difficulty,[25] but the conference sorely disappointed him. It ended in early October with no significant agreement reached on any issue.

Dulles met with his Commission on a Just and Durable Peace immediately upon his return from London. He explained his version of the first council meeting in "off the record" remarks. The Italian treaty, he said, was the first item discussed in London. On every aspect of the proposed treaty, the United States delegation discovered conflict with the Soviet Union. Regarding the ultimate boundary of Italy, the United States operated on the ethnic principle. Generally, this principle favored Yugoslavia on the border between the two countries. Yet since Trieste was overwhelmingly Italian, Americans believed that it should be Italy's possession. Vyacheslav M. Molotov, of the Soviet Union, disagreed and supported Yugoslavia's claim to the territory.

With respect to reparations in Italy, the United States, Great Britain, and France agreed that Italy "had no capacity to pay except in terms of relatively minor foreign assets and some armament equipment and machinery." The Soviets asked for $600 billion, including the proposal to strip North Italy of factories and machinery. Later, the proposal was cut in half in the understanding that "the United States, Great Britain and France would make no claim to participate." The American delegation pointed out that the United States and Great Britain were already paying more than $350 million in food to the Italian people as it was. If Italy were stripped of her machinery, the West would be paying Italy's reparations. Molotov responded that the Soviets deserved the reparations. If the Italians starved because of it, they brought it on themselves.

The other major disagreement with the Soviet Union over Italy arose concerning the issue of trusteeship for Italian colonies. The United States suggested an international trusteeship. The Soviets objected and laid claim on Tripolitania. Molotov also wanted rights in the Dodecanese Islands and a generally enhanced position in the Dardenelles. In any trusteeship, Molotov claimed, Soviets should be the trustees. British and Chinese

---

[25]See Ward, *The Threat of Peace,* 21; see also Byrnes, *Speaking Frankly,* 261; John Gaddis, *The U.S. and the Origins of the Cold War, 1941-1947* (New York: Columbia University Press, 1972) 265; and Richard G. Hewlett and Oscar E. Anderson, Jr., *A History of the Atomic Energy Commission: The New World, 1935-1945* (University Park: Pennsylvania State University, 1966).

delegates accepted the American position. The French rejected both positions. Ultimately, the only agreement reached concerning the Italian peace treaty came after twelve meetings. It granted freedom of speech, religious worship, political belief, and public meeting.[26]

Concerning Rumania and Bulgaria, Byrnes decided that unless free elections were allowed, the United States would withhold recognition. During the meetings Dulles told Byrnes that he doubted the "efficacy of nonrecognition in such a situation as Rumania." He told the secretary that "it seemed like starting all over again our policy of nonrecognition of the USSR—and on much the same grounds—which had proven a barren policy."[27] Byrnes, however, held firm. When Molotov claimed that the United States hoped "to encircle the Soviet Union with hostile governments" unfriendly to Moscow, Byrnes replied that the attitude of the American government toward Finland, Poland, and Hungary "clearly showed that there was no such pattern."[28]

Byrnes's obstinacy concerning democratization for Rumania and Bulgaria led to a breakup of the meeting as Russia, probably in retaliation, questioned the right of the French and Chinese even to participate in the discussions. The Soviets argued that such participation was counter to the agreement reached at Potsdam. Byrnes was ready to compromise on French and Chinese participation, but Dulles insisted that "France and China would not only be publically [sic] humiliated, but would also be alienated from the United States and Great Britain."[29] Dulles recommended ending the conference rather than accommodate the Soviets on this point. He urged Byrnes to give in to Molotov only if Moscow agreed to enlarge the treaty process, an enlargement that would "include all the nations which had been at war."[30] Molotov would not agree to this unless the Americans agreed to a Soviet share in the occupation of Japan. Since no one was seriously willing to effect a compromise, the impasse re-

---

[26]JFD, "Off the Record," 4-6, 8 November 1945, DP, Box 26.

[27]Quoted in Ward, *The Threat of Peace,* 32.

[28]JFD, "Off the Record," 10.

[29]Ward, *The Threat of Peace,* 40.

[30]Quoted in Pruessen, *The Road to Power,* 282.

mained and the conference adjourned without even issuing a traditional protocol.

Dulles, in later years, was much harsher in his assessment of the London Conference than he was immediately afterwards. With the publication of his two articles on Soviet foreign policy published in *Life* in June of 1946, Dulles began to assert that, at London, Americans placed their "foreign policy on the right track."[31] Americans had abandoned willingness to cooperate with the Soviet Union merely because of that country's valiant war efforts. In Dulles's view, "it was good riddance."[32] According to Dulles, and his recollections concerning the significance of London hardened with each passing year, when Byrnes refused to give in concerning France and China, the "postwar policy of 'no appeasement' was born."[33] At that point, Americans made the "memorable decision" that "in time of peace," the United States would not carry on in the tradition of "Tehran and Yalta, making concessions in order to buy from Soviet leaders a facade of harmony and of agreement." When Soviet leaders realized this, "they dropped the pretense of friendliness and opened up the cold war with full fury."[34]

This tougher rhetoric regarding Soviet behavior at the London meeting did not really characterize Dulles's initial reactions to the conference. Immediately following the meeting, Dulles voiced his opinion that the results of the first Foreign Ministers Council were consistent with what American leadership had anticipated. Those results might have come "as a shock to the American people," but, Dulles reasoned, it was good that the difficulties regarding successful peace settlements were now out in the open.[35]

> They [the Soviets] knew that we were anxious quickly to conclude peace with Italy. They wanted to find out how much of our principle we

---

[31]JFD, "Thoughts on Soviet Foreign Policy and What to Do about It," *Life* 20 (3 June 1946): 124.

[32]JFD, *War or Peace* (New York: The Macmillan Company, 1950) 32.

[33]Ibid., 30.

[34]JFD, "Statement of Senator John Foster Dulles," 1, 22 July 1949, DP, Box 43.

[35]Quoted in Pruessen, *The Road to Power,* 282; see also JFD, "Opening Statement at Cambridge Conference," 4, 4 August 1946, DP, Box 30.

would sacrifice to attain these goals. They found out that the United States was not willing to sacrifice its principles or its historic friendship with China and France. In every important negotiation . . . there comes a moment when the negotiators test one another out. It was inevitable that the time would come when the Soviet Union would want to test us out.[36]

Hence closer to the actual event, Dulles viewed Soviet action in London as the natural move for any great nation to make when beginning tough negotiations with other great powers. This assessment is confirmed by other speeches delivered by Dulles in the fall of 1945. In November, for example, he spoke at the Riverside Church in New York City, where Henry P. Van Dusen was being honored as the recent choice for president of Union Theological Seminary. In his address he emphasized that "fellowship, and not fear, is the cement with which world order must be built." Soviet actions must be viewed in the light of "the distrust, the differences of moral judgment" that "are just as great today as they were six months ago at San Francisco."[37]

Dulles was obviously discouraged by the dismal outcome of the London Conference; yet he was not quite ready to write off the possibility of successful fellowship with the Soviet Union. However, he was aware of the difficulties involved in maintaining it.

To secure unity, it may be necessary to compromise ideals. On the other hand, it may be possible to maintain ideals but only at the expense of a division of the world into spheres of influence. The choice between these alternatives is not an easy one.[38]

World events during the next few months would convince him that the latter alternative was the only option open to Americans.

In January of 1946, the first session of the United Nations General Assembly met in London. Dulles served as an alternate delegate. When he returned from the meeting, he delivered a speech before the Foreign

---

[36]Quoted in Brian Gardner, *The Year That Changed the World: 1945* (New York: Coward-McCann, Inc., 1963) 284.

[37]JFD, "The Atomic Bomb and the Moral Law," 5, 15 November 1945, DP, Box 27.

[38]JFD, "Off the Record," 15; see also JFD, "The Statement of Action on Four Fronts of Peace," 2-3, 28 December 1945, DP, Box 26.

Policy Association in which he attempted to evaluate the assets and liabilities of the first session of the United Nations.

On the asset side of the ledger, Dulles listed four items. First, both
Canada and New Zealand were willing to sacrifice their respective can-
didacies to the Security Council and the Economic and Social Council.
Second, the General Assembly made progress toward forming an international trusteeship over orphaned colonies. Third, relief operations to
provide food and clothing to depressed economic areas seemed headed
for speedy implementation. And last, France agreed to a total withdrawal
of her troops in Syria and Lebanon.

On the liabilities side of the ledger, Dulles listed four major setbacks,
all in one way or another attributable to the Soviet Union. First, and most
important, the Soviet Union insisted on using the Security Council for its
own purposes, thus causing it to be seriously divided. In Dulles's view,
the Soviet Union exploited the fact of British troops in Greece and Java
as encouragement for violent independence movements against colonial
powers. Second, the Soviets hoped to embarrass France by seeking a
strong condemnatory resolution concerning the troops stationed in Lebanon and Syria. The underlying motivation for this Soviet action, Dulles
reasoned, stemmed from the fact that the French Minister of Foreign Affairs headed the strongest anti-Communist party in France. Third, the
Communist-controlled countries sought special privileges for the World
Federation of Trade Unions. Aware of the union's influence on many
governments, the Soviets hoped to have it dominate the General Assembly and the Economic and Social Council. And last, the "member states
which did not believe in free political thinking and talking wished to purge
the refugee camps of political thinkers unfriendly to their established political order."

Obviously, concluded Dulles, the total of the liabilities "rather out-
weighs the assets." This was, for him, a distressing sign. That the liabilities could all be attributed to the Soviet Union distressed him even
more.

> It was particularly hard to find ways to work with the Soviet Union, for
> it seems not to want that. . . . It never accepted the adverse verdict of
> a committee, even a full committee of 51 nations.

The Soviet representatives at the meeting "almost uniformly" avoided
"friendly and communicative relations with foreigners." They "refused

to join the international economic, financial and cultural understandings which have been launched since the war." Soviet leaders, it seemed to Dulles, wanted to establish "barriers which are normally invoked against an unfriendly and dangerous outer world. It will not be easy to break those barriers down."[39]

Up to this point, Dulles still entertained some hope that the barriers could be overcome. He emphasized that "the needs of the Russian people are great." Not only are the Russian people "inherently friendly," he continued, but they have many "social goals" in common with the American people.[40] All these things must be considered when anyone attempts to assess Soviet foreign policy.

> The Soviet Union, with its 200 million, faces the economic consequences of the devastation of its richest agricultural and industrial lands. The misery there is undoubtedly intense. This may be the clue to much in Soviet policy that is hard to understand. It may be that Soviet leaders maintain barriers against the outer world so that their own people will not know of the better conditions of working people elsewhere; and so that Soviet sympathizers abroad will not be disillusioned by seeing the realities that are in Russia today.[41]

By admitting the possibility that "the motives" behind the Soviet Union's policies were "mixed," Dulles demonstrated that he did not yet view all Soviet action as illustrative of an ideological creed bent on world domination. Before long, however, such subtle distinctions disappeared altogether.

One thing that particularly bothered Dulles was the behavior of Mr. Andrei Vishinsky, the Soviet delegate to the United Nations. "His words," he later wrote, "even when uttered in a language that is not understood, strike with the force of bullets from a machine gun."[42] Especially disturbing was Vishinsky's statement at the opening session concerning the refugees who fled Russia during the war. "In words that were powered

---

[39]JFD, "Foreign Policy Association Speech," 25 February 1946, 3-6, DP, Box 30.

[40]Ibid., 7.

[41]JFD, "Address before the Federal Council of Churches," 3, 5 March 1946, DP, Box 293.

[42]JFD, *War or Peace*, 27.

with deep hatred, . . . Mr. Vishinsky proclaimed the resolve of the Soviet Government to scour the face of the earth to find . . . [and] seize them."[43] In response to an appeal for tolerance made by someone in the Assembly, Vishinsky reportedly exclaimed, "Tolerance? Away with it! We have had too much tolerance."[44]

The fervency with which Vishinsky commented sparked Dulles to evaluate his own delegation's commitment to American ideals. By comparison, the Americans "were apathetic." "Cold logic," he declared, "does not restrain those who are passionately dedicated to some great purpose. . . . The very fact that we were so reasonable shows the low level of our faith and of our purpose."[45] This realization marked the beginning of the end for Dulles's cooperation with the Soviet Union on international matters; any accommodation of American ideals in order to reach settlement was becoming a thing of the past. What America needed, urged Dulles, was a renewal of its once "great faith."[46] Only then could America meet head-on the increasingly clear dogmatism of the Soviet Union. Expanding this call for revival would soon occupy a great majority of Dulles's time.

Education and Proclamation

Diagnosing the Problem. The two London meetings held in late 1945 and early 1946 created within Dulles an urgent desire to learn more about Soviet aims and purposes. Thus upon his return from the meeting of the General Assembly, he began to take an intensive look at Soviet foreign policy. By May he was certain he had learned something that needed to

---

[43]JFD, "Faith of Our Fathers," 8, 28 August 1949. This speech is published in Henry P. Van Dusen, ed., *The Spiritual Legacy of John Foster Dulles* (Philadelphia: The Westminster Press, 1960) 5-12.

[44]JFD, "Remarks," 2, 14 April 1952, DP, Box 307; this anecdote is also found in the following places: JFD, "Thoughts on Soviet Foreign Policy and What to Do about It," 113; and "Dulles Address and Interview," 1 March 1946, quoted in Pruessen, *The Road to Power,* 279.

[45]JFD, "The United Nations: Its Challenge to America," 1, 22 February 1946, DP: Additional Papers, Box 1 (of 3).

[46]Ibid.

be shared. He wrote to the members of the Commission on a Just and Durable Peace and informed them of his feeling that the commission had "been derelict in not facing up to the Russian problem." Accepting "primary responsibility for the delay," he said,

> Until recently I have not felt clear enough in my own mind about Russian foreign policy to feel like giving leadership in any particular direction. As a result of the opportunities which I have had over the last year and more, I now feel that I have a clear understanding of the fundamentals, at least, of Soviet foreign policy.[47]

This letter is the start of his concentrated attempt to provide a meaningful interpretation of the events that marked the beginning of the Cold War.

Dulles's first contribution in this area consisted of a series of two articles written for *Life* magazine entitled "Thoughts on Soviet Foreign Policy and What to Do about It." They were published in back-to-back issues during the first two weeks of June. From this point on, Dulles's developing perception of the Soviet challenge was to clearly dominate all he said and did in the public sphere. He carefully watched for new signs that might lead to a clearer understanding of what motivated leaders behind the Iron Curtain. Large blocks of his time went into analyzing Soviet behavior and then constructing a course of action based upon his deepening "understanding" of the Soviet threat. The possibility that his analysis could be wrong never entered his mind. During the next five to six years, his perception of the Soviet Union developed purely in one direction.

Just ten days before his *Life* articles appeared, Dulles addressed the Presbyterian General Assembly in Atlantic City. His topic, of course, was the threat to freedom posed by the Soviet system. Under it, he declared, "absolute authority is vested in a few leaders who are committed to promote the welfare of the many." Now the Soviet leaders "seek worldwide acceptance of their system." This particular speech is interesting because it reveals that at least at this point in time, Dulles didn't argue that "worldwide acceptance of their system" meant a monolithic machine seeking the destruction of individual freedom as its main goal. Rather, the desire behind the Soviet goal was "in part" the natural result "of a

---

[47]JFD to all members of the Commission on a Just and Durable Peace, 8 May 1946, Box 29.

nationalistic desire to enlarge their domain and protect it." It was also due "in part" to the Communist belief that individual human freedom constituted "a basic cause of human discord and inefficiency and that if it was taken away," it would "increase man's material welfare." The Soviets, Dulles continued, are convinced that "their experience at home has proved that to be so, and that if their system were given worldwide application[,] that would best assure worldwide peace and security." "To achieve that," he concluded, "is the basic goal of Soviet foreign policy."[48]

The first *Life* article provides a hint of Dulles's developing attitude toward the Soviet threat. Natural nationalistic expansion began to be overshadowed by what Dulles came to perceive as a burgeoning international conspiracy against freedom. The serious tone of the article was designed to impress upon the reader the importance of the subject. The "primary purpose" of Soviet foreign policy, he confidently asserted, "is to achieve peace, security and opportunity for the Soviet Union." "These," he continued, "are the usual goals of every foreign policy." Had he not qualified this statement in any way, he would not have had much to tell his readers other than to say that the Soviet leaders represented a national power and were doing what leaders of national powers do. However, Dulles believed that in the Soviet case the matter was a little more complicated than what one might see on a first glance.

Because, in the Soviet mind, "the world is one world" and "peace is indivisible," the twin goals of peace and security "are considered by them to depend upon eradicating the non-Soviet type of society." Thus establishment of peace and security for Soviet leaders means "eradication" of these qualities for the Free World. World harmony, in the Soviet understanding of the term, will only come into existence through the creation of "a great political calm which will be the Pax Sovietica."[49]

The goal of Soviet foreign policy, therefore, as Dulles presented it, was to create governments according to the Soviet model. In *Life* he wrote, "Soviet foreign policy is powerful because it is a national projection abroad of Soviet domestic policy."[50] The Soviets are "attempting in

---

[48]JFD, "Freedom through Sacrifice," *The Commercial and Financial Chronicle* 163 (30 May 1946): 2912 and 2955.

[49]JFD, "Thoughts on Soviet Foreign Policy," 113.

[50]Ibid., 123.

foreign affairs to do precisely what they have been doing at home for nearly thirty years."[51] Or, as he stated in a speech given during the same month that the article was published, "It does little good to have destroyed the mosquitos on your own land if they are breeding in surrounding lands and flying in."[52]

To believe that the Soviets were intent on destroying all dissent from their viewpoint represents a very important evolution in Dulles's thought concerning the motivations behind Russian actions. Prior to 1945, he continually expressed his belief that the Russian Revolution may have "swept away the Czars and all their institutions," but "the foreign policy of the USSR today is that of Peter the Great." Earlier, Dulles claimed that national interest, not some ideological universalistic faith, motivated Soviet leadership in the foreign arena. He argued that "nations that have the power to do so will usually seek strategic boundaries unless satisfied that their security can equally or better be served in some other way."[53] However, as he expressed it in this *Life* article, the Soviet intentions in foreign affairs went far beyond national-interest considerations; he was now convinced that the Soviet leadership was motivated by a desire for world domination. Foreign policy as practiced by the Soviets could no longer be viewed as Russian, it was Communist.

In order to clarify the situation for his readers, Dulles explained that the Kremlin had sectioned the world into three zones: the "Inner Zone," the "Middle Zone," and the "Outer Zone." The inner zone represented territory already incorporated into the USSR "on the basis of historic, strategic or ideological considerations."[54] The middle zone was "territory which surrounds the inner zone which is not yet ripe for incorporation into the USSR, but which is close enough to it to be amenable to the influence of Soviet military power." According to Dulles, most of this

---

[51]JFD to A. J. Muste, 17 June 1946, DP, Box 30.

[52]JFD, "State Control versus Self Control," 2, 19 June 1946, DP, Box 30.

[53]JFD to Thomas Dewey, 26 June 1944; and JFD, "America's Role in the Peace," quoted in Pruessen, *The Road to Power,* 272.

[54]JFD, "Thoughts on Soviet Foreign Policy," 113. The inner zone included Finland, Esthonia, Latvia, Lithuania, Eastern Poland, Eastern Czechoslovakia, Bessarabia, Bukovina, Tanna Tuva, Port Arthur, Southern Sakhalin, and the Kurile Islands.

zone "is, or recently has been, occupied by the Soviet army."[55] The outer zone "comprises the balance of the world."

As Dulles defined it, the outer zone required special techniques of the Soviet policymakers. These techniques differed according to the part of the world in which they were to be applied. In the colonial world the Soviets "encourage revolution" and provide independence movements with "moral leadership." In Europe the goal is to keep France, Belgium, Holland, and the United Kingdom divided so they "won't rival Soviet influence in the middle zone." To some degree, according to Dulles, vibrant Communist party operations at work in France and Italy served this purpose. In Latin America the Communist party was at work attempting to break up "hemispheric solidarity." To a lesser extent, Soviet leadership seemed to be successfully "wooing" the Arabs as well. Strong support was also given by Moscow to the World Federation of Trade Unions as a mechanism for furthering Communism. Further, smear methods were used to discredit foreign leaders.[56] In Dulles's view, these represented just a few of the weapons in the Soviet arsenal.

Dulles's study of the Soviet Union led him to one simple conclusion: Communism was of one mind, and that mind was determined to control the entire world. "Soviet diplomats and private agents abroad," he wrote, "are the pieces who move as directed by the master mind." Because the Soviet system demands conformity, it must, Dulles wrote, be considered as "ruthless."[57]

Offering a Solution. The second article in *Life* dealt specifically with suggesting a program for handling the Soviet challenge. In this article Dulles followed up on the theme he had sounded in his speech to the Presbyterian General Assembly a few weeks before: "[The Soviet] challenge derives its greatest power from the weaknesses which have developed in our society of freedom and which have caused a widespread

---

[55]Ibid., 114. The middle zone, according to Dulles, included Hungary, Rumania, Yugoslavia, Albania, Spain, the remainder of Czechoslovakia, France, the remainder of Poland, East Germany, Finland, Sinkiang, Azerbaijan, Outer Mongolia, North Korea, Manchuria, Eastern Austria, and Bulgaria.

[56]Ibid., 116-18.

[57]Ibid., 123-24.

lack of faith."[58] As he expressed this concern in *Life,* he emphasized that "at this critical juncture," there is need for

> an affirmative demonstration that our society of freedom still has the qualities needed for survival. We must show that our free land is not spiritual lowland, easily submerged, but highland that, most of all, provides the spiritual, intellectual and economic conditions which all men want.[59]

This rhetoric did not mean a willingness to resort to military force. On the contrary, Dulles believed that the United States would be mistaken to "coerce Soviet leaders into abandoning their ambitions." For if that were done, "the Soviet experiment would then seem to have succumbed, not to our merit but to our might." Any dependence upon a display of "military and economic power" would only cause "new disciples of that faith [to] spring up everywhere."[60] Therefore, Dulles suggested an approach of a different kind.

> The most significant demonstration that can be made is at the religious level. The overriding and ever-present reason for giving freedom to the individual is that men are created as the children of God, in His image. The human personality is thus sacred and the State must not trample upon it. This is what our forebears believed.[61]

"The truth is," Dulles told the Presbyterian General Assembly, "that a society of freedom *cannot* persist, and probably *ought not* to persist, except as a religious society."[62] This assertion reflects Dulles's presupposition that a free society with a religious foundation is virtually immune to developing into an authoritarian state. Dulles assumed a priori that a religious society would be committed to the principles of the moral law. Such a commitment would naturally encourage the citizenry to exercise

---

[58]JFD, "Freedom through Sacrifice," 2955.

[59]JFD, "Thoughts on Soviet Foreign Policy," 120.

[60]JFD, "Freedom through Sacrifice," 2955.

[61]JFD, "Thoughts on Soviet Foreign Policy," 120.

[62]JFD, Freedom through Sacrifice," 2955. See also JFD, "State Control versus Self Control," 8.

"the self-restraint, the self-discipline and the self-sacrifice" necessary for the maintenance of a free society.[63]

As Dulles envisioned a solution to the problem posed by the emerging Soviet threat, he emphasized the need for Americans to formally rededicate themselves "to the faith of [their] fathers." What America needs, Dulles said, is a good old-fashioned "spiritual revival." Such a renewed faith would "heal the sores of the body politic" and "make apparent the futility of any world program based on the suppression of human freedom."[64] As Dulles termed it, unless Americans renewed their faith successfully, "dictatorships will grow throughout the world" and, as a result, an "alien faith will isolate us and press in upon us to a point where we shall be faced with surrender or with new war."[65]

Obviously these are strong words. They point to an attitude that would later become even more explicit. As Dulles began to emphasize a spiritual revival, he came close to equating freedom with the moral law. When, over the course of the next year, he began to contrast the religious commitments of the Free World with Communist party atheism, this equation between freedom and the moral law became a matter of conscious expression.[66]

Dulles's call for an American renewal of faith is a theme he returned to consistently during the next several years.[67] This particular expression provided Dulles with the justification for refusing further collaboration with the Soviet Union. Obviously, a renewed faith cannot be

---

[63]JFD, "Thoughts on Soviet Foreign Policy," 120, and JFD, "Freedom through Sacrifice," 2955; see also JFD, "State Control versus Self Control," 9-12.

[64]JFD, "Thoughts on Soviet Foreign Policy," 122; see also JFD, "State Control versus Self Control," 10.

[65]Ibid.

[66]The fact that this equation constitutes a profound transformation in Dulles's thought will be discussed below as that thought becomes more explicit.

[67]See, for example, the following: JFD, "World Brotherhood through the State," 8 September 1946, DP, Box 293; JFD, "Draft," 11 March 1948, DP, Box 37; JFD, "Moral Force in World Affairs," *Presbyterian Life* 1 (10 April 1948): 28; JFD, "The Atlantic Pact," 4 May 1949, DP, Box 43; JFD, "Speech," 12 October 1949, DP, Box 298; JFD, *War or Peace,* particularly 253-61; JFD, "Universal Bible Sunday Broadcast," 20 November 1950, DP, Box 50; JFD, "A New Foreign Policy," 19 May 1952, DP, Box 57; JFD, "Our Foreign Policy: Is Containment Enough?" 8 October 1952, DP, Box 59.

compromised. Thus, for Dulles, accommodation was no longer acceptable. It seems as if the consistent and forceful adherence to the party line
exhibited by Communists throughout the fall of 1945 and the spring of
1946 taught Dulles that Americans should be equally committed to their
ideals. Dulles reasoned that a revival of faith in the American tradition
would result in a vibrant spiritual commitment to freedom that Communism would never be able to break.

Reasoning of this type would be revised in the not-too-distant future.
At least through the spring of 1948, Dulles claimed that the Soviets were
successful in their expansion, not because they forced their system upon
others, but because the actions of the West had created a "moral vacuum" that made Communism seem inviting.[68] He freely admitted that
world war and economic crisis had largely dominated the scene for the
last twenty-five years in a world largely led by the Western democracies.
Such a world had successfully crushed the spirit of the individual. "It is
not surprising," he wrote, "that the resultant chaos and destitution should
give rise to a strong reaction." Many in the world, he continued, "are
tempted to gamble on new leadership and many rise to the lure of a new
and radical experiment."[69]

When Dulles spoke of the need for a religious revival, he hearkened
to the days when "Western ascendency was not so much the work of
generals as it was of diplomats, merchants, and missionaries."[70] The crisis of the present day, he offered, could best be met by a return to the
days when American example showed through the works of the missionaries. An objective contemporary observer might have reminded Dulles
that in his desire to return to the traditional understanding of the "good
old" American sense of mission, he seemed to overlook the more imperialistic and narrow-minded aspects of the work done by these missionaries. To extol the work of the nineteenth-century American
missionaries without qualification was to approve tacitly their attempts
to export American culture and values. In earlier years, Dulles would have

---

[68]"Draft," 17.

[69]JFD, "Freedom and Sacrifice," 2955; see also JFD, "State Control versus Self Control," 4.

[70]JFD, *War or Peace,* 75; see also JFD, "Evolution or Revolution," 3, 12 February
1949, DP, Box 43.

winced at such presumption. Now, however, he praised such action as constituting a worthy end.

> [The missionaries] had a sense of mission in the world, believing it their duty to help men everywhere to get the opportunity to be and to do what God designed. . . . Through missionary activities and the establishment of schools and colleges, American ideals were carried throughout the world.

As this later speech indicates, by 1948 "American ideals" were synonymous with helping "men everywhere to get the opportunity to be and to do what God designed." In the emerging context of the Cold War, Dulles felt that Americans needed to return, with renewed determination and dedication, to such a vision.[71]

> It takes work to get religion and keep it, and no community will bear the imprint of righteousness unless the people get together in worship, to pray, to sing hymns, to hear the reading and preaching of the Holy Word and to plan to spread the truth. Without that, a society inevitably becomes rotten. . . . What America needs now is a religious revival.[72]

The righteous faith sought by Dulles beginning in 1946 was considerably different from the one he had hoped Americans would develop during the war. In Dulles's mind, the image of "manifest destiny" was replacing the earlier emphasis on America as a "light to the nations." In the earlier period, Dulles emphasized a righteous faith that would be free from seeing "the defects in others and only the virtues in yourself."[73] It was a righteous faith that required "a sense of values conceived in terms of the general welfare rather than that of our particular nation, race, or class."[74]

---

[71] JFD, "Draft," 2, 11 March 1948.

[72] JFD, "Religion in American Life," 2, 4 November 1951, DP, Box 55; see also JFD, "Evolution or Revolution," 5; and JFD, "Our International Responsibilities," 5, 4 June 1950, DP, Box 50.

[73] JFD, "CBS: The People's Platform," 19 December 1942, DP, Box 21.

[74] JFD, "Christianity in This Hour," 21-22; see also JFD, "The American People Need Now to Be Imbued with a Righteous Faith," in *A Righteous Faith for a Just and Durable Peace,* ed. with an intro. by John Foster Dulles (New York: The Commission to Study the Bases of a Just and Durable Peace, 1942) 9-10; and JFD, "A Righteous Faith," *Life* (28 December 1942): 50-51.

By 1946, however, the righteous faith he urged was only compatible with the Western economic system. It could flourish only where people were free in the same way as Americans were free. "Personal freedoms . . . in fact . . . disappear with the disappearance of free economic opportunity."[75]

At this point, it should be noted that Dulles refused to condemn the attempt made by the "so-called Western democracies of Europe" to "find a compromise which, while reducing economic freedom through state socialism, will still preserve a considerable measure of spiritual, intellectual and political freedom." Nevertheless, he did express his fear that such an experiment "leaves freedom with but a precarious hold in the world."[76] By 1950 this fear became hardened into the view that the British experiment was analogous to "the captain and crew [who] often act as though they were in charge of a derelict drifting to no discernible haven, with no dependable means of propulsion and only limited supplies of food and water."[77]

The two London Conferences contributed to at least one significant change in the way Dulles viewed American policymaking vis-à-vis the Soviet Union. By underlining the need for renewed commitment to American traditions and values, Dulles came to espouse a position of noncooperation in the international arena concerning issues that inspired Soviet and American disagreement. In February of 1947, in a speech appropriately titled "Ideals, Not Deals," Dulles emphatically stated that "peace lies not in compromising, but in invigorating, our historic policies."[78] As he expressed it a few months earlier, "It is a good initial approach to say that if you pat the dog he will not bite you. If, however, after several times patting the dog he still nips you then it is necessary to think of another approach."[79]

---

[75] JFD, "Thoughts on Soviet Foreign Policy," 122.

[76] JFD, "Freedom through Sacrifice," 6.

[77] JFD, *War or Peace,* 159.

[78] JFD, "Ideals, Not Deals," 7, 10 February 1947, DP, Box 33; see also JFD, "Europe Must Federate or Perish," *Vital Speeches of the Day* 13 (1 February 1947): 234.

[79] JFD to Irving Fisher, 23 September 1946, quoted in Pruessen, *The Road to Power,* 288.

According to Dulles, Hitler and others would have followed a different course if the United States had let them know early on that it would act to stop international aggression. In his words: "By not making apparent, in time, our devotion to our ideals, we were guilty of contributory negligence."[80] Such a mistake, he warned, must be avoided when dealing with the aggressiveness of the Soviet Union.

> We have the ideals, we have the know-how, and we have the power. We should put all three to work in harness. . . . Now there is danger that the peace will reflect not the high *ideals* of the Atlantic Charter, but the secret *deals* of Teheran and Yalta. . . . Our nation was never destined to become involved in cheap intrigue with foreign rulers. We do not do that well. . . . We have a different destiny. It is to forge spiritual alliances with the peoples of the world.[81]

In two short years Dulles had moved from the realistic posture of "Ideals Are Not Enough,"[82] a speech in which he emphasized the need for compromise among nations, to the nationalistic posture expressed in his speech "Ideals, Not Deals," which emphasized the need to avoid any plan that would involve compromising national ideals. This shift in emphasis began to perplex some of the churchmen who had learned to respect and admire the work of Dulles. Frank Laubach, a Presbyterian pastor writing to Dulles in late 1946, complained that the Dulles speeches of the preceding months were "too much on the side of the toughness of a lawyer and not enough like Jesus Christ."[83] Conversely, the more conservative leadership in both religious and secular circles that had once opposed Dulles now began to appreciate him, though inevitably they felt the change was a little late in coming. One former critic wrote, "Not until June, 1946, did Mr. Dulles make an outright assault on Moscow's purposes and methods. . . . It required an intensive direct education by Molotov, Vishinsky and Gromyko to crack the crust of his illusion."[84]

---

[80]JFD, "Ideals, Not Deals," 7.

[81]Ibid., 10-11. Emphasis is that of Dulles.

[82]JFD, "Ideals Are Not Enough," *International Conciliation* no. 409 (March 1945): 131-41.

[83]Frank Laubach to JFD, 17 November 1946, DP, Box 29.

[84]See "Is Dulles Fit to Be Secretary of State?" 4, DP, Box 61.

By 1947 it was obvious that Dulles had begun to question whether national interest or an ideological commitment to a universalistic faith guided Russian foreign policy. Even though his position on the Soviet Union had hardened considerably, it had not hardened enough to completely satisfy his good friend, Senator Arthur Vandenberg. Reflecting on a special preview copy of the *Life* articles, referred to by Vandenberg as Dulles's "Russian Tome," Vandenberg told Dulles that he [Dulles] was "a philosopher up in [an] ivory tower." "I am," he wrote, "a sadist who thirsts for a practical showdown. Perhaps you had best stay in your tower—and not let me tempt you to toss bricks."[85] Dulles was not long for his ivory tower. Events over the next year would soon cause him to "toss bricks" with the best of the "sadists."

---

[85]Vandenberg to JFD, 7 April 1946, DP, Box 30.

9

From Noncooperation
to Prevention,
1946-1949

While Dulles was chairing an International Conference of Church Leaders at Cambridge in August of 1946, he received a cablegram from Kenneth Leslie, the editor of *The Protestant,* a left-wing Christian publication. The text of the cablegram contained an editorial written for the journal that asked for Dulles's resignation from his chairmanship due to alleged fascist connections.[1] Dulles and his friends in the churches viewed this particular incident as a "communist inspired" attempt to smear Dulles's name in retaliation for his recent articles on Soviet foreign policy. A few American church leaders were officially serving as sponsors of *The Protestant* at the time the editorial appeared. Among those who resigned from their positions as a result of the article were President Ed-

---

[1]"Cablegram," Kenneth Leslie to JFD, 6 August 1946, DP, Box 30; see also "Dulles Asked to Resign to Save Protestantism," *Los Angeles Times,* 6 August 1946.

win McNeill Poteat of Colgate-Rochester and President John A. Mackay
of Princeton Theological Seminary.[2] Alleged "communist" smearings of
Dulles's good name were beginning to become routine. It was not long
before he began to note them with a certain pride and sense of accomplishment.

One significant result of the Cambridge meeting, which was held under the cosponsorship of the World Council of Churches and the International Missionary Council, was the decision to form a new church
commission. This newly formed commission, The Church Commission
on International Affairs, marked the end of the Dulles Commission on a
Just and Durable Peace, for its wartime influence had waned. Dulles's increased involvement in the political arena had left him less and less time
to spend in the work of the commission.

At Cambridge Dulles's position was one of moderation compared to
that of Swiss theologian Emil Brunner, who urged delegates to recognize
that totalitarianism is "Anti-Christian" and could not be accepted in any
form. Dulles chose to emphasize America's need to pledge noncoercive
methods in its foreign policy. According to the *Christian Century,* "It was
remarked that his statements were less open to anti-Soviet interpretation than were his recent articles in *Life.* "[3] Most Christian leaders, however, had applauded even those articles. Morrison, of the *Christian
Century,* wrote shortly after the Dulles articles were published: "There
is no panic in them, and no war mongering. But there is sober appraisal
of an exceedingly serious and dangerous situation."[4] Reinhold Niebuhr,
while at Cambridge, urged that Protestants must not "join the Vatican in
a holy war on Russia."[5] On this point, at this time, Dulles would not necessarily have disagreed with Niebuhr's plea for a moderate approach to
the rising Soviet problem.

Dulles's noncooperative stance hardly constituted a holy war. It
merely meant that America should not be a party to policies that ulti-

---

[2]Henry S. Leiper to JFD, 6 November 1946, DP, Box 30.

[3]Robert Root, "World Council of Churches Launches a New Commission for Global
Peace," *Christian Century* 63 (28 August 1946): 1040.

[4]Charles C. Morrison, "Dulles Proposes a Russian Policy," *Christian Century* 63 (12
June 1946): 740.

[5]Root, "World Council," 1040.

mately result in the loss of individual, political, and religious freedom for some population elsewhere in the world. The fact that differences between the two super powers existed could not be ignored. But, in Dulles's view, the differences didn't justify a holy war. The events of the next two to three years would, however, move Dulles a step closer to the Vatican's perception of the Soviet Union.

During the next few years, Dulles attended three Foreign Ministers' Conferences and two General Assembly meetings of the United Nations. Each of these head-to-head meetings seemed to harden Dulles a little more until, finally, he advocated a hard line completely. In his own assessment of the effects of these meetings, Dulles said:

> For nearly three years we had explored the way of peace. I myself attended seven international conferences involving negotiations with the Soviet Union. I can testify, without reserve, that we had earnestly sought peace and had, indeed expected it. We were, perhaps, naive. We thought that Soviet leaders could value, and not deliberately destroy, the friendship which had developed when our peoples were comrades in arms.[6]

What caused the eventual total estrangement between the Soviet Union and the United States? Dulles came to believe that the fault lay totally with the Soviet Union. However, after looking at the justification given by American policymakers as they responded to Soviet action during these years one could claim that faulty moral reasoning on their part might have had as much to do with the end result as Soviet aggression. Dulles provides an interesting example of this aspect of the problem.

Increased Soviet aggression pushed Dulles further and further away from being attuned to the faults of American action in the world arena. Directly related to his increasing tendency to overlook American selfishness in international diplomacy was a corresponding tendency to view the moral expression of the Free World as *the* moral law. Soviet aggression caused Dulles to adopt a defensive posture that led him to defend particular Western moral concepts as universally applicable. The moral law, previously defined as transcendent and independent of any nation's finite expressions of it, soon became a moral law that was exclusively identified with Western moral traditions as they are expressed in Western re-

---

[6]JFD, "Not War, Not Peace," 1, 5 January 1948, DP, Box 36.

ligious, political, and economic institutions. At this point one might question the moral reasoning Dulles utilized in this process. When American policy is formulated by leaders who identify the moral law with American moral expressions, it is likely that such policy will be offensive to those who do not share those expressions.

Soviet Obstructionism
and the Problem of Germany

The second part of the First Session of the United Nations was convened in New York on 23 October 1946. During these meetings Soviet obstruction of trusteeship agreements greatly disturbed Dulles. He believed that the Communist strategy included blocking the establishment of the Trusteeship Council because

> if there were no Trusteeship Council, the non-self governing peoples would feel abandoned by the United Nations and that the only way to realize their aspirations was to take matters into their own hands and use violence under the leadership of the Soviet Union.[7]

This development made Dulles uneasy. After the session held in London earlier in the year, Dulles thought that "the barriers" erected by the Soviet Union with regard to the West could be broken down, though it would "not be easy."[8] In New York he grew less optimistic that such fellowship could ever be achieved: "The climate so far has not been very good. There has been a clash between East and West which, if it continues, will make it impossible for the United Nations to grow up as planned."[9]

As Ronald Pruessen has pointed out, "Among the basic facts of U.N. life which Dulles generally chose to ignore after mid-1946 was the behavior of his own country."[10] The United States was itself tardy in submitting its mandated territories to U.N. trusteeship. When finally these

---

[7]JFD, *War or Peace* (New York: The Macmillan Company, 1950) 83.

[8]JFD, "Foreign Policy Association Speech," 6, 25 February 1946, DP, Box 30.

[9]JFD, "Script," 6, 21 October 1946, DP, Box 30.

[10]Ronald W. Pruessen, *John Foster Dulles: The Road to Power* (New York: The Free Press, 1982) 410.

territories were submitted, they were submitted "with the United States as the administering authority."[11] This "single nation" administration hardly indicated confidence in the newly established Trusteeship Council. Of course, the administering nations could also build military bases within their own trust territories as they saw fit. As Pruessen concludes, "United States resistance to real limitations on its sovereignty and freedom of movement was one of the factors that prevented the emergence of a viable international organization after 1946."[12]

Dulles preferred to blame the Soviet Union for the failure of the U.N. to achieve significant results. Since public opinion in the U.N. generally supported the United States, he was anxious to use that support to good advantage. As early as his "Ideals, Not Deals" speech of early 1947, Dulles urged that Americans "should begin to use the United Nations to mobilize world opinion against international injustices."[13] This excerpt constitutes the first instance of a later concerted effort to use the U.N. as an effective tool in the Cold War against the Soviet Union.[14]

Shortly after the close of the first complete session of the U.N. General Assembly, Dulles delivered an address before the National Publishers Association. The topic of this speech concerned recommendations for needed reform to help guarantee a peaceful Europe in the future. Throughout World War II Dulles was a consistent advocate of a federated Europe. This address accords with that conviction. Yet, more specifically, the address dealt with the problem of Germany. How could Germany be successfully unified without causing concern among its European neighbors? Of course, the other important aspect of the problem involved the question of how to keep a unified Germany from falling into the Soviet sphere.

According to Dulles, the Soviet challenge was "double-barreled." On the one hand, the Soviets hoped to foster "social revolution throughout the world." On the other, they desired "nationalistic expansion." Germany offered opportunity in both of these areas. Dulles believed that the

---

[11]JFD, *War or Peace,* 84.

[12]Pruessen, *The Road to Power,* 413.

[13]JFD, "Ideals, Not Deals," 9, 10 February 1947, DP, Box 33.

[14]See ch. 10 for an explanation of this later development.

United States should see that no Soviet inroads were made in either category.

As Dulles looked at the German problem, "the central problem of Europe," he emphasized that the solution would come through thinking "more in terms of the economic unity of Europe and less in terms of the Potsdam dictum that Germany shall be 'a single economic unit.' " The solution that Dulles hoped would be effected in a German peace treaty included a proposal for the decentralization of Germany, that is, some "form of joint control which will make it possible to develop the industrial potential of Western Germany in the interest of Western Europe, including Germany." The core of Dulles's suggestion concerned an internationalization of the basin of the Rhine. If the Ruhr valley were left totally under the control of a unified Germany, that economic power could make the "Germans the master of Europe."[15]

Through his proposals concerning Germany, Dulles made it clear that he desired "reform of the political economy of Europe." Equally clear were his "grave doubts about the trustworthiness of Germany" along with his "attentiveness to the traditional needs of the United States."[16] These proposals emerged as much out of his historic concern for a more unified Europe as from his newer fear of Soviet expansionism.

Development of a Preventive Program

In the address on Germany that he made before the National Publishers Association, Dulles urged the continuation of bipartisan cooperation in foreign affairs. The praise he heaped upon Democratic leadership for their willingness to extend an ear to Republican suggestion was not ignored by the Democratic administration. An election year was just around the corner. Truman could be vulnerable to Dewey. It could not hurt to continue Dulles's participation in foreign policymaking. Such a move could head off criticism of campaign issues in the international sphere. Less than a month after Dulles's address, Secretary of State Marshall invited Dulles to the State Department for a meeting.

---

[15]JFD, "Europe Must Federate or Perish," *Vital Speeches of the Day* 13 (1 February 1947): 234-36.

[16]Pruessen, *The Road to Power,* 337-38.

During this meeting Dulles reiterated his program for the economic recovery of Europe. He argued that a program such as he described was necessary in order to prevent a "Soviet-type" of economy from taking over. Marshall ended the meeting by asking Dulles to accompany him as a delegate to the Moscow Foreign Ministers' Conference.[17]

Vandenberg expressed that it was really too bad that Marshall had invited Dulles to Moscow because the conference was bound to fail and would have made good ammunition for the upcoming campaign. Even the administration felt that the conference would do no more than "reduce and clarify the issues."[18] Dulles accepted the administration's invitation knowing ahead of time that not much would be accomplished.

Even though Dulles was not expecting much from the Moscow Conference (10 March to 25 April), he was still disappointed when his expectation became reality. The results of the Moscow Conference made the prospect of the Soviet Union and the United States ever being able to "work hand in hand in the post-war world" seem much "more doubtful."[19] When he returned from Moscow, he began to articulate a program that he later characterized as the "preventive phase" of American post-war policy. The program was designed to "encourage and help those peoples of Europe who were yet free, so that they would find new strength out of new unity." Primarily, Dulles hoped to prevent peacefully further Soviet expansion. According to Dulles, as a direct result of the Moscow Conference, "There gradually began to emerge, in broad outline, the vision of a way whereby, without war, the free societies might frustrate the Soviet design" by filling the vacuum of Western Europe with "native and friendly processes," designed primarily to prevent the intrusion of "alien despotism."[20]

Why would the Moscow Conference, which was not expected to yield much in the way of significant results anyway, cause Dulles to formulate a new approach to the Soviet menace? The answer to that question is that in Moscow the American delegation saw several problems more

---

[17]JFD, "Memorandum," 3, 26 February 1947, DP, Box 31.

[18]Ibid.

[19]JFD to William G. Coxhead, 4 June 1947, DP, Box 42.

[20]JFD, "The Atlantic Pact," 2, 12 July 1949, DP, Box 43; see also JFD, *War or Peace*, 101; and JFD, "Report on Moscow Meeting," 2-11, 29 April 1947, DP, Box 31.

clearly. First, the uncertainty of French stability became obvious. Communists held thirty percent of the votes as well as a number of important political offices. Second, the Soviets wanted a unified Germany in the hope that "they could get control of Germany by getting control of that central power." Obviously, the Soviets were fearful of a reunited Germany, which, as Dulles proposed, would be integrated into Western Europe. Third, the Moscow Conference heightened American sensitivity to the scope of Soviet ambitions in Europe, particularly with regard to France and Germany. And fourth, this increased anxiety level brought to American leadership a more urgent desire to provide economic aid for Europe. In sum, Dulles wrote,

> The Moscow Conference was, to those who were there, like a streak of lightning that suddenly illumined a dark and stormy scene. We saw as never before the magnitude of the task of saving Europe for Western civilization. We saw the need of economic and moral support and the need of a program that would be both comprehensive and creative. [21]

Thus, after Moscow, Dulles envisioned a program composed of two pillars, one pertaining to the economic aspects of the problem and the other attending to moral concerns. Secretary of State Marshall addressed the economic problem shortly after the delegation returned from Moscow. In his now-famous Harvard commencement address on 5 June, Marshall unveiled the administration's plan for the economic recovery of Europe. The Marshall Plan was born. Paul Hutchinson, the new editor of the *Christian Century,* publicly speculated that Dulles was at least partially responsible for the shift from the military emphasis of the Truman Doctrine—announced by the president to the Congress in an address on 12 March—to the economic emphasis of the Marshall Plan. [22] Dulles indicated privately that Hutchinson's suspicion was indeed correct. [23]

The Marshall Plan represented a very realistic reaction to the situation in Europe. To whatever extent Dulles helped to encourage a move in that direction, he should be given credit. However, his actual involve-

---

[21]JFD, *War or Peace,* 105.

[22]Paul Hutchinson, "Backing Away from the Truman Doctrine," *Christian Century* 64 (25 June 1947): 790-91.

[23]JFD to Paul Hutchinson, 24 June 1947, DP, Box 32.

ment in the development of the plan was negligible. The Marshall Plan was completely devised without his knowledge. The plan did, however, follow the pattern of his earlier proposals concerning Europe. On the whole, the plan serves as an excellent example of enlightened self-interest in action: it coupled the moral aspect of alleviating human suffering with the national-interest aspect of using economic means to prevent the spread of Soviet Communism into the vacuum created by World War II.

The Marshall Plan contributed significantly to providing an economic support structure for Western Europe. Dulles, therefore, concerned himself with the question of how the corresponding moral support structure might be implemented. In a secret memorandum Dulles expressed his finally hardened belief that "there is a world-wide struggle primarily ideological between Western (Christian) civilization and Communism, the former led by the U.S.A. and the latter led by the U.S.S.R."[24] This realization led Dulles to a more aggressive expression of Western moral principles. He believed that American leadership needed to shift from a passive role in international affairs to a more active expression of moral principles which, he emphasized, should be attached to tangible programs designed to frustrate Soviet expansionism. In other words, simple noncooperation was no longer adequate. "We cannot afford to feel complacent," he wrote, "merely because, at conferences, we have stopped surrendering our principles."[25]

Philosophical Foundations
for a New Policy

Dulles felt that the first step toward more active opposition might best be achieved through educating the American people regarding the urgency of the situation. Once that urgency were made clear, he believed that support for more serious preventive measures would be forthcoming. In order to pinpoint the nature of the problem facing the Free World, Dulles endeavored to assess the ideological differences between the United States and the Soviet Union. Thus he concentrated on trying to

---

[24]JFD, "Secret Memorandum," 1, 7 March 1947, DP, Box 31.

[25]JFD, "Report on Moscow Meeting," 11.

provide the average American citizen with a philosophical understanding of the differences between the two faiths claiming international jurisdiction, those of democracy and Communism. Such an understanding would, after all, be entirely consistent with his call for spiritual revival and, in all likelihood, would contribute to its success. Before American faith could be revived, Americans needed to understand the essentials of the vital faith represented in their heritage and to appreciate how those essentials differed from the dangerous new faith of the Soviet Union.

Recapturing the American Tradition. Upon his return to the United States from Moscow, Dulles immediately set to work on a document that was later adopted and published by the Commission on a Just and Durable Peace. The document was the last one published by the commission. Dulles titled the essay "Crossroads of American Foreign Policy." The "basic international issue" dividing the present world, he wrote, was "simply the issue of the free society versus the police state."

> By a free society we mean a society in which human beings, in voluntary cooperation, may choose and change their way of life and in which force is outlawed as a means to suppress or eliminate spiritual, intellectual and political differences between individuals and those exercising the police power. The police state denies these rights. [26]

As Dulles interpreted it, the heritage of the United States demonstrated the best aspects of the free society. Over the next several years, Dulles devoted himself to illustrating forcefully the ramifications of this observation. Christ, in his day, had emphasized that "the truth shall make you free." "Every one of the intervening years sustains that utterance. The church spires which silhouette the skyline of America symbolize acceptance of his way."[27] Americans, as members of a spiritual society, have consistently espoused freedom for the individual. As a result, the American nation has become "known" and "loved" the world over "as the exponent of international righteousness."[28]

To Dulles, it seemed that Americans had lost touch with the rich heritage that had earned the respect and love of the rest of the world. Amer-

---

[26]JFD, "Crossroads of American Foreign Policy," 3, 1 July 1947, DP, Box 32.

[27]JFD, "Speech," 5, 12 October 1949, DP, Box 298.

[28]JFD, "A New Look at Foreign Policy," 6, 4 October 1952, DP, Box 63.

icans were clearly experiencing a crisis in faith. Why was this the case? The answer to that question, Dulles believed, lay with the failure of Americans "to see the connection between our faith and our institutions." Several factors contributed to this cultural and spiritual blindness. First of all, "the older people," he explained, "have failed to pass on dramatically to the younger people recognition of the quality of [American] institutions which justifies that faith and sense of mission."[29]

Second, Dulles harkened to the days of his youth when history was taught "so as to emphasize the best in [the] great American tradition." Unfortunately, he lamented, "historians today seem to take pride in trying to find defects in our great national figures and to show hypocrisy in our national conduct."[30] This particular statement indicates a marked departure from statements of earlier years in which he warned that biased history contributed to the erection of insurmountable barriers between the peoples of the world. These days, however, Dulles was much more interested in seeing that those barriers held up. The foe on the other side of those barriers represented too great a threat to relax them.

Finally, Dulles argued that the churches have "contributed to breaking the connection between our faith and our practices by emphasizing the imperfection of what is."[31] This belief also clearly contradicts his earlier emphasis, as a leader in the churches, on the need for Americans to acknowledge their own abuses of the moral law before pointing out the abuses of other nations. Obviously, his viewpoint had changed considerably.

> Some think that peace can be assured if we see only the good that is in others and the evil that is in ourselves. I believe that involves blurred vision rather than clear vision and that peace requires our seeing clearly what there is of righteousness in our own institutions and defending that, not with arms, but with faith.[32]

---

[29]JFD, "Address to the Chaplain's Association of the Army and Navy," 11 May 1948, DP, Box 295.

[30]JFD, "Address before the Watertown Chamber of Commerce," 2, 30 April 1952, DP, Box 307.

[31]JFD, "Christian Responsibility for Peace," 6, 4 May 1948, DP, Box 38.

[32]Ibid. Compare this with his statement of 1942 that Americans needed to develop "a sense of values conceived in terms of the general welfare rather than that of our particular nation, race, or class" ("Christianity in This Hour," 22, 21 April 1941, DP, Box 20).

For Dulles, this meant a return to that faith which developed "an area of spiritual, intellectual and economic vigor the likes of which the world had never seen."[33] Such a faith was needed in order to combat effectively the growing Communist challenge. Americans would need the "alert and effective use . . . of moral power" so characteristic of American citizens in the past whenever the country was at war. "The world will never have peace," he exclaimed, "so long as men reserve, for war, the finest human qualities."[34] "Only war itself," he wrote elsewhere, "brings out our keenest vision, our highest competence and our most enobling [sic] spirit."[35]

The American churchmen who worked with Dulles in earlier years, especially those who had received admonishing letters from him concerning their overzealous emotionalism during World War II, must surely have been surprised by these statements. Any emphasis on the imperfections and immoralities of the American past, so often an integral part of Dulles's earlier expressions, had disappeared altogether. Dulles now believed that for their own sake, and for the sake of the rest of the world, Americans should remember that they were "predominantly a moral people, who believe that [their] nation has a great spiritual heritage to be preserved."[36] That fact is what has made America "great in the true sense of the word."

> That belief translates itself into a society of individuals who love God and their fellow man, and who fear only God and not any man; who work hard as a matter of duty and self-satisfaction, not compulsion; who gain personal and family security primarily through ability and willingness voluntarily to earn and save; who are self-reliant, resourceful, and adaptable to changing conditions, and for whom life is not merely physical growth and enjoyment, but intellectual and spiritual development. It also translates itself into public organizations, through which men willingly coop-

---

[33]JFD, "Foreign Policy and the National Welfare," 6, 16 February 1952, DP, Box 59.

[34]JFD, "The Churches' Opportunities in World Affairs," 3-4, 6 August 1947, DP, Box 33.

[35]See the *New York Times,* 5 October 1952.

[36]JFD, "Principle versus Expediency in Foreign Policy," 4, 26 September 1952, DP, Box 64; see also JFD, "Our Spiritual Heritage," 1, 21 October 1947, DP, Box 33.

erate, at national and local levels, to do what they cannot well do otherwise.[37]

Such an idealistic view of the American personality sounds as if it came right out of a Presbyterian sermon telling a Calvinist flock what is to be expected from them. For Dulles, the Presbyterian sermons he had so often heard throughout his entire life were now universally applicable. They no longer represented merely a finite and necessarily partial understanding of universal truth; instead, those sermons had come to be taken much more seriously. As a result, any contrary viewpoint was beginning to be regarded as not merely wrong but evil.

The Materialistic Heritage of the Soviet Union. Dulles believed that the American people should not only possess an understanding of their own "spiritual" heritage, but should also learn about the "materialistic" heritage of the Soviet Union. Such an understanding, he believed, would serve to renew faith in the righteousness of American institutions as well as foster support for American policy with regard to the Soviet Union. Dulles felt himself eminently qualified to educate the American public on this subject. Shortly after the Moscow Conference, he seriously set himself to the task at hand.

Dulles was confident that he was suited for this task primarily because he had studied Stalin's *Problems of Leninism,* referred to by Dulles as the "Soviet Bible."[38] Within two years after his 1946 *Life* articles, Dulles began to devote some of his extra time to the reading of Stalin's work. Beginning in the late fall of 1947, his addresses begin to quote freely from two of these books: *Problems of Leninism* and *Dialectical and Historical*

---

[37]JFD, *War or Peace,* 260; see also JFD, "The Churches' Opportunities in World Affairs," 9; JFD, "Our International Responsibilities," 1, 4 June 1950, DP, Box 50; and JFD, "The Free East and the Free West," 6, 29 November 1951, DP, Box 55.

[38]JFD, "Christian Responsibility for Peace," 8; JFD, "U.S. Military Actions in Korea," *Department of State Bulletin* 23 (17 July 1950); and JFD, "Address," 18 September 1952, DP, Box 59. The obvious inference here is that the West adhered to the Bible in the same way that Soviets adhered to Stalin's *Problems of Leninism.* Further, Dulles stated that Stalin's book was "a pattern, much as *Mein Kampf* was a pattern of Hitler" (JFD, "The Republican Outlook," 5, 11 December 1947, DP, Box 31; see also JFD, *War or Peace,* 7; and JFD, "The Strategy of Soviet Communism," 1, 14 March 1950, DP, Box 50).

Materialism.[39] He often quoted portions of both these books from memory. As Hoopes has pointed out, Dulles "kept a heavily underlined and well-thumbed copy [of *Problems of Leninism*] on his desk and another at his bedside."[40] Consequently, Dulles felt that he understood Communist ideology as well as any man could. With that understanding, he would dogmatically instruct any audience willing to listen to him.

Dulles contrasted the great "spiritual heritage" enjoyed by Americans with the thoroughly "materialistic" tradition of the Soviet Union. For Dulles, the hallmark of America's heritage, that which made it spiritual, was its emphasis on freedom for the individual. Thus the hallmark of the materialistic heritage found in the Soviet Union was exactly the opposite: no individual freedom whatsoever. As early as the 1946 *Life* articles, Dulles began to emphasize that the Soviet Union, "under atheistic leadership," logically and practically treats "human freedoms like the freedoms of wild animals" and intends "to suppress those freedoms so that men, like domesticated animals, will be more amenable and more serene."[41] A year later Dulles embellished the imagery some:

> Under it [Soviet leadership] the people are like a herd driven from pasture to barn, from barn to pasture. The individuals are kept in formation by police dogs. If any stray, they are nipped. If they stray far, they are destroyed.[42]

After 1946 Dulles repeatedly described the Soviet Union as "a police state run by a small group of ruthless men."[43] Soviet leaders, he as-

---

[39]The following addresses serve as a few examples. An exhaustive list would cover several pages: "The Republican Outlook," 11 December 1947, DP, Box 31; "Christian Responsibility for Peace"; "The North Atlantic Treaty and the United Nations," 29 April 1949, DP, Box 43; "The United States and Russia," 18 January 1949, DP, Box 46; "The Blessings of Liberty," 28 December 1949, DP, Box 46.

[40]Townsend Hoopes, *The Devil and John Foster Dulles* (Boston: Little, Brown and Company, 1973) 64.

[41]JFD, "Thoughts on Soviet Foreign Policy and What to Do about It," *Life* (10 June 1946): 120.

[42]JFD, "Draft," 4, 15 August 1947, DP, Box 31. In other addresses Dulles refers to the Soviet population as being "molded into . . . ants and bees" (see JFD, "U.S. Policy in the Face of Aggression," 1, 11 October 1952, DP, Box 64) and relegated to "the status of broken-spirited pack animals" (JFD, *War or Peace,* 175).

[43]See, for example, JFD to Reverend James G. Huggin, 28 July 1947, DP, Box 33.

serted, "believe in, and practice at home, a system of liquidating by force all who disagree with them."[44] Thus Soviet leaders fully intend to "extend the police state system throughout the world."[45] For "established civilization [the free societies of the West]," such an intent represented a challenge "which occurs only once in centuries."[46] The challenge consisted of "an ambitious and well organized program to overthrow the free societies."[47] Dulles's favorite analogy compared the Soviet threat to the threat of Islam in the tenth century.[48]

Throughout these later years Dulles attributed the "great evil" of the Soviet system to the natural result of a philosophy that "puts material things first."[49] In order to substantiate statements like these, Dulles often quoted Stalin's emphasis on the importance of the materialistic society.

> The material world is primary and mind, thought, is secondary. . . . Hence the source of formation of the spiritual life of society should be sought . . . in the conditions of the natural life of society.[50]

Due to the Soviet emphasis on materialism, Communist priorities, in Dulles's view, were exactly opposed to American priorities. This was only to be expected, he wrote, from an ideology that "starts with an atheistic, Godless premise. . . . If there is no God, there is no moral or natural law."[51] For Dulles, the moral law was cemented to the Western concept of God. Thus, any society that defined reality without including this concept of God was incapable of conforming to the moral law and, in fact,

---

[44]JFD to Rowland Rogers, marked *"Personal,"* 25 June 1947, DP, Box 33.

[45]JFD, *Congressional Record, House,* 8363, 3 July 1947, DP, Box 32.

[46]JFD, "World Brotherhood through the State," 1, 8 September 1946, DP, Box 293.

[47]JFD, "Draft," 2.

[48]See, for example, JFD, "World Brotherhood through the State," 1. As Dulles got closer to the 1952 campaign, he amended this thought to say that Soviet Communism represents "the greatest menace that free men have ever had to face" (JFD, "Platform Draft," 1, 20 June 1952, DP, Box 63).

[49]JFD, "Remarks at Founder's Day Luncheon of Presbyterian Hospital in Philadelphia," 2, 14 April 1952, DP, Box 307.

[50]The quotation is from Stalin's *Dialectical and Historical Materialism* (1938). See JFD, "The Blessings of Liberty"; and JFD, "Remarks," 2, 14 April 1952, DP, Box 307.

[51]JFD, *War or Peace,* 8.

must be viewed as opposed to it. "The despots of the Kremlin," he wrote, believe that the world consists of "human beings [who] are without souls and without rights, except as the government chooses to allow them." "Soviet leaders," he continued, "believe in what I call the 'flat iron' method—make it hot and make it heavy and iron out all the wrinkles."[52] During the 1952 campaign, this was one of his favorite ways to express this belief: "The rulers of Russia are cruelly, systematically and with unprecedented terrorism going about the job of liquidating love of God, love of country and sense of personal dignity" within their sphere of influence.[53]

The Moral Law
and Individual Freedom

Dulles, when he addressed the delegates of the First Assembly of the World Council of Churches held in Amsterdam in 1948, strongly emphasized the inherent societal failure brought on by the vices of materialism. In contrast, he spoke about the success that naturally follows when a society expresses its commitments in spiritual rather than material beliefs and consciously attempts to adhere to the dictates of the moral law (by now synonymous in his mind with Western Christian moral principles). Joseph L. Hromadka, of Czechoslovakia, took the other side of the issue as the topic for his address.[54] He cited the failure of the West throughout history ever to deal successfully with the problems facing humankind. In his view, the West was no more successful or unsuccessful than any other civilization in dealing with these problems. Leadership among the Federal Council of Churches believed Hromadka's address came closer to

---

[52]JFD, "Our International Responsibilities," 2; see also JFD, "The Strength of Diversity," 1, 18 May 1950, DP, Box 50.

[53]See, for example, the following addresses: JFD, "Our Foreign Policy—Is Containment Enough?" 4, 8 October 1952, DP, Box 59; JFD, "Foreign Policy and the National Welfare," 6; JFD, "A New Look at Foreign Policy," 1; JFD, "America and the World," 12, 11 October 1952, DP, Box 63; JFD, "A Dynamic Moral Force: America's Opportunity," 4, 10 June 1952, DP, Box 307.

[54]Joseph L. Hromadka, "Our Responsibility in the Post-War World," in *Man's Disorder and God's Design,* vol. 4, with an intro. by Kenneth Grubb: *The Church and the International Disorder* (New York: Harper and Brothers, 1948) 114-42.

hitting the truth. Thus, Amsterdam revealed, in a dramatic way, a division between the thought of the church leadership in America and the newly developed thought of their once highly respected lay leader.

In his address to the gathering, entitled "The Christian Citizen in a Changing World," Dulles attacked the "compulsory enmity, diabolical outrages against the human personality, and . . . wanton distortion of the truth" that characterized the Soviet tactics.[55] The Soviets, he said, "do not believe in such concepts as eternal justice."[56] Hope for the future "leads from the West," as only it possesses the spiritual power to "wrest the initiative from forces of evil, ignorance and despair which exist in every land and which seem to be conspiring to overwhelm mankind with awful disaster."[57]

Though several portions of his mid-1948 speech point to the evil aspects of Soviet materialism, Dulles at least mentioned the need to avoid "identifying righteousness with anything that is" and, thereby, placing "the seal of God's approval upon that which, at best, may be expedient, but which cannot wholly reflect God's will."[58] The logical end of his argument, however, was not lost on his audience. The American way of life logically constituted a challenge to the Christian faith itself in that the spiritualism of American life, as expressed by Dulles, tended to compete for the ultimate loyalty of American citizens.

It was Paul Tillich who at Amsterdam spoke of both democracy and Communism as "secular faiths" that "rival" the historic faith of Christianity. "No Christian evangelism," he admonished, "can be effective within our world that does not take into account that the people who are emancipated from the church have yielded in some way or other to the appeal to these faiths."[59] In the same setting, Reinhold Niebuhr warned against succumbing to the temptation of simplistic generalizations. "It is wrong," he said, "to regard the socialization of property as a cure-all for

---

[55]JFD, "The Christian Citizen in a Changing World," ibid., 95.

[56]Ibid., 91.

[57]Ibid., 74.

[58]Ibid., 102 and 74.

[59]Paul Tillich, "The Disintegration of Society in Christian Countries," in *Man's Disorder and God's Design*, vol. 2: *The Church's Witness to God's Design* (New York: Harper and Brothers, 1948) 52.

every social ill; but it is no more wrong than to regard such socialization as of itself evil."[60]

Such subtleties were lost on Dulles, and for that reason he would soon arrive at the logical end of his analysis, which was equating the American way of doing things with God's way of doing things. As early as the summer of 1947, Dulles wrote, "I believe in the free enterprise system very strongly. . . . I have that economic belief just as I have my own personal religious belief."[61] Before long the attempt to find any distinguishable difference between the two beliefs would be difficult.

In its final report, the Amsterdam Conference stated that "the Christian churches should reject the ideologies of both Communism and laissez-faire capitalism, and should seek to draw men away from the false assumption that these extremes are the only alternatives."[62] This particular statement so dismayed Dulles that he sought to disassociate himself from it. He responded to those who asked him about the resolution by emphasizing that it came up "after" he left the conference.[63] To one friend he admitted, "It is quite true that some of the denominations that are members of the Federal Council of Churches have representatives with the Federal Council who seem to me to be too far to the left, just as to them I seem to be too far to the right."[64] Bringing home his point somewhat more emphatically in a letter written to another friend a few days later, Dulles wrote,

> I think the great difficulty is that many of the Protestant denominations have allowed the church offices and appointments too much to get into the hands of those of Left Wing and Socialist tendencies. That is the real trouble. The Federal Council of Churches merely records the fact.[65]

---

[60]Reinhold Niebuhr, "God's Design and the Present Disorder of Civilization," in *Man's Disorder and God's Design,* vol. 3: *The Church and the Disorder of Society* (New York: Harper and Brothers, 1948) 21-22.

[61]JFD to Rolland J. Hamilton, 15 July 1947, DP, Box 32.

[62]"The Church and the Disorder of Society," Official Report of the First Assembly of the World Council of Churches, DP, Box 51.

[63]See JFD to Charles R. Petticrew, 20 January 1950, DP, Box 51. See also JFD to Allan B. Crow, 22 May 1950, DP, Box 51.

[64]JFD to William H. Fitzgerald, 22 May 1950, DP, Box 51.

[65]JFD to Allan B. Crow, 31 May 1950, DP, Box 48.

The extensive space in the final report devoted to quoting from Hromadka's address, when compared to the two brief quotations from Dulles's speech, is evidence of the more favorable hearing the world's religious ecumenical leadership gave to the Czechoslovakian speaker in Amsterdam.[66] Hromadka's speech, characterized by Dulles as full of "grotesque distortions,"[67] was a remarkably calm and realistically astute analysis of Soviet Communism, especially considering that it was delivered only shortly after the Russians seized Hromadka's homeland of Czechoslovakia. He described the Soviet brand of Communistic atheism as "rather a tool and weapon of an anti-bourgeois or anti-feudal political propaganda than a distinctive faith and metaphysic." He believed that materialism should be defined in terms other than simply the crushing of individual freedoms. Rather, as the Soviets see it, it consists of "struggling for a social system in which all class differences would fade away, the demonic, tyrannical power of money and private property would be crushed, and all human beings would be united on the same ground of human dignity, freedom and love."[68]

It does no good, stated Hromadka, to compare Soviet Communism "with the democratic institutions and processes originated, grown and perfected under an utterly different historical sky." When Americans demand that the Soviets define personal freedoms in exactly the same way they do, the end result merely increases Soviet paranoia and leads to the further entrenchment of the already all too prevalent "violent methods of agitation, threat, deportation, trials and police control."[69] Soviet Communism should rather be viewed as a "historical necessity in a country consisting of multiple ethnic, and in part culturally backward elements, and in a nation which for many reasons had not been privileged to enjoy political liberties and popular education."[70]

The Soviet hatred of religion, Hromadka urged, should be placed in its historical context. It was due to a "kind of humanistic evangelism

---

[66]See "The Church and the Disorder of Society," DP, Box 51.

[67]JFD, "Evolution or Revolution," 12 February 1949, DP, Box 43.

[68]Hromadka, "Responsibility in the Post-War World," 129.

[69]Ibid., 141.

[70]Ibid., 131.

preaching the destruction of the evil caesaro-papistic system" of the czars. The church "was intrinsically associated with the very structure of the pre-revolutionary society."[71] It had helped to transform the poor into "a liturgical, mystical, opiate." Communism originally hoped to do for the poor what the church had failed to do. The church in Russia, through its own action, brought on Bolshevik hatred. In Hromadka's opinion, such an understanding was vastly superior to the simplistic "spiritualism versus materialism" being propounded by Dulles.

The World Council's support for Hromadka's views obviously disturbed Dulles. The support offered to the Czechoslovakian, as Dulles interpreted it, demonstrated the naiveté of the churchmen. He believed that things had grown too complicated for the churchmen to understand. Their commitment to see the best in everyone was clouding their vision.[72] What Dulles failed to see was that his own analysis would soon logically lead him to universalize the conflict and to equate the cause of the "spiritual West" totally and completely with the will of God. Such a move bothered not only churchmen but members of the press as well. As Frank Kingdon of the *New York Post* phrased it: "The outlook for world peace seems to be getting dull, duller, Dulles."[73]

The more Dulles compared the spiritualism of the West with the materialism of Soviet Communism, the more intimately he connected the latter with sin incarnate:

> The only system that is theoretically flawless is one of absolute despotism. . . . Then, in theory, all disharmonies, all imperfections can be removed, all grit can quickly be cleared out, and perfect mechanical harmony can result. However, the attempt to do that creates moral enormities. That is always the case when men indulge in the conceit that they can do better than God.[74]

Equating materialism with sin was the first step toward equating democracy, because of its emphasis on the freedom of the individual, with the cause of righteousness. During World War II Dulles had emphasized

---

[71]Ibid., 138.

[72]See JFD, "Christian Responsibility for Peace," 6.

[73]Frank Kingdon, *New York Post,* 28 July 1947, DP, Box 33.

[74]JFD, *War or Peace,* 260.

that Nazism arose as a reaction to the attempt by the nations in power, including the United States, to preserve the status quo. Now, however, he viewed the violence perpetrated by the Soviet Union in an altogether different light. This new violence arose from Communist ideology. No Western power could be assigned any share of the blame regarding its creation.[75]

During the war years Dulles had advocated a righteous faith, which was defined by the injunction to make the welfare of humankind the highest good. This highest good was something that summoned Americans. It required economic changes, some progress toward the loss of sovereignty, the renunciation of military force as a meaningful tool in international relations, and so on. More and more, after 1947, the highest good came to embody the American way of life. It no longer called Americans to it, for they had already arrived. The emphasis now shifted to interesting every other nation in a societal structure resembling that of the United States. "What is our feverishness about?" asked Dulles. "It is presumably to save mankind from falling under the sway of a materialistic rule that holds that man's chief end is to glorify the state and serve it forever."[76]

Dulles, therefore, believed that the key to peace and progress lay solely in the hands of the Free World. This belief formed the philosophical foundation for Dulles's "preventive phase" as a response to Soviet expansionism. The common enemies of humankind were no longer the abstractions of "intolerance, repression, injustice, and economic want." They were now replaced by the atheistic Communist leaders who perpetuated these abstractions.[77] Essentially, Dulles developed an ideology of the Free World. In his words,

> I saw there could be no just and durable peace except as men held in
> common simple and elementary religious beliefs: belief that there is a God,
> that he is the author of a moral law which they can know, and that he

---

[75]Concerning this point, see E. Raymond Platig, "John Foster Dulles: A Study of His Political and Moral Thought Prior to 1953 with Special Emphasis on International Relations" (dissertation, The University of Chicago, 1957) 270.

[76]JFD, "Leadership for Peace," 16, 8 March 1949, DP, Box 46. The language of the above quotation is drawn from The Westminster Shorter Catechism, 1647.

[77]See Platig, "John Foster Dulles," 305-306.

imparts to each human being a spiritual dignity and worth which all others should respect. Wherever these elementary truths are rejected there is both spiritual and social disorder. That fact is illustrated by fascism and communism.[78]

As expressed here, peace is impossible apart from all nations in the world coming to share the Western religious world view. Those in the West, "those who believe in a spiritual world," are "able to find practices superior to those which derive from a materialistic and atheistic belief." In fact, practices derived from "a spiritual view of the nature of man" are of "infinitely greater worth."[79]

The superior worth of the Western view arose from its emphasis on individual freedom. Is "liberty the fountainhead of welfare?" Dulles asked. Or is "welfare . . . primarily material" with "governmental compulsion" its best dispenser?[80] With these rhetorical questions, Dulles defined the moral law in terms of the American understanding of individual liberty. He attached ultimacy to the concept of individual freedom. All nations were to be judged by adherence or nonadherence to this concept. Thus Dulles redefined what he viewed as the major task of the United Nations. No longer was it to be viewed as an international body which, through tough compromise and negotiation, would arrive at mutual understandings among equally finite nations concerning international problems. "The United Nations," he wrote, "cannot suppress or reconcile the differences between the materialistic and atheistic philosophy of the Communist Party and the spiritual faith that animates the leaders and peoples of the non-communist states."[81] The United Nations must now take sides in the conflict.

These words illustrate that the Dulles of old, a man who clearly recognized the importance of international power structures, was replaced with a new Dulles, a man who no longer recognized those structures unless they worked along with him in behalf of the Free World. He had

---

[78]JFD, "Faith of Our Fathers," in *The Spiritual Legacy of John Foster Dulles,* ed. Henry P. Van Dusen (Philadelphia: The Westminster Press, 1960) 7.

[79]JFD, "The Blessings of Liberty," 21-22.

[80]Ibid., 1.

[81]JFD, *War or Peace,* 185; see also JFD, "Our International Responsibilities," 3.

moved from being concerned with the needs of others, economic as well as spiritual, to being only interested in proselytizing others. His faith was no longer placed in the transcendent God who stands over and above all nations; rather, his faith now rested in the inherent righteousness of free institutions. For Dulles, the very success of God's purposes in the world depended upon the West's ability to win the Cold War. If the Free World were undone, the cause of righteousness would suffer a considerable setback, or perhaps even be overcome completely.

During these later years, Dulles replaced his earlier emphasis upon a moral law that would emerge from negotiation and compromise among the nations of the world with a new understanding of morality that was exclusively defined in terms of individual liberty. Since all men yearn to be free, the moral law possesses the universality that is needed to bring understanding among nations. In Dulles's words, "no policies are sound or will succeed unless they have elements of universality and that means morality, for only morality has universality."[82] In Dulles's mind, if there was to be peace in the world, the Soviet Union must recognize the fundamental truth that morality required individual liberty, and then act accordingly.

In this way, Dulles universalized the confict.[83] It took on cosmic importance. One universalistic faith, that of spiritual American democratic capitalism, was pitted against another universalistic faith, that of materialistic Soviet Communism. That is why Dulles felt that "the basic issue" between America and the Soviet Union "cannot be compromised."[84] In Dulles's mind, at least, no doubt existed as to which faith personified good and which personified evil.

---

[82]JFD, "The Importance of Spiritual Resources," 22, 27 January 1950, DP, Box 48.

[83]For example, consider the following titles of Dulles speeches: "State Control versus Self Control," 15 July 1946, DP, Box 30; "Police State versus Free State," 15 September 1947, DP, Box 33; and "Materialistic Society versus Spiritualistic Society," in *War or Peace,* 258-61. The following speeches are examples of the same theme, though the titles are not quite as graphic: "The Importance of Spiritual Resources," "Address at Seoul National University," 20 June 1950, DP, Box 50; "Universal Bible Sunday Broadcast," 20 November 1950, DP, Box 50; "Republican Foreign Policy," 21 July 1952, DP, Box 59; "Three Propositions," 22 February 1952, DP, Box 63.

[84]JFD, "Our International Responsibilities," 3.

Introducing the Concept
of Selective Change

The increased significance attached to the conflict between the United States and the Soviet Union caused Dulles to modify his earlier concern for the need to recognize change in the international arena. In *War, Peace and Change* (1939), Dulles had argued that the political leadership of the satisfied nations should be willing to accept the change that inevitably accompanies the dynamic impulse of peoples elsewhere in the world. Part of this, he wrote, would involve acceptance of types of government different from those of free societies.[85] Now, he argued that "not . . . all change is desirable." Rather, "change must be selective."[86] Change should be selected on the basis of whether or not it "progressively increases the opportunities for individual growth."[87] As is evidenced by this statement, individual freedom had become the standard by which everything in the international arena was to be measured.

> If peaceful change requires deciding whose judgment is to prevail, and if the judgment of a free, disciplined society is the most reliable and generally acceptable judgment, then the extension of free societies throughout the world is prerequisite to a world-wide institutionalizing of change.[88]

In 1939 Dulles argued that the dynamic, rather than the static, powers provided the impulse toward change. By 1948 he argued that the opposite was true. Only mature peoples can provide for peaceful change.

> Practical experience seems to show that where peoples have a considerable degree of self-discipline, when they recognize duty to fellow men and where they have considerable education, then they can operate political processes which make for change which is peaceful and selective.[89]

---

[85]See particularly, JFD, *War, Peace and Change* (New York: Harper and Brothers, 1939) 22, 29-33, 39-44, 95-96, 135-39.

[86]JFD, "Address at White Plains Church," 4, 12 October 1949, DP, Box 298.

[87]JFD, "The Christian Citizen," 84; see also *War or Peace,* 264.

[88]JFD, "The Christian Citizen," 86-87.

[89]Ibid., 83. Compare this with Dulles's position as presented on 123-32.

Therefore, as Dulles explicitly stated, only the "Western democracies" and their "political institutions" are able to bring about the desired changes in the international arena. "There is no comparable evidence to show that under a despotic or totalitarian form of society there can be sustained change that is peaceful and selective."[90]

The opportunity provided by the inevitability of change has two facets, according to Dulles. On the one hand, "there is the opportunity to make the world more nearly one in which God's will is done on earth as it is in heaven." For Dulles, this meant a change toward democratic government since, as he defined it, that was what most closely approximated God's standards for individual spiritual and intellectual development. On the other hand, change provided "the opportunity for personal growth and development which comes out of grappling with situations and trying to mould them."[91]

Peace and security were therefore defined by Dulles as by-products "of great endeavor and great faith" on the part of Western democracies in order to guarantee that proper selective change occurs.[92] Concurrently, those institutions that provide for peaceful change, "without violating human personalities," are deserving of a great faith. "Such a faith," Dulles believed, "if coupled with works, is the best possible insurance against assault from without."[93] In a rather ironic way, then, the later Dulles argued for selective change, the logical outcome of which is actually tighter security for the existing free societies. His earlier concern that the rights of dynamic powers be heeded dropped from sight entirely.

Was Dulles's moralistic emphasis of these later years merely a practical necessity in order to gain a political following? When seen as part of the total context of Dulles's life, the answer must be "no." Dulles, throughout his life, spoke in terms of the moral law. I would agree with churchman Samuel McCrea Cavert's assessment that Dulles's moralizing was "[not] at all an affectation or just a political gimmick. He had very

---

[90]Ibid., 84.

[91]Ibid., 75.

[92]JFD, *War or Peace,* 175.

[93]JFD, "Christian Responsibility for Peace," 11.

deep moral convictions." In fact, in Cavert's words, Dulles was "essentially a Puritan of the twentieth century."[94]

The former West German minister to America, Albrecht von Kessel, couched his evaluation of Dulles in similar terms:

> Dulles was an American Puritan very difficult for me, a Lutheran, to understand. This partly led him to a conviction that Bolshevism was a product of the devil and that God would wear out the Bolsheviks in the long run. . . . Dulles's approach made him, to a certain point, an immobilist.[95]

Sir Oliver Franks, former ambassador from Great Britain, believed that Dulles resembled the leaders of the Protestant Reformation.

> Like them, in vigorous and systematic reflection, he had come to unshakeable convictions of a religious and theological order. Like them, he saw the world as an arena in which the forces of good and evil were continuously at war. Like them, he believed that this was the contest that supremely mattered.[96]

The religious imagery used in these contemporary characterizations of Dulles provides evidence of the forceful way in which his religious commitments served as the basis of his foreign policy.

The Context for Prevention

The emerging nationalist philosophy, characterizing both Dulles's pronouncements and his policy recommendations after 1947, did not develop in a vacuum. In addition to his attendance at the Moscow Foreign Ministers' Council, Dulles also served as an adviser to the brief London Foreign Ministers' Conference (November-December 1947) which, consistent with other postwar conferences, produced no significant agreement on the hard questions of the peace. Dulles left the council meetings in London on 4 December to check on the political situation in Paris for Secretary Marshall. He conferred with President Auriol, Prime

---

[94]Samuel McCrea Cavert, interview, 37.

[95]Quoted in Roscoe Drummond and Gaston Coblentz, *Duel at the Brink: John Foster Dulles's Command of American Power* (Garden City: Doubleday and Company, 1960) 15.

[96]Ibid.

Minister Schuman, and leading political figures like Leon Blum, on the "left," and General de Gaulle, on the "right."

Dulles was quite disturbed by the "desperate situation in Paris." Because of Communist activity, industry was at a standstill. Electrical power and running water were both shut down. Rail transportation was disrupted. From Paris, Dulles contacted his brother Allen to get word to Vandenberg describing the critical conditions. He told him that the European Recovery Act, at that time in the Senate, "must be passed."[97]

Communist-organized political strikes in France and Italy in the fall of 1947 and the winter of 1948, combined with the dismal results of the Foreign Ministers' Council of 1947, caused Dulles to push harder for the European Recovery Act—which he referred to as generating "a rebirth to moral greatness"[98]—and propose other "preventive" measures to forestall the advance of Communism. He argued that "pacific resistance, i.e. economic resistance" must be used to demonstrate that the "methods of physical destruction . . . which are being used by the Soviet Communist Party in France and elsewhere will fail."[99]

Beginning in London, due to Soviet efforts to "sabotage French recovery,"[100] Dulles began to urge that the three Western zones in Germany be economically unified without the Russian zone.[101] Concerning this point, the Western powers were in agreement. On 2 June, a series of "London Recommendations" were issued that called for an international authority to control the Ruhr, closer economic cooperation (including currency reform) in the three Western zones, preparatory work to be done on a constitution that would establish a new and independent West Germany, and a full West German role in the European Recovery Plan. These proposals constituted a "package of nightmares"[102] for the Soviets. Yet, for Dulles, they were all in line with his concept of "passive resistance."

---

[97]JFD, *War or Peace*, 106; see also JFD, "The Republican Outlook," 5-6.

[98]JFD, "Draft," 1, 11 March 1948, DP, Box 37.

[99]JFD to A. J. Muste, 19 January 1948, DP, Box 36.

[100]JFD, "Not War, Not Peace," 1.

[101]JFD, "The Republican Outlook," 6.

[102]Pruessen, *The Road to Power*, 374.

Throughout the winter and spring of 1948, tension increased at a rapid pace between the super powers. Dulles described the situation as one of "not war, not peace."[103] In February the Russians seized Czechoslovakia. In March the West European countries signed the Brussels defense pact. The Soviets responded a few days later by walking out of the Allied Control Council in Berlin and blocking all military traffic headed for Berlin. With the June announcement of the London Recommendations, the Soviets applied a full and total blockade of Berlin. Economic integration of the three Western zones of Germany had spurred the Soviets to action.

On 19 July, Secretary Marshall asked Dulles to meet with him for a conference concerning the Berlin crisis. Others in attendance that day included Charles Bohlen, George Kennan, and Dean Rusk. Since the Moscow note concerning Berlin called the obstructive measures "temporary," Dulles recommended that the U.S. take steps that would make it easy for the Soviets to back down without sacrificing a serious loss of prestige. He advocated toughness without forcing the Soviet leadership to use military power against the United States in order to save face. He felt such a move might lead to general war. Berlin was not, in his opinion, worth that. He urged that the issue be turned over to the General Assembly in an effort to use world opinion to force a solution.[104]

The Berlin crisis illustrates well the efforts of both Dewey and Dulles not to rock the boat in foreign affairs during the 1948 presidential election. As Robert Divine found in his study of that election, foreign affairs was a nonissue.[105] Dulles's commitment to a bipartisan foreign policy had increased as the differences between the Soviet Union and the United States became more apparent. His recognition that bipartisanship—since it "cuts across our basic constitutional and traditional views"—should be "used only sparingly and where the needs and perils are so great that exceptional measures are demanded," demonstrates that he viewed the postwar problem with the Soviet Union as a great enough "peril" to avoid

---

[103]JFD, "Not War, Not Peace."

[104]For more complete information concerning Dulles's role here, see Pruessen, *The Road to Power,* 374-84.

[105]Robert A. Divine, *Foreign Policy and U.S. Presidential Elections, 1940-1948* (New York: New Viewpoints, 1974) 269; see also Pruessen, *The Road to Power,* 366-74.

rocking the foreign-affairs boat during the 1948 election.[106] "In today's world," he exclaimed, "an America divided is an America imperiled."[107]

Bipartisanship in foreign affairs enabled the American leadership to move from the negotiating position of Yalta to the military preparedness represented by NATO in four short years. NATO represented the crown jewel in the American program that Dulles termed "preventive." For Dulles, the first hint of development toward an Atlantic Pact came in April of 1948. He was on spring vacation at Duck Island when he received a call to attend a meeting on 27 April at Blair House. Others present at the meeting were Secretary Marshall, Under Secretary Lovett, and Senator Vandenberg.

Dulles at first was somewhat hesitant to endorse wholeheartedly the idea of a regional security arrangement to include the United States. In his memorandum recording the meeting, Dulles said, "Any permanent arrangement might seem to guarantee the status quo and make it less likely, rather than more likely, that the Western European democracies would unite to create greater strength themselves."[108] The greater portion of his hesitancy was due to his fear that an Atlantic Pact would provide a divided Europe with the machinery enabling it to remain divided. Dulles had always preferred that Europe federate on the pattern of the United States. Yet Dulles also expressed concern that using Article 51 "to create new groupings for purposes of expediency, . . . might result in frustrating the United Nations."[109]

Whatever reservations he once felt about this issue were quickly overcome. As he phrased it in the spring of 1949, the "Soviet use of the veto power has so far made it impracticable to develop for everybody, the security system that the Charter contemplated."[110] Thus he had de-

---

[106]JFD, *War or Peace*, 122.

[107]JFD, "How Can We Have Peace?" 3, 25 September 1946, DP, Box 28; see also JFD, "Evolution or Revolution," 6 and 9, 12 February 1949, DP, Box 43.

[108]"Memorandum," 2, 27 April 1948, DP, Box 37.

[109]Ibid.

[110]Text of "The United States and Collective Security," an NBC broadcast including interviews with Dr. Philip Jessup, Ambassador at Large, Dean Rusk, Assistant Secretary of State for Political Affairs, and JFD, Representative to 3rd Session of the United Nations, 6, 20 March 1949, DP, Box 43.

cided that something was clearly needed. A speech delivered at the Paris House of the Carnegie Endowment for International Peace illustrates well the transition period. On the one hand, "It would not advance the purposes of the United Nations Charter if the Members organized themselves to solidify antagonisms to others." On the other hand, "If, however, regional and security groupings reflect a natural expanding of common concepts of national conduct, then they can greatly accelerate achievement of the goals of the United Nations."[111] Fortunately, as Dulles analyzed it, he determined that the Atlantic Pact fell into the latter category. So much so that when Mr. Richard Harkness, an NBC Washington correspondent asked him six months later if the Pact represented a "detour" around the United Nations, Dulles replied,

> My answer is a flat No! From a legal point of view, the pact is entirely within the Charter. It is firmly hitched to the Articles of the Charter . . . Article 51 recognizes the inherent right of self-defense, both individual and collective, in case of armed attack.[112]

Dulles's fervent support of NATO is found in nearly every address he delivered between the summer of 1948 and the treaty's final ratification in the Senate on 21 July 1949. Throughout these addresses, Dulles consistently cited Soviet actions since 1945 as the major reason NATO was necessary. In one address, under the heading "The Successes of Violence," he outlined the advance of Communism during this period.

> By coercion and terrorism in Russia, Eastern Europe and Northwest Asia, it has brought some 500,000,000 people of sixteen countries under its rule. Throughout China, Communist generals are extending their sway; in Greece, Communist guerillas are fighting and terrorizing, and in Korea Communist forces amputate the land and threaten civil war. In much of the world, men feel the hot breath of Communist terror; they fear for their wives and children and they toil wearily against economic sabotage.[113]

---

[111]JFD, "The Future of the United Nations," 6, 29 September 1948, DP, Box 39.

[112]"The United States and Collective Security," 4; see also JFD, *War or Peace,* 88-93; and JFD, "The Atlantic Pact," 11, 12 July 1949, DP, Box 43.

[113]JFD, "Evolution or Revolution," 8; see also JFD, "Europe and the Atlantic Pact," 1, 23 March 1949, DP, Box 43.

Since the London Foreign Ministers' Council, Dulles had also come to fear what a totally unified Germany might mean to Western Europe. It was obvious that the Soviets favored such a program in order to gain control of Germany's future. A unified Germany, Dulles was certain, would mean a Communist Germany. However, the Atlantic Pact would enable the three Western sections of Germany to unite and participate fully in Western Europe "without dominating it."[114] Without the guaranteed protection pledged by the United States, France and Italy would never be convinced of the wisdom of allowing a unified West Germany to become a meaningful addition to the European community. As Dulles told the Senate Foreign Relations Committee when he testified on behalf of the Pact, "Germans can be brought into the West *if* that West includes the United States—They cannot safely be brought into the West if the West does *not* include the United States."[115] Dulles believed, therefore, that resistance toward the Soviet Union "cannot be organized except around the United States." Peace was impossible without total American involvement.

Upon returning from the Paris meeting of the General Assembly in the fall of 1948, Dulles, as interim head of the American delegation, reported: "It was clear that every country outside the Soviet bloc feared Soviet power and took comfort in American power."[116] Dulles believed that such foreign reliance upon America brought with it "responsibilities that are immence."

> Of course, we cannot bolster everything, everywhere, that Communism seeks to overthrow. If we attempted that, we would become over-extended materially and discredited morally. We have to be selective. But also we should not be so selective that we ignore the global nature of the struggle and allow Soviet Communism to win great victories by default.[117]

----

[114]JFD, "Memo on the North Atlantic Pact," 3, 11 February 1949, DP, Box 43.

[115]JFD, "The North Atlantic Pact: Statement before the Foreign Relations Committee of the United States Senate," 4 May 1949, DP, Box 43. For further evidence of Dulles's beliefs concerning this issue, see JFD, "Memo on the North Atlantic Pact," 1-4.

[116]"The United States and Collective Security," 2; see also JFD, "The North Atlantic Pact," 3-4.

[117]JFD, "Europe and the Atlantic Pact," 1.

Again, Dulles's words belie his contention that America was involved in a global conflict of good against evil. The immense responsibility that naturally accompanies a war of this magnitude could not be ignored.

> A United States which could be an inactive spectator while the barbarians overran and desecrated the cradle of our Christian civilization would not be the kind of United States which could defend itself.[118]

Further, Dulles wrote, such neglect "would at once be the signal for a revival of the Communist offensive against Western Europe" and "make it utterly impossible to go on from here, as I hope we shall, to develop a program to save Asia from being overrun by Soviet Communism."[119] In Dulles's view, the Atlantic Pact represented a willingness on the part of all involved to move beyond "words of unity" to "deeds of unity."[120]

In early July of 1949, New York's Senator Robert Wagner announced his retirement because of health problems. Governor Dewey turned to Dulles to fill the vacancy. On 8 July, Dulles became a United States senator for the remaining four months of Wagner's term.[121] Four days later, breaking a hallowed Senate tradition regarding the meekness of rookie senators, Dulles delivered an impassioned defense of NATO.[122] In this context, Dulles listed the many programs engendered by the bipartisan approach to foreign affairs:

> There came in quick succession, the European Recovery Plan, the Brussels Pact, the uniting of the British and United States zones of Germany, and, shortly, adding to them the French zone, making possible the creation of the Bonn government of Western Germany, the internationalization of the Ruhr, the joint United States–British airlift, which held Berlin

---

[118]JFD, "Where Are We?" 6, 29 December 1950, DP, Box 50.

[119]JFD, "The Atlantic Pact," 2.

[120]Quoted in Pruessen, *The Road to Power,* 397.

[121]Dulles ran for the Senate seat in November but lost to Herbert Lehman by 196,000 votes in a highly charged political battle. Dulles relentlessly attacked Lehman for alleged Communist support of his candidacy. For a more complete account of this campaign, see Pruessen, *The Road to Power,* 398-403.

[122]JFD, "The North Atlantic Pact."

against the Soviet blockade, the Council of Europe, and now the North Atlantic Treaty.[123]

In Dulles's opinion, this list of accomplishments represented a fairly complete enunciation of the "prevention" mind-set of American foreign policy during these years.

The Senate hardly needed Dulles's defense of NATO to encourage its acceptance of it. Nor was Dulles's help really essential in gaining approval for the Mutual Defense Assistance Act. The Soviets provided more than enough incentive when, five days before the Senate voted on the act, they exploded their first atomic bomb.

For Dulles, NATO tangibly and practically expressed his recent emphasis on the interdependence among peoples of the West. After 1946 Dulles no longer talked about the interdependence of the world as a whole. Rather, as he came to see it, the world was now divided into two irreconcilable faiths. NATO represented the moral law in the conflict. Those nations that opposed NATO, by obvious inference, also opposed the moral law. NATO helped to make the dimensions of the cosmic battlefield more clearly visible. Soon the two sides of the conflict would be locked in physical combat at the 38th Parallel and the preventive phase in American foreign policy would give way to the phase of physical opposition.

---

[123]Ibid., 2.

10

From Prevention
to Opposition,
1949-1952

The philosophy that lay beneath Dulles's "preventive" approach to the Soviet Union has within it the seeds of his later "brinkmanship" trademark.[1] His familiarity with Stalin's works taught him that the Soviets would not retreat unless the situation demanded it. "Most Communists are fanatics," he generalized, who continue an offensive until they meet an effective counterforce.[2] In early 1949 Dulles discussed why he believed that

---

[1]This word was coined by the press and used to describe Dulles's policies after Dulles, in answer to a reporter's question, emphasized that we must have the willingness to go to the "brink of war" with nations holding viewpoints contrary to those of the United States on important issues. Such a willingness, Dulles asserted, would show those with whom we differed that the United States was serious about these issues and would bring about the desired results before such a war could occur.

[2]JFD, "Evolution or Revolution," 10, 12 February 1949, DP, Box 43.

preventive action should be the primary principle behind American foreign policy.

> Stalin emphasizes the importance of "tempo." There is a time to attack and a time to retreat. It is to them all a matter of expediency and to me the important and vital thing is to create conditions such that the continuing use of these methods will seem to Soviet leaders inexpedient and the coming years will seem to them to be good years for retreat.[3]

Dulles believed the United States must provide the counterforce to Soviet expansion. Other countries depended upon it. "That is our opportunity and it is our responsibility," he wrote, "may we not fail."[4] In order to convince the Soviets to retreat, Dulles felt that a willingness to go to the brink of war must be demonstrated.

Policies formulated over the previous year and a half—especially those that resulted from bipartisan cooperation—had, according to Dulles, performed quite admirably in the ongoing fight to curb Communist expansion in Western Europe. The Marshall Plan marked a significant commitment to European economic recovery. NATO, "a living instrument for righteousness and peace,"[5] provided the 1.4 billion dollar Military Assistance Program, which greatly buttressed European defenses. American resourcefulness during the Berlin crisis demonstrated to Europeans that America was willing to spend enormous energy to meet the needs of a beleaguered people.[6] Further, the integration of Western Germany into the general European economy was proceeding at a rapid pace. As a result of programs like these, Communist tactics were "becoming less potent." American reaction to those tactics caused them to become "better known, discovered, exposed, nullified."[7]

In the early to mid-1940s, Dulles made it clear that he viewed Soviet expansion from within the context of traditional Russian foreign policy and

---

[3]JFD to J. Salwyn Schapiro, 7 January 1949, DP, Box 46.

[4]JFD, "Evolution or Revolution," 11.

[5]JFD, "The North Atlantic Pact: Statement before the Foreign Relations Committee of the United States Senate," 1, 4 May 1949, DP, Box 43.

[6]JFD, *War or Peace* (New York: The Macmillan Company, 1950) 31.

[7]JFD, "The United States and Russia," *New York Herald Tribune,* 18 January 1949, DP, Box 46.

the quest for an understandable national security. However, by the late 1940s, he had altered his view considerably. "By now," he wrote, "most of Russia's historic goals have been achieved. The great goals which remain are those of the Soviet Communist Party."[8]

By defining the problem in this way, Dulles was able to maintain a consistency with his earlier statements regarding Soviet expansionism. Unquestioned control of policymaking now rested securely in Communist party hands. Party goals, fundamentally antireligious in nature, exceeded traditional national-interest considerations.[9] The fact that the Communist party was separate from the Russian government did not escape Dulles; yet he viewed the Russian government as "a tool of the Communist Party." Had not Stalin written in the Soviet "Bible" that "not a single important political or organizational question is decided by our Soviet . . . without guiding directions from the Party"?[10] Because of this relationship, "you can no more make a 'deal' with Communism to limit itself to certain areas than you can make a 'deal' with Christianity to limit itself to certain areas."[11]

Dulles's emphasis on the connection between the Russian government and the Communist party caused him to change his earlier belief that the threat posed by the Soviet Union was double-barreled in that they sought social revolution throughout the world as well as a traditional nationalistic expansion. Now the threat was a single one: the Soviets' desire "to take over the domination of the world."[12] "The question of questions," wrote Dulles, is "do the Soviet leaders plan to use their army for conquest?"[13] Dulles feared, at least as far as Europe was concerned, that the answer to that question was affirmative. NATO, in his mind, helped to counteract the possibility of it becoming a reality.

----

[8]JFD, "Not War, Not Peace," 5, 5 January 1948, DP, Box 36; see also JFD, "The United States and Russia."

[9]See JFD, *War or Peace*, 5 and 114.

[10]Quoted ibid., 11.

[11]JFD, "The United States and Russia."

[12]See especially JFD, "A Policy for Peace Insurance," *Department of State Bulletin* 22 (29 May 1950): 863 and 873.

[13]JFD, *War or Peace*, 110.

There is always a risk that the Russian government with its military establishment might be used as a tool to accomplish ends which go beyond
the actual historical ambitions of the Russian nation. . . . I believe that
we must try to conduct ourselves so as always to make that unlikely.[14]

Successes of a "Preventive" Mentality

From all indications, the attitude of tough prevention served the
United States well in Western Europe. Dulles viewed the resolution of
the Berlin crisis as an example of its success. In early May of 1949, the
crisis was peacefully settled when Moscow lifted the Berlin blockade. Two
weeks afterward, the Council of Foreign Ministers met in Paris. It was
the first meeting for this group since the ill-fated Moscow Conference
broke up in December of 1947. Once again, the State Department called
upon Dulles to serve as an adviser. The delegates to Paris did not really
accomplish much. The reunification of Germany served as the main topic
of discussion. Yet the division of the country into East and West had already progressed to the point of no return.

The only significant agreement reached at Paris was a Soviet promise not to reimpose the Berlin blockade. Dulles viewed Soviet willingness to concede this point as representative of "a very marked change
in Soviet policy which I think results from the very good policy we've been
carrying out ourselves over the last eighteen months." Further, he believed that this concession indicated that the Soviet Union had passed
"from the offensive to the defensive," which might mean "the end of the
cold war in Europe."[15] In another context, he expressed a similar assessment of the Paris meeting.

The difference in two years has been tremendous. There had been a very
great transformation. . . . I realize that many aggravations, many dangers surely remain, and that Soviet policy can be changed overnight; but

---

[14]JFD, "The United States and Russia"; see also JFD, "U.S. and Russia Could Agree
but for Communist Party's Crusade," *U.S. News and World Report* 26 (21 January 1949):
32-36.

[15]JFD, Script from CBS "Capital Cloakroom," with Griffin Bancroft, Eric Sevareid,
and Edward Murrow, 1, 29 June 1949, DP, Box 46.

> I say that the program along which we have been moving has begun to show tentative results. [16]

Thus Dulles's feeling concerning the international situation was generally optimistic in mid-1949.

Dulles reminded his hearers that success in policy did not translate into relaxed efforts. Just because "the free world ha[d] gained a certain immunity to the Communist Party poison,"[17] the battle was not yet over. Dulles refused to believe "for a minute that Soviet Communism . . . renounced its objectives for good." As he interpreted Soviet strategy, the Soviets were merely shifting their attention from Western Europe, where they had encountered persistent opposition, to East Asia where conditions conducive to Communist infiltration were much more prevalent.

Spewing Out the Lukewarm Nations

In the late fall-early winter of 1949-1950, Dulles dedicated himself to the task of writing in order to make clear his concern over the shift in Soviet strategy from Europe to Asia. He felt that the Truman administration was dangerously lulled to sleep by the Soviet concessions in Europe. No one on the inside was listening to his warnings concerning the development of an "Asia first" strategy in the Kremlin, so Dulles decided to force the issue by taking it to the public. These efforts culminated in the publication of his second book. [18]

Dulles's transformation from prophet of realism to priest of nationalism is graphically illustrated by comparing this later book, *War or Peace,* to his earlier book, *War, Peace and Change.* The former work is an unemotional examination of the causes of war. Through it Dulles hoped to

---

[16]JFD, "The North Atlantic Pact," 2.

[17]JFD, "Where Are We?" 1, 29 December 1950, DP, Box 50.

[18]When the president of Macmillan Co., George Brett, first saw the outline of the book, he wrote Dulles that "more or less directly or certainly by implication one will get the idea from reading the book that the present administration has been derelict in its duties to the people in that it has not built up the gigantic and all powerful psychological warfare program which I am sure you and I believe is the only chance we have of avoiding a third world war" (George Brett to JFD, 18 January 1950, DP, Box 47).

point humankind toward universal rather than national values.[19] In order to concretize his concern for world peace, he suggested a prophetic program containing both ethical and political solutions.[20] The program he suggested naturally arose out of the realistic observations he made concerning the behavior of nations in international politics. In this latter work, the earlier detached philosophical analysis was replaced by a journalistic style; moreover, thematically, the book treated American values as an ultimate concern.

In *War or Peace,* Dulles acted as if America had arrived at the destination set forth in *War, Peace and Change.* Americans are considered representative of the universal values defined as "good." The task that faced American leadership was whether it could "contribute decisively to the peaceful frustration of the evil methods and designs of Soviet Communism."[21] Salvation for the " 'civilized' part of mankind" depended upon the success of this endeavor.[22] The obvious implication was that wherever Communism was in control, people were uncivilized. More directly, the Communists were "under the control of a despotic group fanatical in their acceptance of a creed that teaches world domination."[23] "Soviet Communism starts with an atheistic, Godless premise," asserted Dulles. "Everything else flows from that premise." In short, the Soviet government represented, so far as Dulles was concerned, the universal value defined as "evil."

Differences between the two Dulles books, particularly in the areas of style, emotion, and methodology, are great enough to cause one to wonder whether they could possibly be written by the same author. On closer examination, however, the thread of continuity becomes clear. Both books emphasize the existence of a moral law. Yet, in the interim between publication dates, Dulles's definition of it had drastically

---

[19]JFD, *War, Peace and Change* (New York: Harper and Brothers, 1939) 134-35.

[20]See ch. 6.

[21]JFD, *War or Peace,* 261; see also 140.

[22]Ibid., 186.

[23]Ibid., 2.

changed.[24] Historical contingencies moved Dulles to reduce the judg-
mental and transcendent moral law to an agreeable shadow of its former
self. The altered moral law served as divine sanction for American aims
and purposes in the international arena.

War or Peace represents a snapshot of Dulles's prevention-oriented
mind-set. In the first four chapters he explained the dire danger that faced
the world. As titles like "Know Your Enemy" and "No Appeasement"
imply, Dulles stressed the importance of understanding the limitless ambition and ruthlessness of the Soviet Union, along with the importance of
resolution in meeting the Soviet threat. The book began with the words:
"War is probable—unless by positive and well directed efforts we fend it
off."[25]

In succeeding chapters, Dulles reviewed the course of international
affairs and American foreign policy since 1945. He attempted to determine the gains and losses for both sides in the Cold War and ultimately
to explain "Why Soviet Communism Wins." In the final section of the
book, Dulles returned to a detailed analysis of "what needs to be done"
in order to stop the Soviet winning streak. At this point, he related his
concern for bipartisanship, collective security organizations, adequate
Asian policies, and especially, America's "spiritual need."

Because he universalized the conflict between the Soviet Union and
the United States, Dulles logically had to take the next step toward, as
he phrased it, "ending neutrality." The Cold War did not involve a "typical 'great power' struggle" between two nations intent on dominating the
world. Neutrality would be the proper response to such a conflict. In the
case of this particular struggle, the issue was primarily moral. The United
Nations had proved that. Through the work of that international agency,
"Soviet propaganda" was "uncovered and the nature and magnitude of
the danger" was "revealed." The processes of the United Nations had,
according to Dulles, also made it "clear that the United States had no lust
for more power, but only a desire to safeguard institutions that re-

---

[24]As Townsend Hoopes has observed, even comparisons between *War or Peace* and
the 1946 *Life* articles reveal "that four years had measurably toughened his anti-Communism, deepened his pessimism, and enlarged his self righteousness" (Townsend
Hoopes, *The Devil and John Foster Dulles* [Boston: Little, Brown and Company, 1973]
83).

[25]JFD, *War or Peace*, 2.

spected human liberty."[26] Clearly, the nations of the world must "reject neutrality and prefer to stand together against aggression, direct or indirect."[27] Individual populations must "be active participants" in the struggle. "They must realize that 'they' are in this struggle, it is their values that are at stake."[28]

Early in his term as secretary of state, Dulles betrayed a lack of enthusiasm for providing foreign aid to nations that refused to choose sides in the Cold War. This serves as a good example of the way in which Dulles secularized the biblical injunction, "Because you are lukewarm, and neither cold nor hot, I will spew you out of my mouth" (Revelation 3:16). Dulles seemed to ignore the possibility that world peace might be better served if nations, rather than committing themselves to either side in the Cold War, concentrated on acting against aggression wherever it arose. As Pietro Quaroni, the former Italian ambassador to Paris, remembered Dulles, "He believed in the ideals of the West with the same intensity as Khrushchev believed in Communism."[29] Such intensity did not allow him to consider the "lukewarm" stance an appropriate one.

Dulles's desire to "end neutrality" left him willing to use the United Nations as a tool of the West. In the spring of 1950, for example, he stated that the "United Nations Meetings give the representatives of free peoples a chance to strip Communist propaganda of the veneer that makes it dangerous."[30] Such a suggestion obviously contradicted his earlier commitment to the United Nations as a truly universal community that transcended national purposes. Circumstances, however, had changed and so had Dulles's perception of the United Nations' function. Ronald Pruessen's insight into the character of this change is worth quoting.

If he [Dulles] had once pictured U.N. members as rival tribal chieftains

---

[26]JFD, "The North Atlantic Pact," 2; see also JFD, "The North Atlantic Treaty and the United Nations," 9, 29 April 1949, DP, Box 43.

[27]JFD, *War or Peace,* 71-73; see also JFD, "State Control versus Self Control," 11, 19 June 1946, DP, Box 30.

[28]JFD, "Capital Cloakroom," 5.

[29]Roscoe Drummond and Gaston Coblentz, *Duel at the Brink: John Foster Dulles's Command of American Power* (Garden City NJ: Doubleday, 1960) 14.

[30]Quoted in Ronald W. Pruessen, *John Foster Dulles: The Road to Power* (New York: The Free Press, 1982) 427.

gathered round a campfire to talk hesitantly about the possibility of future harmony, he came to see one of those chieftains as bent on destroying all the others.[31]

As Pruessen's assessment indicates, Dulles's early realism concerning the behavior of nations, and the consequent effect such behavior would have on the United Nations, had dissipated. He lost sight of the fact that the United Nations would necessarily be elemental in the beginning. The part of his philosophy that had given him his prophetic vision, namely his formulation of a transcendent moral law, was now acting as a blinder that inhibited him from seeing events realistically. When his former colleagues in the churches condemned America's use of the United Nations for its own purposes, Dulles admonished them, stating "I think it is important that a church gathering should think about Christian responsibility, and not concentrate upon criticism of others."[32] Such a remark must have seemed strange to those who had worked so closely with a different Dulles a decade earlier.

For Dulles, by 1949, the free nations had come to embody the very essence of the moral law. "The only tie which dependably unites free peoples is awareness of common dedication to moral principles." No longer was there "any conflict between the national interest of any free state and the welfare of all mankind."[33] As Dulles expressed it in *War or Peace,*

Experience in the United Nations shows that there is considerable agreement about what is right. That is particularly true between those who are influenced by one or another of the great religions. All the great religions reflect to some degree the moral or natural law, and that makes it possible to find some common denominators of right and wrong.[34]

---

[31]Ibid., 411.

[32]JFD to Walter W. Van Kirk, 16 February 1949, DP, Box 41.

[33]E. Raymond Platig, "John Foster Dulles: A Study of His Political and Moral Thought Prior to 1953 with Special Emphasis on International Relations" (dissertation, The University of Chicago, 1957) 308.

[34]JFD, *War or Peace,* 87; see also JFD, "The Christian Citizen in a Changing World," in *Man's Disorder and God's Design,* vol. 4, with an intro. by Kenneth Grubb: *The Church and the International Disorder* (New York: Harper and Brothers, 1948) 104; and JFD to Right Reverend Edwind Berggrav, bishop of Norway, 9 May 1949, DP, Box 46.

In the fall of 1951, Dulles made an even clearer identification between the West and the moral law when he proclaimed that "truth and righteousness" were qualities that are "the peculiar possession of minds and spirits that are free."[35] This expression obviously indicates a turning away from his thought in the early 1940s when he consistently reiterated that no "adequate and world-accepted definitions of right and wrong conduct" were to be found.[36] "There are always lacking," he had said, "any such common mores throughout the world as are the necessary condition to common rules being understood and deemed reasonable."[37] Further, he had consistently warned Americans of the dangers of being "dogmatic." "Our particular ideals and sense of vital interest are not the only ones in the world."[38] In short, his earlier belief had emphasized that no single nation or group of nations embodied the moral law. After 1949 such an assertion was, in his mind, no longer applicable.

Accompanying this jingoism was his equally fervent belief that the resolution of international conflict largely depended on humankind adopting the values of the West. Wherever the "simple and elementary religious beliefs" of the West "are widely rejected," he reasoned, "there is both spiritual and social disorder."

> That fact is illustrated by fascism and communism. These are, in the main, atheistic and antireligious creeds. Orthodox communists believe that there is neither God nor moral law, that there is no such thing as universal and equal justice, and that human beings are without soul or sacred personality. They are free of the moral restraints and compulsions which prevail in a religious society, and they think it quite right to use force and violence to make their way prevail.[39]

---

[35]JFD, "Can We Stop Russian Imperialism?" 6, 27 November 1951, DP, Box 55.

[36]JFD, "The Churches and a Just and Durable Peace," *The Biennial Report of the Federal Council of Churches of Christ in America* (1944) 28.

[37]JFD, "Toward World Order," in *A Basis for the Peace to Come,* ed. Francis· J. McConnell, et al., Merrick-McDowell Lecture Series (New York: Abingdon-Cokesbury Press, 1942) 46.

[38]JFD, "America's Role in the Peace," *Christianity and Crisis* 4 (22 January 1945): 5.

[39]JFD, "Faith of Our Fathers," in *The Spiritual Legacy of John Foster Dulles,* ed. Henry P. Van Dusen (Philadelphia: The Westminster Press, 1960) 7; see also JFD, "The North Atlantic Treaty and the United Nations," 2; JFD, "The Importance of Spiritual Resources," 19, 27 January 1950, DP, Box 48; JFD, *War or Peace,* 187; JFD to Walter W. Van Kirk, 20 October 1950, DP, Box 48.

People in the West "have such high moral standards that they voluntarily refrain from using bad methods to get what they want." However, "atheists can hardly be expected to conform to an ideal so high."[40]

Of utmost significance to Dulles was his belief that those who ignore the moral law must pay the consequences of their actions. Can "Russian imperialism" be stopped? "Yes," Dulles replied, "evil is never irresistible." Since the moral law "has been trampled by the Soviet leaders, . . . they can and should be made to pay."[41] As I have demonstrated, so far as Dulles was concerned, the United Nations should act as the collection agency. "We must see the United Nations as a place where the moral conscience of the world can drive the nations into following policies of justice, righteousness and concord."[42] The General Assembly, therefore, should be used to "expose the facts and by so doing . . . build up a moral judgment so strong that no nation will ignore it."[43] The moral law does not "of itself bring order and well being into human affairs." It does not automatically produce "moral force" just as "waterfalls do not of themselves produce electrical power." The moral law needs help. The United States, through the United Nations, would supply that help by using "ideas as weapons."[44]

> No political or social system should prevail unless it is the means whereby men are consciously trying to bring human conduct into accord with moral law and to enlarge the opportunity of men to exercise their human rights and fundamental freedoms.[45]

In short, Communism deserved nothing less than extinction.

---

[40]JFD, *War or Peace*, 19.

[41]JFD, "Can We Stop Russian Imperialism?" 6, 27 November 1951, DP, Box 55; see also JFD, "A New Foreign Policy," *Life* 32 (19 May 1952): 11.

[42]JFD, "The Churches' Opportunities in World Affairs," 10, 6 August 1947, DP, Box 31.

[43]Quoted in Pruessen, *The Road to Power*, 423; see also JFD, "The Churches' Opportunities in World Affairs," 8.

[44]JFD, "A New Foreign Policy," 12.

[45]JFD, "Moral Leadership," *Vital Speeches of the Day* 14 (15 September 1945): 706.

The Communist Plot in East Asia

Phase One: Turning China "Red." Two events in the Far East caused
Dulles to press even harder for the United Nations to more actively fight
against Communism. The first of these events involved the so-called
"loss" of China, which occurred in the fall of 1949; the second, of course,
was the Korean War, which began in June of 1950.

Throughout *War or Peace,* Dulles emphasized Stalin's interest in the
Far East. Quoting once again from the Soviet Bible, Dulles warned of
Stalin's belief that the "road to victory over the West" ran through China.[46]
The Soviets ultimately desired encirclement of the West. "In this phase
of encirclement," Dulles reminded his countrymen, "Asia has a priority
claim on Soviet intention."

> The people of Asia, it is thought, can most easily be "amalgamated" into
> the Soviet orbit because they have had no great experience in political
> and civic freedom, their economic standards are often lower even than
> those of Russia, and the Asians fear the West because of its colonial rec-
> ord.[47]

Indicting administration policy concerning Asia became one of Dulles's
favorite pastimes after the 1948 presidential election. His criticisms occupied particularly safe political ground since no bipartisanship had yet
developed regarding Asian policy.[48] During the summer of 1949, while
admitting that the Chinese were largely responsible for problems in Asia
at that time, Dulles charged that "with resourcefulness we could have
found policies that would have improved conditions considerably."[49] As
the 1952 election neared, his criticism naturally increased. "Since Germany surrendered in 1945," Dulles observed, "our Secretaries of State
have taken 17 trips to Europe, involving 457 days of time." During the

---

[46]JFD, *War or Peace,* 232; see particularly 224-32.

[47]JFD, "A Positive Foreign Policy," 4-5, 15 May 1952, DP, Box 62.

[48]See JFD, "The Balance of Power," 10 March 1950, DP, Box 50.

[49]JFD, "Capital Cloakroom," 7.

same period, he continued, "no Secretary of State has even visited a Pacific or Asian nation."[50]

Mao's success in China provided Dulles with new ammunition as well as a seriously intensified concern. Events in China in 1949 confirmed Dulles's belief that Communism was a monolithic threat centered in Moscow. The Soviet Union, he contended, had installed "Mao-tse-Tung as the Kremlin's first 'president' of China."[51] As he put it in his first Senate speech, "The Soviet Communists' purpose . . . was no less than world domination to be achieved by gaining political power successively in each of the many areas that had been afflicted by war so that in the end the United States . . . would be isolated and closely encircled."[52]

> Thus the 450,000,000 people in China have fallen under leadership that is violently anti-American, and that takes its inspiration and guidance from Moscow. . . . Soviet Communist leadership has won a victory in China which surpassed what Japan was seeking and we risked war to avert.[53]

In another context, Dulles explained the causes for his "reservations as to the genuine Chinese character" of the new regime. First of all, Mao obviously won his power "with Russian aid." Second, his regime does "violence to every Chinese instinct" as it "embraces the traditional enemy of China and insults and attacks those who have been the traditional friends of China."[54]

The position represented in these statements differed considerably from that of the pre-1946 Dulles. As Pruessen recognized, "In 1938 he [Dulles] had called Mao-tse-Tung an 'agrarian reformer,' and during World War II had dubbed Mao's followers 'the so-called Red Army faction,' both terms implying some appreciation for the indigenous roots of the Chinese Communist Party."[55] In February of 1945, Dulles had emphasized that

---

[50]JFD, "A Positive Foreign Policy," 7; see also JFD, "Foreign Policy Needs," 9, 12 May 1952, DP, Box 307.

[51]JFD, "The Free East and the Free West," 29 November 1951, DP, Box 55.

[52]Quoted in Pruessen, *The Road to Power*, 439.

[53]JFD, *War or Peace*, 147.

[54]JFD, "Mr. Chairman," 19, 3 December 1950, DP, Box 51.

[55]Pruessen, *The Road to Power*, 441.

"the net result of the last eight years has been to cause the Chinese people to doubt the value of foreign friendships. There is danger that postwar China will be anti-foreign."[56] This statement also indicates an awareness of environmental factors as most important in China's turn toward governmental structures of its own making.

Dulles's former associates in the Federal Council were not satisfied with Dulles's later assessment of the situation. "We find it difficult," wrote Sir Kenneth Grubb, the chairman of the Commission of the Churches on International Affairs (a commission Dulles had a hand in forming), "to see that the single assumption that Communism has been imposed on China by force is adequate as a basis for policy." Many of the churchmen, Grubb continued, "are inclined to think Communism was inevitable, and, indeed, welcome to many Chinese."[57]

For Dulles, however, there was never any question, especially after Mao's Moscow visit in February of 1950 resulted in the thirty-year treaty of friendship, that Mao operated simply "as a puppet of Moscow."[58] Therefore, for the last nine years of his life, Dulles supported Nationalist China's claim to be representative of the true desires of the Chinese people. "The liberation of China," he wrote in 1951, "must remain one of the . . . major United States policies."[59] Obviously, his 1943 statement that "China . . . must work out her own salvation" was no longer applicable in a world threatened by monolithic Communism.[60]

Phase Two: Turning Korea "Red With Blood." After the Soviet explosion of the atomic bomb in 1949, the Alger Hiss perjury conviction regarding Communist ties in early 1950, and the arrest of Klaus Fuchs as a traitor in London, the more conservative elements of the Republican party, led most notably by Senator Joseph McCarthy, began to make vicious attacks on the Democrats. Dean Acheson and his State Department became one of the favorite targets. Pruessen writes that Dulles, "in this kind of environment[,] . . . may have thought he had much to offer

---

[56]JFD, "Appraisal of United States Foreign Policy," 8, 5 February 1945, DP, Box 27.

[57]From Sir Kenneth Grubb to Frederick Nolde, 23 April 1952, DP, Box 62.

[58]JFD, "Draft," 1 May 1951, DP, Box 304.

[59]Ibid.

[60]JFD, "Statement of Foreign Policy," *Confidential,* 1943, DP, Box 22.

the Democrats."[61] More fervently than ever, Dulles believed in the importance of bipartisanship. Though in many ways Dulles was as dedicatedly anti-Communist as McCarthy, he was more concerned with developments in the Far East than he was with the slight evidence indicating Communist infiltration in American government. Dulles possessed more political sophistication than did McCarthy. The developing Communist threat in Asia lay behind Dulles's continued advocacy of bipartisanship throughout the McCarthy period. "Solid unity in the nation," rather than the "dissemination of rumors and suspicions," promised the only hope of producing "foreign policies adequate to meet the grave peril we face."[62]

Truman's Democratic administration did not overlook Dulles's commitment to bipartisanship. During a time when Republican barbs were particularly relentless, Dulles's presence in the State Department could prove a definite asset. On 6 April 1950, following a letter from an ailing Senator Vandenberg encouraging such a move, Secretary Acheson appointed Dulles an adviser to the State Department. Shortly after Dulles arrived there, Walter Butterworth, who since March had been working on the Japanese Peace Treaty with Acheson, left for a new post as ambassador to Sweden. As soon as the administration decided on this transfer of duties for Butterworth, Acheson, Butterworth, and Dean Rusk met to discuss who should be given the duties involved in the preparation and negotiation of the peace treaty. They "all agreed that John Foster Dulles was the man."[63] According to Acheson, "he was competent, ambitious . . . close to Vandenberg, and in good standing with both the Dewey and Taft wings of the Republican Party. These qualities would lead him to do a good job and to get the treaty through the Senate."[64] Dulles took over the work on 18 May.

Secretary of Defense Louis Johnson announced in May that he and General Bradley were embarking on a thirteen-day inspection of Amer-

---

[61]Pruessen, *The Road to Power,* 435.

[62]JFD to Secretary Acheson, 29 March 1950; quoted in Pruessen, *The Road to Power,* 435.

[63]Dean Acheson, *Present at the Creation* (New York: W. W. Norton and Company, Inc., 1969) 432.

[64]Ibid.

ican bases in the Pacific. As Acheson tells it, Johnson hoped to influence General MacArthur, the Supreme Allied Commander in Tokyo, to side with the Defense Department against the State Department by urging a delay in negotiating a Japanese peace treaty. Defense wanted to retain an American presence in Japan, something that more than likely would be given up if a peace treaty were negotiated.[65] Acheson believed that Dulles and his assistant, John Allison, should make a similar trip of their own "to serve warning that discussion of a peace treaty was no longer premature."[66]

Before flying on to Tokyo, Dulles and Allison made a stop in South Korea. On the 18th of June, Dulles had his picture taken with South Korean officers at the 38th Parallel. One week later those officers were fighting for their lives as North Korea invaded South Korea. When the war started, "Dulles and his wife were sightseeing in Kyoto."[67] He returned immediately to Tokyo where he found a confident General Douglas MacArthur who was certain that the South Koreans could handle the attack by themselves. Dulles was not so sure.

Even though Dulles was well aware of North Korean troop movements while he was in South Korea, the attack took him by surprise. He did, however, take account of the imminent danger of invasion in his 19 June address to the South Korean parliament. He informed the people of South Korea that they were "today . . . in the front line of freedom, under conditions that are both dangerous and exciting." "Soviet Communism, . . . north of the 38th parallel," he continued, "seeks, by terrorism, fraudulent propaganda, infiltration, and incitement to civil unrest, to enfeeble and discredit your new Republic." Thus the Koreans were forced to participate in "the constant struggle between good and evil," which "has no limits in space or time." He assured them that they were "not alone" in this struggle. "You will never be alone, so long as you continue to play worthily your part in the great design of human freedom."[68]

---

[65]Ibid., 432-35.

[66]Ibid., 432.

[67]Hoopes, *The Devil,* 97.

[68]JFD, "The Korean Experiment in Representative Government," *Department of State Bulletin* 23 (3 July 1950): 12-13.

When North Korea launched the invasion six days later, Dulles and Allison urged strong action. They cabled the following message to Acheson:

> It is possible that South Korea may themselves [*sic*] contain and repulse attack and if so this is the best way. If, however, it appears they cannot do so then we believe that U.S. forces should be used even though this risks Russian counter moves. To sit by while Korea is overrun by unprovoked attack would start [a] disastrous chain of events leading most probably to world war.[69]

The use of large numbers of U.S. troops was not, however, particularly appealing to Dulles. When the idea first arose, he expressed reservations to Acheson.[70] In the first week of July, Truman sent troops into action and permitted American planes to attack North Korean targets. Dulles gave Walter Lippmann his initial reaction to those developments: "I had doubts as to the wisdom of engaging our land forces on the continent of Asia as against an enemy army that could be nourished from the vast reservoirs of the U.S.S.R."[71]

As Pruessen has recently indicated, Dulles's doubts "were not evidence of some basically temperate approach to the Korean conflict. They were part of a very specific tactical debate that never translated into disagreement about the overall direction and goals of U.S. policy."[72] Dulles viewed American response to the invasion as absolutely necessary; the only question was how the response should be carried out. "If the free peoples," he wrote for the *New York Times,* "act quickly, largely and unitedly to translate their freedom into strength of moral purpose and material might, they may yet save humanity from the deep abyss."[73]

The Security Council of the United Nations did, indeed, act quickly. Its swiftness of action was due primarily to the fact that the Soviet Union was boycotting the Security Council at the time. Soviet leaders were angry over the Security Council's refusal to replace the Nationalist Chinese

---

[69]JFD and Allison to Acheson and Rusk, 25 June 1950, DP, Box 49.

[70]See Pruessen, *The Road to Power,* 455.

[71]JFD to Walter Lippmann, 13 July 1950, DP, Box 48.

[72]Ibid., 456.

[73]JFD, "To Save Humanity from the Deep Abyss," 5, 30 July 1950, DP, Box 50.

representative on the council with one from "Red" China. This turn of events enabled the Security Council to act without any threat of veto.[74] On 7 July it passed a resolution authorizing a United Nations command in Korea under the leadership of the United States. General Douglas MacArthur was named as the United Nations commander.

Dulles described the valiant efforts of the United Nations forces in words reminiscent of the Christian crusades. "We have borne a Christian witness," he said in a radio address. "We need have no remorse. Also we need not despair. We have acted as God gave us to see the right."

> Any soldiers who fight in response to a United Nations appeal can be pretty sure that they are fighting for a just cause and that they are not sacrificing their lives merely to satisfy the ambitions of rulers who think it would be exciting to be a conquering hero. . . . It involves a big moral advance when we put armed force at the service of the United Nations Organizations so that the force will only be used for a cause which is determined by the United Nations itself to be a just and righteous cause.[75]

To impress upon his hearers the spiritual nature of the American call to duty in Korea, Dulles appealed to Scripture:

> For ourselves, let us heed the words of Paul: "Now no chastening for the present seemeth to be joyous, but grievous; nevertheless afterward it yieldeth the peaceable fruit unto them which are exercised thereby. Wherefore lift up the hands which hang down, and the feeble knees; and make straight paths for your feet."[76]

During the following months, Dulles exhorted Americans "not [to] be afraid to live sacrificially and even dangerously in a righteous cause."[77]

---

[74]JFD, "Korean Attack Opens New Chapter in History," *Department of State Bulletin* 23 (7 August 1950): 209.

[75]JFD, "Universal Bible Sunday Broadcast," 3-4, and 6, 20 November 1950, DP, Box 50.

[76]Ibid., 4. The quoted passage is from Hebrews 12:11-13, a passage that Dulles attributed to Paul. Of course, today Paul's authorship is discounted by most biblical scholars.

[77]JFD, "The Interdependence of Independence," *Department of State Bulletin* 23 (17 July 1950): 92.

For a man with Dulles's presuppositions, the origin of the Korean conflict was no mystery. From the time of the occupation of North Korea in 1945, the Russians "made it their first business to develop a trained, tough and well-equipped North Korean army."[78] Now that the Soviets had exhausted every avenue of indirect aggression, they decided to "explore the possibilities of direct aggression."[79] Korea was picked because it represented a country "that could be exploited without an open use of Soviet forces."[80] For Dulles, there was never any doubt that "the dangerous moment had to come."[81] In spite of the fact that the dangerous moment had arrived, Dulles was confident "that we shall find the ways to paralyze the slimy, octopus-like tentacles that reach out from Moscow to suck our life blood."[82] With such colorful language, Dulles's crusade approach made a strong impression upon his listeners.

Since MacArthur's forces were more and more successful in pushing the North Koreans back, Truman and his advisers, including Dulles, decided that the United Nations' forces ought to attempt a complete reunification of Korea that they could then place under United Nations' supervision. In a memorandum written for the State Department, Dulles argued that "the North Korean army should be destroyed . . . even if this requires pursuit. . . . There must be a penalty to such wrong doing unless we want to encourage its repetition."[83] Late in November, MacArthur pushed north to the banks of the Yalu River near the border of China's Manchuria. In response, on 26 November, thousands of Chinese troops pushed across the Yalu River to fight the surprised Americans. The Chinese forces successfully forged deep into South Korean territory before MacArthur was finally able to regroup his troops and force the Chinese back to the 38th Parallel.

---

[78]JFD, "America and the World," 6, 11 October 1952, DP, Box 63.

[79]JFD, "Korea," 1, 31 July 1950, DP, Box 50; see also JFD, "Korean Attack Opens New Chapter," 207.

[80]JFD, "Korea," 2.

[81]Ibid.; see also JFD, "U.S. Military Actions in Korea," *Department of State Bulletin* 23 (17 July 1950): 90.

[82]JFD, "The Challenge of Today," *Department of State Bulletin* 24 (11 June 1951): 936.

[83]Quoted in Pruessen, *The Road to Power,* 456.

The actions of the Communist Chinese reinforced Dulles's impression that Moscow controlled Mao. "What has happened shows that our policies have been sound in so far as they have recognized the impossibility of separating the Chinese and Soviet Communist."[84]

> These foreign policies of Mao-tse-Tung are utterly irreconcilable with the interests of the Chinese people. . . . No one in his senses could assert that it is in China's interest to shovel its youth and material resources into the fiery furnace of the Korean War to gain South Korea, an area which means little to China, but which, since the Czars has been coveted by Russia because of its strategic value against Japan.[85]

Dulles overlooked the obvious threat posed to Communist China by the loss of North Korea as a buffer zone if the United Nations' forces successfully had unified Korea under the supervision of the United Nations, an organization that refused membership to Communist China.

Communist China's invasion of North Korea caused Dulles to reassess his support for that nation's membership in the United Nations organization. In *War or Peace,* Dulles argued that "we ought to be willing that all nations should be members without attempting to appraise closely those which are 'good' and those which are 'bad.' " "Already," he wrote, "that distinction is obliterated by the present membership of the U.N."[86] After the Communist Chinese invasion of Korea, however, Dulles actively argued against granting United Nations membership to China.

Accompanying his hardened attitude concerning U.N. membership was an equally hardened stance toward the extension of diplomatic recognition to China. Again, he altered the opinion he had expressed in *War or Peace.* In that book, he had written that "as between nations, diplomatic recognition involves no element of moral approval."[87] After Korea,

---

[84]Memorandum, JFD to Acheson, "Secret: Estimate of the Situation," 1, 30 November 1950, DP, Box 47; see also JFD, "Draft," 1 May 1951, DP, Box 304.

[85]*Department of State Bulletin* 24 (28 May 1951): 844; see also JFD, "Mr. Chairman," 4-5.

[86]JFD, *War or Peace,* 190.

[87]JFD, *War or Peace,* 209. This position was consistent with that expressed years earlier with regard to Costa Rica (see JFD, "Political and Economic Conditions in Costa Rica," 9-10, 21 May 1917, DP, Box 1), the Soviet Union (see JFD to James G. McDonald, 15 November 1926, and JFD to Esther Everett Lape, 16 March 1933), and with regard to the definitions of recognition generally expressed in his earlier book, *War, Peace, and Change* (see particularly 88).

Dulles wrote that the policy of nonrecognition serves "our national interest, our friendship for China, and the historic dedication of our nation to the cause of human freedom."[88] Suddenly moral approval became all-important in determining whether diplomatic recognition should be extended toward Communist China. If the United States recognized "Red" China, it would be equivalent, in Dulles's view, to abandoning the moral dictates of the American heritage. In addition, recognition would "give moral support to a regime" that Dulles believed was "doomed to failure."[89]

Throughout his tenure as secretary of state, Dulles held to this non-recognition policy. One of the clearest examples of the breach that had developed between Dulles and his former colleagues in the churches resulted from Dulles's steadfastness on this particular issue. Dulles addressed the National Council of Churches at the 1958 Study Conference held in Cleveland. A few hours after the address, the group passed a resolution calling for American recognition of Communist China. As his sister, Eleanor Lansing Dulles, recalled it,

> It was to him a real and deeply felt hurt when the group . . . to whom he had talked, and with many of whom he had worked, voted to recommend the recognition of Communist China after his talk. . . . He left for his rest at Duck Island with a feeling of sadness that some of the churchmen had weakened in the face of pressures.[90]

It is not clear just what pressure the churchmen were facing that could have made them formulate a resolution on recognition. Something else is clear, however. Those churchmen, with whom Dulles had worked many years before, were no doubt equally saddened that their former friend and leader had himself "weakened in the face of pressure" and abandoned the prophetic posture so characteristic of his earlier years.

---

[88]*Department of State Bulletin* 24 (28 May 1951): 845.

[89]JFD, "Capital Cloakroom," 9. Compare this statement with his earlier statement that moral judgment of this type was "of dubious value" and represented an "Alice in Wonderland" kind of mentality; see 99.

[90]Eleanor Lansing Dulles, *John Foster Dulles: The Last Year* (New York: Harcourt, Brace and World, 1963) 197-98.

The Aftermath of Korea:
Militaristic Considerations
to the Fore

Korea must be viewed as the pivotal factor at work behind Dulles's more militaristic approach to Soviet expansionism. He articulated this move as a shift from the preventive phase to one that he termed the "phase of opposition."[91] This represented a move from deterrence primarily reliant on moral indignation to an increased reliance on military might. As Dulles expressed it: "Since international Communism may not be deterred by moral principles backed by potential might, we must back those principles with military strength-in-being, and do so quickly."[92]

Such a shift represented a significant change in Dulles's outlook. Throughout his long career, he had warned of the inherent dangers in policies that placed too heavy an emphasis on military considerations. Now, however, military considerations were all-important. Korea "surely invalidates the assumption that we can continue still for a time to live luxuriously, without converting our economic potential into military reality."[93] Dulles was obviously and sincerely frightened by Communism's willingness to resort to arms. America, he believed, must develop a new strategy in order to deal with that willingness. Part of Dulles's personal strategy involved securing Japan's position in the Free World. The remainder of his strategy depended on increased military strength. A word about the former is in order before discussing the latter.

The Japanese Peace Treaty. The Korean War affected Dulles's work on the Japanese Peace Treaty. As previously mentioned, Dulles was in Tokyo when the Korean conflict started. Acheson reports that Dulles "returned to Washington with the conviction that the negotiation of a

---

[91]JFD, "New Phase of American Foreign Policy," *Department of State Bulletin* 23 (17 July 1950): 90-91.

[92]JFD, "To Save Humanity from the Deep Abyss," 3.

[93]Ibid., 4. Compare these statements with those of the earlier Dulles discussed on 130-31.

treaty with Japan had become more rather than less important."[94] Both the secretary and Dulles agreed that the attack on Korea "would be regarded by the Japanese as aimed at them." Therefore, the need to maintain "a Japan independent of Soviet influence" became much more pressing.

Dulles and Acheson immediately set to the rather formidable task of obtaining the Defense Department's support of the desire to proceed rapidly. Fortunately for the State Department, General Marshall replaced Secretary Johnson as the secretary of defense. The only remaining obstacle involved the Joint Chiefs of Staff who, under General Bradley's leadership, believed that "a favorable resolution of the military situation in Korea" should precede the peace settlement with Japan.[95] The president, however, sided with the State Department and he proceeded to help in the removal of any remaining in-house obstacles to the treaty.

Dulles worked extremely hard between 8 September 1950, the day the president actually assigned him to the task, and 8 September 1951, the day the signing ceremonies took place. He particularly relished the task since it gave him a practical avenue through which he could constructively vent his anti-Communism. The guiding principle of his work was to insure that Japan would be completely integrated into the Free World as a sovereign nation. As Dulles defined his approach, "It is not merely a matter of liquidating the old war with Japan but of building a strong bulwark against the threat of Communist aggression from the East."[96] If Americans were not careful, Dulles warned, they "could, indeed, lose more in Japan than can be won in Korea."[97] In order to provide Dulles with the credentials necessary to successfully secure Japan's allegiance and friendship, President Truman, in January of 1951, designated him as a "Special Representative of the President with the Personal Rank of Ambassador."[98]

---

[94]Acheson, *Present at the Creation,* 434.

[95]Ibid., 435; see also Pruessen, *The Road to Power,* 457.

[96]JFD, "Laying Foundations for Peace in the Pacific," 1, 1 March 1951, DP, Box 54; see also JFD, "The Free East and the Free West," 29 November 1951, DP, Box 55; JFD, "Far Eastern Problems," 1, 5 May 1952, DP, Box 64.

[97]JFD, "Korea," 4.

[98]See President Truman to JFD, 10 January 1951, DP, Box 56.

Dulles's efforts did not disappoint Truman. Shortly after Dulles handed him the final draft, Truman sent Acheson a handwritten note that simply read, "The document is a jewel."[99] Once Dulles had the approval of both the Japanese and the Truman administration, he still faced a significant obstacle in assuring countries like the Philippines, New Zealand, and Australia that a completely sovereign Japan was in their best interests. Dulles overcame the problem by negotiating several mutual-security agreements. Three basic security arrangements resulted from the negotiations, all of which included the United States as the common denominator.

Bilateral pacts were signed between the United States and Japan and between the United States and the Philippines. Finally, the United States, Australia, and New Zealand agreed to a trilateral security pact. These agreements demanded less than the NATO pact in that, rather than requiring immediate military action in the event of an attack upon one of the signatories, they simply stated that each would "act to meet the common danger in accordance with its constitutional processes."[100] In spite of the somewhat ambiguous wording, the pacts assured the anxious Pacific nations that the United States would stand by them in the event of armed aggression.

One final minor hurdle remained. The manner in which Dulles crossed it once again reveals his anti-Communism. Great Britain proposed in March of 1951 that the Communist Chinese be invited to sign any peace treaty reached with Japan since they were the legitimate ruling power on mainland China. Dulles was seriously opposed to the idea. "Signature by Commie regime," he wrote, "is absolutely out."[101] As a sop to the British, however, Dulles suggested that Nationalist China be included in the peace-treaty process at some time separate from the other Allies. London remained unsatisfied. Therefore, Dulles negotiated a compromise that left the choice between the two Chinas up to the sovereign discretion of Japan. As a point of fact, however, Dulles and the Truman administration were seriously opposed to the possibility of Communist Chinese participation. Personal feelings of antagonism were too strong to allow

---

[99]President Truman to Dean Acheson, 1951, DP, Box 56.

[100]Quoted in Pruessen, *The Road to Power,* 481.

[101]Ibid., 487.

it. Previous to working out the compromise, Dulles had received assurances from Prime Minister Yoshida that, "under no circumstances," would Japan choose Communist China.[102]

Once all obstacles were overcome, Dulles invited more than forty nations to San Francisco for a gathering during which they would hear a few speeches and apply their respective signatures to the peace treaty. Absolutely no negotiation was to take place. Since Dulles had spent the last eleven months negotiating across the globe, most of the invited nations accepted this arrangement. Only the Soviets and two of their satellites, Poland and Czechoslovakia, attempted to renegotiate the treaty. Ronald Pruessen describes what happened:

> When Andrei Gromyko rose at the first plenary session to urge that Peking be invited to send a delegation forthwith, presiding officer Dean Acheson ruled him out of order because an Anglo-American motion on procedural rules was already on the floor; after adoption of the previous motion, Gromyko tried again, but was now told that he was out of order because his proposal was not allowable under the rules just approved: it was an absurd Catch-22 which the vast majority of delegations endorsed when an appeal was made to overturn the ruling of the chair. Toward the end of the conference the Soviets tried to introduce "amendments" that would have struck out provisions of basic significance to the United States. They were told that amendments could not be entertained, and found themselves outvoted 46 to 3 when they appealed for a counter-ruling by the delegates.[103]

One can only imagine the expression of delight on Dulles's face as these events transpired. In his view, "The Soviet Union and its satellites suffered their most humiliating defeat in conference history."[104] Dulles attributed this defeat to the fact that "the Conference became the expression of dynamic and righteous faith" as "all the delegates at San Francisco who accepted a religious view of the world, whether Christian, Buddhist, or Moslem, found inspiration from the fact that the treaty invoked the principle of the moral law." Such an assessment once again il-

---

[102]Ibid., 488.

[103]Ibid., 490.

[104]JFD, "Three Propositions," 4, 22 February 1952, DP, Box 63.

lustrates Dulles's complete disregard for the national-interest considerations of other nations as a primary motive for their political action in international affairs. In this instance, Dulles simply placed motivations under the rubric of "religious" and "anti-religious" impulses.

The "Uniting for Peace" Resolution. One way Dulles revealed his new reliance on military strength was through his support of the American campaign north of the 38th Parallel. Soon, Dulles's support for a proposal dealing with U.N. military powers would reveal even further his dedication to increased military tactics. The success of the unification campaign in Korea depended upon further U.N. action. Acheson wondered just how such action might best be fostered. Since the Soviet delegate had returned to his seat on the Security Council in August, a veto of further action was almost certain. Therefore, Acheson chose to turn to the General Assembly.

In his "Uniting for Peace" speech of 20 September, Acheson proposed that the existing Charter's system of collective security be strengthened. Since, in the event of a paralyzing veto in the Security Council, Articles 10, 11, and 14 gave the General Assembly the authority to maintain international peace, Acheson offered a plan designed to increase the assembly's ability to carry out that task. If the Security Council could not act due to a veto, Acheson suggested that an emergency session of the General Assembly be called within twenty-four hours. According to Acheson's plan, the assembly would then have the right to enlist a peace patrol "to provide immediate and independent observation wherever international conflict might threaten."[105] Further, a special committee would be established that would possess the power to use the armed forces that each member nation would be required to make available for United Nations service.

Administration officials had opposed such a development in 1945 in San Francisco. Now, in 1950, the American secretary of state proposed that such machinery be put in place. Happy with the General Assembly's present makeup, the British Foreign Office was cool to the idea of any potential change. In Acheson's view, however, "present difficulties outweighed possible future ones."[106]

---

[105]Acheson, *Present at the Creation,* 450.

[106]Ibid.

It should be emphasized at this point that Dulles in 1945 had criticized the reliance placed on force by the planners at Dumbarton Oaks. He wrote that "the Dumbarton Oaks Proposals seem to make force a primary and independent means of assuring peace."[107] In Dulles's opinion, such an approach was undesirable. The "essential" strategy involved the attempt to design an international organization that would "quickly become the nucleus of a cooperative effort which will give all the people a sense of creative fellowship."[108] Relying on military action usually blinds the parties involved so that more creative solutions are overlooked. In Dulles's view, events since the Treaty of Versailles had clearly demonstrated the "impotence of force." He warned against the temptation "to oversimplify the problem of peace by thinking that if only we can have enough force then we will have peace." "No amount of force," he continued, "can assure [peace]."[109]

Yet, five years later, Dulles expressed an entirely different viewpoint. He viewed the Uniting for Peace Resolution as necessary in order to cut "the noose of the veto that would strangle us."[110] In Dulles's unhesitating and complete endorsement of the Uniting for Peace plan, he asserted that the United Nations would be able to decide whether or not a given cause was "just and righteous" through reliance on "the moral principles we find in our Bible." These principles, of course, were clearly synonymous with the hopes and aspirations of the Free World. In his words,

> Experience has shown that when the United Nations meets, and particularly when the General Assembly meets, it registers the moral judgment of the free world. . . . Because the moral law is a natural law

---

[107]JFD, "The Churches and a Just and Durable Peace," 25.

[108]"Comments on Current Discussions of International Order," *Christian Century* 61 (4 October 1944): 1148.

[109]JFD, *Six Pillars of Peace: A Study Guide Based on "A Statement of Political Propositions,"* ed. with an intro. by John Foster Dulles (New York: Commission to Study the Bases of a Just and Durable Peace, 1943) 59-60; see also JFD, *War, Peace and Change* where Dulles urged Americans to "demote force from its role of supreme arbiter of change" (97).

[110]JFD, "Statement," 31 October 1950, quoted in Pruessen, *The Road to Power,* 429.

imbedded in the conscience of all men, there is a surprising amount of agreement as to what is right and what is wrong. [111]

When one considers how the later Dulles redefined the moral law as a "natural law imbedded in the conscience of all men," it is not hard to understand why he viewed the Soviets as "evil" in that they could so easily ignore their consciences and hence dismiss the dictates of the moral law. Any one of the leaders of the American Federal Council of Churches might have reminded Dulles that the moral law had been formulated by Jews and Christians attempting to understand the nature of their environment—one that differed vastly from that of their counterparts in the Eastern Hemisphere.

Acheson's Uniting for Peace proposal was adopted by the General Assembly on 3 November 1950 by an overwhelming vote of 52 to 5. Given Dulles's revised definition of the moral law, it comes as no surprise that he viewed the resolution as "a great moral advance." The new achievement in morality, he wrote Walter Van Kirk, his former associate in church endeavors, was "made possible by the fact that there exists a world-wide judgement of what is right and what is wrong." Such judgment, he continued, "is primarily a reflection of religious beliefs."[112]

As Dulles became more and more confident of a universal standard of right and wrong (one that was imbedded in every human conscience yet interpreted only with the aid of religious beliefs), he became equally convinced of the evil present in every Soviet action. The Soviets had no religious beliefs and therefore had no conscience. The negative vote cast by the Soviets on the Uniting for Peace proposal had nothing to do with national-interest considerations or with the Soviet fear that such power in the General Assembly might be directed solely against them; rather, in Dulles's mind, the negative vote was cast simply because the Soviets opposed righteousness in whatever form it appeared.

Massive Retaliation: A New Strategy for Peace. The roots of Dulles's infamous concept of "massive retaliation" were nurtured during the Korean crisis. Prior to the Korean conflict, Dulles had argued that the atomic

---

[111]JFD, "Universal Bible Broadcast," 7-8.

[112]JFD to Walter W. Van Kirk, 20 October 1950, DP, Box 51.

bomb was not a factor in relations with the Soviet Union.[113] Dulles concluded after Korea that the Free World, in order to be secure, must develop the will and the ability to use massive force. Dulles came to believe that security for the Free World depended upon destroying any feelings of security in the other half of the world. In November of 1951, after America had successfully tested the hydrogen bomb, Dulles began to provide the philosophical rationale behind the increasing development of nuclear technology.

> Let the free nations combine to create a striking force of great power and then rely more and more upon the deterrent of that punishing power, and less and less upon a series of local area defenses. That means having . . . the capacity to hit Russia's interior lines of communication with such disruptive power that its highly centralized despotic police state will fall apart.[114]

As the 1952 election drew closer, Dulles emphasized his theory of deterrence much more aggressively. No longer did he talk simply of destroying "lines of communication." Rather, he talked openly of "retaliatory blows so costly that aggression will not be a profitable operation."[115] He advocated developing "a community punishing force" to be used in response to "any armed aggression." This Free World retaliatory force would use "*weapons* of its own choosing against *targets* of its choosing at *times* of its choosing."[116] According to Dulles, the West could "not afford to live without" such military power.[117]

As secretary of state, Dulles received "a flood of letters" from "men with whom as a leading lay churchman, he had long worked closely, upbraiding him for his announcement" of this policy of "massive retalia-

---

[113]JFD, "Improving Relations with Russia," *U.S. News and World Report* 26 (8 July 1949): 31.

[114]JFD, "Can We Stop Russian Imperialism?" 4.

[115]JFD, "A Positive Foreign Policy," 18.

[116]JFD, "A New Foreign Policy," 9 (emphasis is that of Dulles).

[117]Ibid.; see also JFD, "Foreign Policy and the National Welfare," 1, 16 February 1952, DP, Box 59; JFD, "Foreign Policy: Text of Foreign Policy and National Defense Planks of Republican Party Platform," 9, 10 July 1952, DP, Box 62; JFD, "America and the World," 10; and JFD, "A Dynamic Moral Force: America's Opportunity," 3, 12 May 1952, DP, Box 307.

tion." Reportedly, "He was shocked that they construed his formula as immoral." The reactions on both sides merely illustrate the vast differences of viewpoint that had developed between his former associates and himself during the previous five to seven years.[118] Much to the dismay of his former church associates, during that time Dulles had sired twins named "Brinkmanship" and "Massive Retaliation," thus becoming the father of modern-day theories of deterrence.

Liberation versus Containment. Though all the themes he had developed over the previous six years were put to good use,[119] as the 1952 presidential election drew near, Dulles relied heavily on the concepts of "massive retaliation" and the "liberation of captive peoples" in order to distinguish the Republican party from the Democratic administration in the minds of the American constituency. The former concept urged a "bigger bang for the buck" and was therefore perfectly consistent with the Republican image of fiscal conservatism. The latter concept reflected the general anti-Communism of the party and provided the added bonus of appealing to voters' ethnic loyalties.

As early as 1949 Dulles began to talk about "liberation" for people behind the Iron Curtain. In *War or Peace* he stated that "it is time to think in terms of taking the offensive in the world struggle for freedom and of rolling back the engulfing tide of despotism." He did not envision that offensive as an encouragement to captive peoples to take up arms. Such a move, he said, could only lead to "massacre." Instead, he supported measures that would keep "alive in them love of God and of country, faith in human fellowship and belief in the dignity and worth of human personality" until such time as the weaknesses of Communism could be exploited enough to bring about a change of government.[120] Dulles believed that since it happened in Yugoslavia with the emergence of "Titoism," it could happen elsewhere given the proper encouragement.[121]

---

[118]See Drummond and Coblentz, *Duel at the Brink,* 69.

[119]To name a few: renewed appreciation for the moral nature of Western (particularly American) civilization, spiritualism versus materialism, free state versus police state, and Soviet encirclement of the West by way of Asia.

[120]JFD, *War or Peace,* 175 and 249. Pages 242-52 deal exclusively with the theme of liberation.

[121]See, for example, JFD, "Can We Stop Russian Imperialism?" 5; JFD, "Our Foreign Policy: Is Containment Enough?" 7, 8 October 1952, DP, Box 59; and JFD, "Address before the World Affairs Council of Seattle," 5, 18 September 1952, DP, Box 59.

Though Dulles's program of liberation rarely contained anything more than glittering generalities, it was symptomatic of his sincere belief that the Democratic party's program of containment was basically "immoral."[122] He compared it with trying to "keep a bear in a cage." Such an endeavor is hardly "amusing if friends and relatives are caught inside with the bear."[123] To him, containment represented a "sell out" of the captive peoples in order to "make a deal with Stalin—as Roosevelt did at Yalta."[124] In that particular case, the government had been "willing to violate principle in order to gain what it thought were immediate practical advantages." "That," Dulles charged, "was non-moral diplomacy."[125] In light of experience gleaned over the past seven years, Dulles had become convinced that collaboration should not be considered a viable tactic when dealing with the Soviets.

A little more than a week before the 1952 presidential election, Dulles received a letter from George Kennan, the author of the administration's containment policy. Kennan was the American ambassador to Moscow at the time. The letter had nothing whatsoever to do with the subject of containment versus liberation. Rather, it dealt with the role of morality in foreign policy. A few weeks earlier Dulles had sent Kennan a copy of one of his recent speeches and its moralistic tone had obviously bothered the ambassador. Kennan, in response, sent a "thank-you" for the speech accompanied by a copy of remarks drawn up "for another purpose," which seemed to him relevant to Dulles's speech.

Dulles's speech had simply reiterated his belief that there are "certain basic moral concepts which all people and nations can and do comprehend, and to which it is legitimate to appeal as providing some common standard for judging international conflict."[126] These basic moral con-

---

[122]JFD, "Republican Foreign Policy," 4, 21 July 1952, DP, Box 59.

[123]JFD, "Our Foreign Policy," 1.

[124]JFD, "Road to Peace," 3, 10 October 1952, DP, Box 62.

[125]JFD, "Principle versus Expediency in Foreign Policy," 2, 26 September 1952, DP, Box 64. Compare this statement with his 1945 praise of Roosevelt's administration for its willingness to "work in such mire as much of the world is today" even though it might result in unfair criticism because "some of the mire" adhered "to its hands and feet" in the process (JFD, "America's Role in the Peace," 3).

[126]JFD to George Kennan, 29 October 1952, DP, Box 61.

cepts, of course, were clearly exemplified in the American tradition. Kennan's reply took issue with this expression of morality. Other nations, he wrote, "have no obligation to promote the moral principles on which *our* national society was founded." Americans "should refrain from attempting to insert our . . . moral concepts into the differences between third states and from intervening in those differences on the basis of conclusions we arrive at in this manner." A rather lengthy segment of his remarks is worth quoting here since, as a criticism of Dulles's moral position, it helps to pinpoint just what that position was.

> We are not apt to be good judges of who is right and who is wrong. When others quarrel, let us be vigilent [*sic*] to see whether our own interests are being affected and take action if they are; but let us have the honesty to do this on the basis of something we have reason to understand, which is an enlightened view of our own interest, rather than on the basis of a subjective system of moral-political values which others might or might not share. . . . In short then, let us keep our morality to ourselves. With regard to other nations let us not judge, that we be not judged. Let us not attempt to constitute ourselves as the guardians of everyone else's virtue; we have enough trouble to guard our own. I can assure people who may be worried that there are many things, in the conduct of our national affairs, to which other peoples would take exception if they were to attempt to apply their own moral concepts to us; and I am sure that many of these are things which the United States public has not the slightest intention of altering to suit the moral concepts of anybody else. [127]

Kennan's written remarks are indicative of the prophetic realism characteristic of the earlier Dulles. [128] In the years since World War II ended, Dulles had abandoned his previous posture. Kennan's letter attempted to show Dulles the error of his ways. Dulles responded by reaffirming his belief in a universal moral law. Further, after his appointment as secretary of state, Dulles failed to reassign Kennan to another diplomatic position after he was declared *persona non grata* by Moscow. Dulles's inaction forced Kennan's premature retirement from a long ca-

---

[127]George Kennan to JFD, 22 October 1952, DP, Box 61.

[128]Kennan, after all, once described Reinhold Niebuhr as "the father of us all" (See Kenneth W. Thompson, *Ethics, Functionalism, and Power in International Politics: the Crisis in Values* [Baton Rouge: The Louisiana State University Press, 1979] 45).

reer of distinguished public service. [129] Such a slight on the part of a secretary of state regarding a diplomat of Kennan's stature was virtually unheard of and could be interpreted as due to a personal dislike of Kennan, perhaps resulting from Kennan's rather different understanding of the dynamics of international morality.

Dulles began his tenure as secretary of state in January of 1953. He was one month shy of his sixty-fifth birthday. Some forty-six years earlier, while at Princeton University, he had written an award-winning senior thesis in which he expressed his opinion that in life, "our view of the world does change and . . . we may be led to affirm what will cause us to completely revolutionize our view of the world."[130] During the years immediately prior to his installation as secretary of state, Dulles went through just such an experience. His ideological expressions were more than merely his way of providing window dressing for an otherwise conventional approach to world events; indeed, his moralistic rhetoric, though occasionally embellished for maximum political effect (especially during election years), fundamentally revealed the true nature of the man behind it: a determined Calvinist who was transformed as events led him to translate his tradition's long-held belief in the reality of a moral universe into a belief in the moral virtue of his own nation.

-----

[129]Kennan's recall was demanded by Moscow in early November. While in Berlin, Kennan responded to a reporter's question regarding the quality of life in Moscow by drawing a comparison with his internment by Hitler during the war. His words were ill chosen (see Acheson, *Present at the Creation,* 697).

[130]JFD, "The Theory of Judgement," 17, 1907, DP, Box 279.

Conclusion

As World War II ended, most interpreters and leaders believed that the worst was over. The 1930s, and particularly the 1940s, had been difficult decades indeed. Those years seemed almost to demand a compromising spirit so that people of entirely different cultural backgrounds and political ideologies could band together to defeat the obvious ᴄ ʲl of Fascism.

The delicate balance between moral and material resources was not easy to maintain. Such a balance never is. And there were abuses; for many churchmen of the time, the saturation bombings, along with Hiroshima and Nagasaki, were prime examples. Nonetheless, the interpenetration between spirit and power seemed fairly stable during those years. The United Nations, though it had an extremely limited beginning, at least provided a new forum for international justice.

After 1945 the tension in international affairs became, if possible, even more intense. The actions of the Soviet Union were frightening. Nearly all Americans were shocked by the seemingly endless atrocities committed in Eastern Europe. Few political leaders in the West were capable of assessing the events dispassionately. Freedom was being trampled. When Vishinsky delivered the speech calling for an end to tolerance in the United Nations, Americans rightfully became concerned. Dulles, as he witnessed these events, reported them to the public accurately.

Stalin's policies were certainly not harmless or in any way benign. Yet neither were they those of a person intent on controlling the world through masterminding revolution or taking direct military action. As many diplomatic historians have pointed out, even if the Soviet Union had been intent on world domination, it hardly possessed the resources at this time to carry it off. There can be no doubt, however, that Soviet actions under Stalin certainly caused a large measure of anxiety for Americans.

To remain prophetic in an anxious age requires stern concentration. In many respects, the prophet during times of crisis must be hard-hearted, even callous. When people are hurting or scared, they want comfort and assurance. When things are unstable, people want answers that promise stability. Prophets are not generally known as providers of these commodities.

John Foster Dulles gave up his prophetic role after 1945 in order to become a statesman. Being a statesman and being a prophet are not nec-essarily mutually exclusive vocations. Abraham Lincoln serves as an ex-ample of one statesman who was extremely prophetic. Yet, for Dulles, the prophetic dimension that had been so evident in his work with the churches disappeared completely from his work as a statesman.

The natural question to ask is "Why?" Obviously, the role of a public leader does not make the prophetic task an easy one to fulfill. Political leadership naturally involves protecting the national unity and security of one's own country. Right and wrong for statesmen is quite often deter-mined not by seeking some objective and universal standard but by at-tempting to secure safety and security for present and future generations in their own country. Yet sufficient numbers of statesmen in the past have demonstrated that such protection can be had without actually believing the best about one's own country while believing the worst about those countries with competing policies and ideologies. Further, at times in American history, the nation has pursued moral purposes in diplomacy that are not completely explained by self-interest. Becoming a political leader, therefore, does not automatically transform an individual into an uncompromising zealot.

As the preceding pages have demonstrated, most of Dulles's actions after 1945 are representative of the nationalism he decried during his earlier years. In many ways, his actions in the international arena indi-cate more an uncompromising zealot than they do a diplomat. He re-ported the atrocities of the Soviet Union accurately, but he misunderstood the motivations behind them. The historical insecurity and traditional economic instability of the Soviet Union escaped his recollection, as did the reasons underlying the Communist party's distrust of religion. To Dulles, Communism became a monolithic, antireligious machine primar-ily bent on destroying the entire Free World. Once he became convinced of this, most of the complexities, the compromises, the subtleties, the intricacies of international relations were no longer relevant. Gray areas, for Dulles, no longer existed.

So, we return to the original question: why the change? Both political and religious factors were involved. Certainly, the actions of the Soviets in international conferences and in Eastern Europe provided much of the impetus for Dulles's transformation. In this respect, Dulles was not alone in his changed world view. Many, if not most, American leaders underwent a similar change in their perceptions of the Soviet Union during these years. A number of them became self-critical, in the same way that Dulles did, of their pre-1945 naiveté with regard to the Soviet Union.

The Soviets, as exemplified in the actions of Molotov and Vishinsky, seemed unwilling to become responsible members in a world community. The failure of all the postwar conferences, the ruthless and reckless activity of the Soviets in Eastern Europe, the Communist revolution in China, the Korean War—all these elements in combination seemed to indicate an overall design for domination planned and executed by Kremlin leadership. What determined the future of America's interaction (or perhaps better phrased, the lack of it) with the Soviet Union was the American conclusion that Soviet foreign policy was merely an extension of Soviet domestic policy. This conclusion was not necessarily a substantiated one, yet it came to be the major presupposition of American foreign policy. As exemplified in the document known as NSC-68, drafted in 1950 by State and Defense Department officials under the leadership of Paul Nitze (successor to George Kennan as the head of the Policy Planning Staff), it provided the American rationale for the development of the hydrogen bomb and the vastly increased military spending in general. "The Kremlin is inescapably militant," the document reads,

> It is inescapably militant because it possesses and is possessed by a world-wide revolutionary movement, because it is the inheritor of Russian imperialism, and because it is a totalitarian dictatorship. . . . It is quite clear from Soviet theory and practice that the Kremlin seeks to bring the free world under its dominion by the methods of the cold war.[1]

---

[1]Daniel Yergin, *Shattered Peace: The Origins of the Cold War and the National Security State* (Boston: Houghton Mifflin Company, 1977) 402.

As this statement indicates, in an attempt to understand Soviet militarism, the foreign policy establishment in America came to view Communism as a "world-wide revolutionary movement" centered in Moscow. With this document, the connection between Soviet domestic policy and the formation of Soviet foreign policy became firm. As Daniel Yergin has pointed out, "The only significant disagreement came from the two experts on the Soviet Union, [George] Kennan and [Chip] Bohlen, neither of whom at this point believed the Soviets had a world design."[2] Yet neither of these men was able to convince anyone in leadership positions in America that while admittedly the Soviets had imperialistic aims, they were concerned equally with keeping what they already possessed. Moreover, in large measure, they were reacting to the actions of the United States.

The justifications given in NSC-68 are also present, as we have seen, in Dulles's expressions. The very practical questions dealing with Soviet militarism and expansionism were definitely involved in his transformation. Still, as I have argued throughout, the transformation of Dulles's world view was in the main a religious one. Throughout his life Dulles was committed to articulating and actualizing the concerns of the moral law. What changed after 1945 was not his commitment to the moral law but rather his understanding of where the United States stood in relation to it.

For most Americans, as a perceptive article by John Smylie pointed out only four years after Dulles's death, the nation operates as "the organ through which God makes his ultimate historical demands and offers his fullest earthly rewards." This is particularly true for America, argued Smylie, because in America there is no singular "church." No single denominational church can claim to speak "as the Christian church either to the nation or to other national churches." Through a gradual process, "the nation emerged as the primary agent of God's meaningful activity in history." This further led to the nation assuming "the churchly function in becoming the community of righteousness."[3] Most American leadership not only shared this presupposition but also used it to good advantage

---

[2]Ibid., 402.

[3]John E. Smylie, "National Ethos and the Church," *Theology Today* 20 (October 1963): 313-21.

both before and after 1945. Thus, even though many postwar American leaders had changed their perception of the Soviet Union, they did not change their fundamental world view in the same way that Dulles did.

Dulles operated from different presuppositions prior to 1945. This makes his transformation all the more important. The religious reasons behind his change are most certainly rooted in the practical questions raised by Soviet behavior. As Dulles sought answers to these questions, he came upon the antireligious, clearly materialistic, nature of the Soviet Union. The more he studied this particular dimension of Soviet ideology, the more he became convinced that the Soviets were bent on the destruction of all religious expression. Since, for Dulles, commitment to the moral law was a religious commitment, he came to view Soviet attacks on religion as direct attacks on the moral law. Conversely, since the United States defended religious expression and religious freedom, he came to understand American policy as a defense of the moral law.

This process of reasoning led Dulles, borrowing Smylie's terminology, to merge the traditional purpose of the church with the purpose of the nation. In the face of the very real crises of post-1945, America assumed the role of God's redemptive agent in the world. This process was made easier by the way in which he analyzed Soviet behavior. The Soviet dedication to antireligious materialism made American commitment to religious principles seem pale by comparison. He developed a renewed appreciation for the religious heritage of the American republic—a heritage that seemed to have resulted from the permeation of Christian principles in the democratic institutions of American government. Since Dulles viewed the principles as the primary foundation for American democratic institutions, he saw no contradiction in his developing identification between the moral law and American policies.

In an important way, the Cold War acted as a revelatory event for America. Dulles's reaction to it exemplifies its impact. He saw in its development a new incarnation of the will of God for the world. It revealed God's purposes for the nation and provided the nation with a clear mission to fulfill in much the same way as the American Revolution did. As Dulles interpreted this revelatory event, it also led him to call for American rededication to fulfilling this mission. Soviet behavior caused Americans to take stock of themselves and particularly caused Dulles to call for spiritual revival, that is, a return to faith in God and in democratic institutions as instruments of his will. The power of the Soviet threat was

254

a reminder to Americans of their general tendency to take American institutions for granted and a warning about where such apathy might lead them.

History always tends to be a harsh judge. From the perspective of almost forty years later, it is always easy to criticize. Churchmen like Reinhold Niebuhr and John C. Bennett certainly maintained their prophetic voices in the Cold War era, but they had possessed a solid and studied theological grounding that Dulles lacked. Dulles's quest for an ideal world beyond the present one is not to be faulted. His commitment to bringing that world into being showed dedication and sacrifice. Yet from the point of view of prophetic Protestantism, during the years after World War II, Dulles failed to distinguish between the universal he sought and the policies of the country he served. Thus, as John Foster Dulles assumed the office of secretary of state, his new vision of the task ahead resembled the earlier perspective of Josiah Strong, who once wrote: "Not America for America's sake; but America for the World's sake."[4]

---

[4]Josiah Strong, *Our Country: Its Possible Future and Its Present Crisis* (New York: Baker and Taylor, 1885) 218.

Selected Bibliography

General Sources

Acheson, Dean. *Present at the Creation.* New York: W. W. Norton and Company, Inc., 1969.

Adler, Mortimer J. *How To Think about War and Peace.* New York: Simon and Schuster, 1944.

"Ambassador Dulles Returns to Japan for Peace Treaty Consultation." *The Department of State Bulletin* 24 (23 April 1951): 654.

"The American Churches in Time of War." *Federal Council Bulletin* 24 (January 1941): 6-7.

"Backing Away from the Truman Doctrine." *The Christian Century* 64 (25 June 1947): 790-91.

Bailey, Thomas A. *A Diplomatic History of the American People.* 4th ed. Foreword by Dixon Ryan Fox. New York: Appleton-Century-Crofts, Inc., 1950.

Baruch, Bernard M. *The Making of the Reparation and Economic Sections of the Treaty.* New York: Harper and Brothers, 1920.

Bennett, John C. "An International Christian Round Table." *Christianity and Crisis* 3 (26 July 1943): 1-2.

_____. "John Foster Dulles." *Christianity and Society* 18 (Winter 1952-1953): 4-5.

Berding, Andrew H. T. *Dulles on Diplomacy.* Princeton: Van Nostrand, 1965.

Bergson, Henri. *Creative Evolution.* Translated by Arthur Mitchell. New York: Henry Holt and Company, 1911.

Bulletin of the Commission to Study the Organization of Peace 2 (January/February 1942).

Burnett, Philip Mason. *Reparation at the Paris Peace Conference from the Standpoint of the American Delegation.* Foreword by John Foster Dulles. New York: Columbia University Press, 1940.

Byrnes, James F. "The London Conference." *Vital Speeches of the Day* 12 (15 October 1945): 3-7.

_____. *Speaking Frankly.* New York: Harper and Brothers, 1947.

Chamberlain, John. "John Foster Dulles: A Wilsonian at Versailles, This Famous Lawyer May Be Dewey's Secretary of State." *Life* 17 (21 August 1944): 84.

"Christian Standards and Current International Developments." *International Conciliation* 409 (March 1945): 142-49.

"The Churches and the Current International Situation." *International Conciliation* 409 (March 1945): 150-66.

"The Churches and the Forthcoming Peace Conference." *Federal Council Bulletin* 27 (January 1944): 10-11.

"Churchmen Speak on Atomic Bomb." *Federal Council Bulletin* 28 (September 1945): 6.

"Churchmen Urge World Organization." *Federal Council Bulletin* 27 (May 1944): 8.

Comfort, Mildred H. *John Foster Dulles, Peacemaker.* Minneapolis: T. S. Denison, 1960.

"Comments on Current Discussions of International Order." *The Christian Century* 61 (4 October 1944): 1148.

The Commission on the Churches on International Affairs: 1946-1947 through 1956-1957. New York: The Commission on the Churches on International Affairs, 1958.

"Community Indestructible." *The Christian Century* 60 (28 July 1943): 861-62.

"Crossroads of U.S. Foreign Policy." *Federal Council Bulletin* 30 (September 1947): 8.

De Conde, Alexander. *A History of American Foreign Policy.* New York: Charles Scribner's Sons, 1963.

"Developing a Positive Peace Policy." *Federal Council Bulletin* 23 (May 1940): 11-12.

Devine, Michael J. *John W. Foster: Politics and Diplomacy in the Imperial Era, 1873-1917.* Athens: Ohio University Press, 1981.

Dilks, David, ed. *The Diaries of Sir Alexander Cadogan, O.M. 1938-1945.* New York: G. P. Putnam's Sons, 1971.

Divine, Robert. *Foreign Policy and the United States Presidential Elections, 1940-1948*. New York: New Viewpoints, 1974.

_____. *Second Chance: The Triumph of Internationalism in America during World War II*. New York: Atheneum, 1967.

Douglas, Paul H. Review of *War or Peace*, by John Foster Dulles, in *The Saturday Review of Literature* 32 (27 May 1950): 14-15.

"Draft Peace Treaty with Japan and Japanese Declarations." *The Department of State Bulletin* 25 (23 July 1951): 132-38.

Drummond, Roscoe, and Gaston Coblentz. *Duel at the Brink: John Foster Dulles's Command of American Power*. Garden City: Doubleday, 1960.

"Dulles: a Fisherman, a Sailor, a Cook." *Newsweek* 38 (10 September 1951): 36-37.

"Dulles a Senator." *New Times* (20 July 1949).

"Dulles as Demagogue." *The Nation* 169 (15 October 1949): 361.

"Dulles in the Gutter." *The New Republic* 121 (24 October 1949): 6.

Dulles, Allen Macy. *The True Church*. New York: F. H. Revell, 1907.

Dulles, Avery. *A Church to Believe In*. New York: Crossroad, 1982.

Dulles, Eleanor Lansing. *American Foreign Policy in the Making*. New York: Harper and Row, 1968.

_____. *John Foster Dulles: The Last Year*. New York: Harcourt, Brace and World, 1963.

Dunn, Frederick S. *Peacemaking and the Settlement with Japan*. Princeton: Princeton University Press, 1963.

Eden, Anthony. *Full Circle*. Boston: Houghton Mifflin, 1960.

Edwards, Margaret Dulles. "Tomorrow's Legacy." *Bible Society Record* (January 1964): 1.

Finer, Herman. *Dulles over Suez*. Chicago: Quadrangle Books, 1964.

Fitch, Robert E. "Reinhold Niebuhr's Philosophy of History." In *Reinhold Niebuhr: His Religious, Social, and Political Thought*. Edited by Charles W. Kegley and Robert W. Bretall. New York: The Macmillan Company, 1961.

Fosdick, Harry E. *The Living of These Days*. New York: Harper and Brothers, 1956.

Foster, John W. *Diplomatic Memoirs*. 2 vols. Boston: Houghton Mifflin Company, 1909.

Fox, William T. R. Review of *War or Peace*, by John Foster Dulles, in *The American Political Science Review* 44 (September 1950): 751-53.

Freeman, J. M. "John Foster Dulles—Christian Statesman?" *The Protestant* 7 (June/July 1946): 40-44.

"Freshman with a Reputation." *Time* 54 (18 July 1949): 17.

Gaddis, John. *The United States and the Origins of the Cold War, 1941-1947.* New York: Columbia University Press, 1972.

Gardner, Brian. *The Year that Changed the World: 1945.* New York: Coward-McCann, Inc., 1963.

Geyer, Alan. *Piety and Politics: American Protestantism in the World Arena.* Richmond: John Knox Press, 1963.

Gilkey, Langdon. "Reinhold Niebuhr's Theology of History." In *The Legacy of Reinhold Niebuhr.* Edited by Nathan A. Scott, Jr. Chicago: The University of Chicago Press, 1975.

Goold-Adams, Richard John Morton. *The Time of Power: A Reappraisal of John Foster Dulles.* New York: Appleton-Century-Crofts, 1962.

Graebner, Norman A. *The New Isolationism: A Study in Politics and Foreign Policy since 1950.* New York: Ronald Press, 1956.

Guhin, Michael A. *John Foster Dulles: A Statesman and His Times.* New York: Columbia University Press, 1972.

Harsch, Joseph C. "John Foster Dulles: A Very Complicated Man." *Harpers Magazine* 213 (September 1956): 27-34.

Hartmann, Frederick H. Review of *War or Peace,* by John Foster Dulles, in *The Journal of Politics* 13 (November 1951): 716-21.

Heller, Deane and David Heller. *John Foster Dulles: Soldier for Peace.* New York: Holt, Rinehart and Winston, 1960.

Herberg, Will. *Protestant-Catholic-Jew: An Essay in American Religious Sociology.* Garden City: Doubleday and Company, Inc., 1956.

Hewlett, Richard G. and Oscar E. Anderson, Jr. *A History of the Atomic Energy Commission: The New World, 1935-1945.* University Park: Pennsylvania State University, 1966.

Hoopes, Townsend. *The Devil and John Foster Dulles.* Boston: Little, Brown and Company, 1973.

Hull, Cordell. *Memoirs.* 2 vols. New York: The Macmillan Company, 1948.

Hutchinson, Paul. "Proposed Bases for a Lasting Peace." *The Christian Century* 59 (18 March 1942): 360-62.

Ickes, Harold L. "Enough of Dulles." *The New Republic* 122 (16 January 1950): 16.

"In Justice to Mr. Dulles." *The New Republic* 111 (20 November 1944): 647.

"John Foster Dulles." *The Christian Century* 61 (25 October 1944): 1224-25.

"John Foster Dulles Appointed Consultant to the Secretary of State." *The Department of State Bulletin* 22 (24 April 1950): 662.

Jones, John Paul. "Advance from Cleveland." *Social Progress* 35 (March 1945): 2-4ff.

Keim, Albert. "John Foster Dulles and the Federal Council of Churches, 1937-1949." Dissertation, The Ohio State University, 1971.

Kennan, George F. *American Diplomacy, 1900-1950*. Chicago: The University of Chicago Press, 1951.

_____. *Memoirs*. 2 vols. Garden City: Doubleday, 1955-1956.

_____. *Realities of American Foreign Policy*. Princeton: Princeton University Press, 1954.

_____. *Russia, the Atom, and the West*. New York: Harper and Brothers, 1958.

_____. "The Sources of Soviet Conduct." *Foreign Affairs* 25 (July 1947): 566-82.

La Feber, Walter. *America, Russia, and the Cold War*. New York: John Wiley and Sons, Inc., 1967.

Le Fever, Ernest. *Ethics and the United States Foreign Policy*. Cleveland: The World Publishing Company, Meridian Books, 1957.

Leiper, Henry Smith. *World Chaos and World Christianity: A Popular Interpretation of Oxford and Edinburgh, 1937*. Chicago: Willett, Clark and Company, 1937.

Leslie, Kenneth. "Cable to Dulles." *The Protestant* 7 (August/September 1946): 5-6.

McIntire, Carl. *Twentieth Century Reformation*. Collingswood NJ: Christian Beacon Press, 1944.

Mackay, John A. *The Presbyterian Way of Life*. Englewood Cliffs: Prentice-Hall, Inc., 1960.

"Marshall Asks Dulles to Go to Moscow." *The Christian Century* 64 (12 March 1947): 323-24.

Marty, Martin E. *The New Shape of American Religion*. New York: Harper and Brothers, 1958.

Meyer, Donald B. *The Protestant Search for Political Realism, 1919-1941*. Berkeley: The University of California Press, 1960.

Miller, William Lee. "The 'Moral Force' behind Dulles's Diplomacy." *The Reporter* 15 (9 August 1956): 17-20.

_____. *Piety along the Potomac: Notes on Politics and Morals in the Fifties.* Boston: Houghton Mifflin Company, 1964.

_____. *The Protestant and Politics.* Philadelphia: The Westminster Press, 1958.

"Moral Offensive for Freedom." *America* 82 (24 December 1949): 363.

Morgenthau, Hans J. *In Defense of the National Interest: A Critical Evaluation of American Foreign Policy.* New York: Alfred A. Knopf, 1951.

_____. *Politics among Nations: The Struggle for Power and Peace.* 2d ed. New York: Alfred A. Knopf, 1954.

Mosley, Leonard. *Dulles: A Biography of Eleanor, Allen and John Foster Dulles and Their Family Network.* New York: The Dial Press/James Wade, 1978.

Mulder, John M. "The Moral World of John Foster Dulles." *The Journal of Presbyterian History* 49 (Summer 1971): 157-82.

_____. *Woodrow Wilson: The Years of Preparation.* Princeton: Princeton University Press, 1978.

Muller, Dorothea R. "The Social Philosophy of Josiah Strong: Social Christianity and American Progressivism." *Church History* 28 (June 1959): 183-201.

Niebuhr, H. Richard. *Christ and Culture.* New York: Harper and Brothers, 1951.

_____. *The Responsible Self.* New York: Harper and Row, 1963.

Niebuhr, Reinhold. "American Power and World Responsibility." *Christianity and Crisis* 3 (5 April 1943): 4.

_____. *The Children of Light and the Children of Darkness: A Vindication of Democracy and a Critique of Its Traditional Defense.* New York: Charles Scribner's Sons, 1944.

_____. "The Christian Perspective on the World Crisis." *Christianity and Crisis* 4 (1 May 1944): 2.

_____. *Christian Realism and Political Problems.* New York: Charles Scribner's Sons, 1953.

_____. *Christianity and Power Politics.* New York: Charles Scribner's Sons, 1940.

_____. *Faith and Politics: A Commentary on Religious, Social, and Political Thought in a Technological Age.* Edited by Ronald H. Stone. New York: George Braziller, Inc., 1968.

_____. *An Interpretation of Christian Ethics.* New York: Harper and Brothers, 1935.

_____. *The Irony of American History*. New York: Charles Scribner's Sons, 1952.

_____. "Is There a Revival of Religion?" *The New York Times Magazine* (19 November 1950).

_____. *Man's Nature and His Communities*. New York: Charles Scribner's Sons, 1965.

_____. *Moral Man and Immoral Society: A Study in Ethics and Politics*. New York: Charles Scribner's Sons, 1932.

_____. "The Moral World of John Foster Dulles." *The New Republic* 139 (1 December 1958): 8.

_____. *The Nature and Destiny of Man*. 2 vols. New York: Charles Scribner's Sons, 1943.

_____. *Pious and Secular America*. New York: Charles Scribner's Sons, 1958.

_____. "Plans for World Reorganization." *Christianity and Crisis* 2 (19 October 1942): 3-6.

_____. "The Pride of a Righteous Nation." *The Lutheran* 31 (4 May 1949): 17.

"Offer Japan 'Peace of Reconciliation.' " *The Christian Century* 68 (18 April 1951): 484-85.

Oldham, J. H., ed. *The Oxford Conference: Official Report*. New York: Willett, Clark and Company, 1937.

Paterson, Isabel. Review of *War, Peace and Change,* by John Foster Dulles, in *New York Herald Tribune* (7 January 1939).

Paterson, Thomas G., J. Garry Clifford, and Kenneth J. Hogan. *American Foreign Policy*. Vol. 2: *A History since 1900*. 2d ed. Lexington: D. C. Heath and Company, 1983.

Platig, E. Raymond. "John Foster Dulles: A Study of His Political and Moral Thought Prior to 1953 with Special Emphasis on International Relations." Dissertation, The University of Chicago, 1957.

"Policy during War Urged on Churches." *New York Times* (11 December 1942).

"Preliminary Report of the Commission to Study the Organization of Peace." *International Conciliation* 369 (April 1941): 193-204.

Pruessen, Ronald W. *John Foster Dulles: The Road to Power*. New York: The Free Press, 1982.

Rauch, Basil. Review of *War or Peace,* by John Foster Dulles, in *Political Science Quarterly* 65 (December 1950): 592-94.

Reston, James B. "John Foster Dulles and His Foreign Policy." *Life* 25 (4 October 1948): 131.

_____. Review of *War or Peace,* by John Foster Dulles, in *New York Times Book Review* (23 April 1950).

Shafer, Luman J. "American Approaches to World Order." *The International Review of Missions* 33 (April 1944): 174-82.

Shotwell, James T. *At the Paris Peace Conference.* New York: The Macmillan Company, 1937.

"Six Pillars of Peace." *Christianity and Crisis* 3 (28 June 1943): 6-8.

"Six Pillars of Peace." *Christianity and Crisis* 3 (12 July 1943): 6-7.

Stang, Alan. *The Actor: The True Story of John Foster Dulles.* Boston: Western Islands, 1968.

Stettinius, Edward R., Jr. *Roosevelt and the Russians, the Yalta Conference.* Edited by Walter Johnson. Garden City: Doubleday and Company, Inc., 1949.

Straight, Michael. *Make This the Last War.* New York: Harcourt, Brace and Company, 1943.

Tarr, Dennis L. "The Presbyterian Church and the Founding of the United Nations." *The Journal of Presbyterian History* 53 (Spring 1975): 3-32.

Thompson, Kenneth W. *Ethics, Functionalism, and Power in International Politics: the Crisis in Values.* Baton Rouge: The Louisiana State University Press, 1979.

_____. *The Moral Issue in Statecraft: Twentieth-Century Approaches and Problems.* Baton Rouge: The Louisiana State University Press, 1966.

_____. *Political Realism and the Crisis of World Politics: An American Approach to Foreign Policy.* Princeton: Princeton University Press, 1960.

Tillich, Paul. *The Protestant Era.* Chicago: The University of Chicago Press, Phoenix Books, abr. ed., 1957.

Tracy, David. *The Analogical Imagination.* New York: Crossroad, 1981.

Truman, Harry S. *Memoirs.* 2 vols. Garden City: Doubleday and Company, 1955-1956.

U.S. Senate Committee on Foreign Relations. *Hearing, Nomination of John Foster Dulles Secretary of State Designate.* 83rd Congress, 1st Session, 1953.

Vandenberg, Arthur H. *The Private Papers of Senator Vandenberg.* Edited by Arthur H. Vandenberg, Jr. Boston: Houghton Mifflin Company, 1952.

Van Dusen, Henry P. "The Six Pillars of Peace." *Christianity and Crisis* 3 (22 March 1943): 1.

Van Kirk, Walter W. "British and American Post-War Aims." *The Federal Council Bulletin* 25 (September 1942): 10.

Ward, Patricia Dawson. *The Threat of Peace: James F. Byrnes and the Council of Foreign Ministers, 1945-1946.* Kent: Kent State University Press, 1979.

World Council of Churches. *Man's Disorder and God's Design.* The Amsterdam Assembly Series. New York: Harper and Brothers, 1948.

Yergin, Daniel. *Shattered Peace: The Origins of the Cold War and the National Security State.* Boston: Houghton Mifflin Company, 1977.

Yinger, J. Milton. *Religion in the Struggle for Power: A Study in the Sociology of Religion.* New York: Russell and Russell, Inc., 1961.

Works by John Foster Dulles

"The Aftermath of the World War." *International Conciliation* 369 (April 1941): 265-71.

"The Allied Debts." *Foreign Affairs* 1 (15 September 1922): 116-32.

"Allied Indebtedness to the United States." *The Annals of the American Academy of Political and Social Science* 96 (July 1921): 173-77.

"The American Churches and the International Situation." *Biennial Report of the Federal Council of the Churches of Christ in America* (1940) 21-27.

"The American People Need Now to Be Imbued with a Righteous Faith." In *A Righteous Faith for a Just and Durable Peace.* Edited by John Foster Dulles. New York: The Commission to Study the Bases of a Just and Durable Peace, 1942.

"America's Role in the Peace." *Christianity and Crisis* 4 (22 January 1945): 2-6.

America's Role in World Affairs. New York: The Federal Council of the Churches of Christ in America, 1940.

"Analysis of Moscow Declarations in Light of the 'Six Pillars of Peace.'" *The Annual Report of the Federal Council of the Churches of Christ in America* (1943) 157-60.

"Answer to Soviet Charges against Japanese Treaty." *The Department of State Bulletin* 25 (17 September 1951): 461-63.

"As Seen by a Layman." *Religion in Life* 7 (Winter 1938): 36-44.

"The Blessings of Liberty." *Vital Speeches of the Day* 16 (1 February 1950): 231-36.

"Business and Finance Will Benefit Most Quickly from Treaties." *League of Nations News* 2 (November 1925): 3-4.

"Can We Guarantee A Free Europe?" *Collier's* 121 (12 June 1948): 20ff.

"Can We Stop Russian Imperialism?" *The Department of State Bulletin* 25 (10 December 1951): 938-41.

"Challenge of the Little Assembly." *The New York Times Magazine* (4 January 1948).

"Challenge of Today." *The Department of State Bulletin* 24 (11 June 1951): 935-37.

"Chinese Communist Intervention in Korea." *The Department of State Bulletin* 23 (18 December 1950): 990-93.

The Christian Forces and a Stable Peace. New York: Committee on Public Affairs, National Board, Young Men's Christian Association of the United States, 1941.

"The Churches and a Just and Durable Peace." *The Biennial Report of the Federal Council of Churches of Christ in America* (1944) 22-29.

"The Churches' Contribution toward a Warless World." *Religion in Life* 9 (Winter 1940): 31-40.

"Collaboration Must be Practical." *Vital Speeches of the Day* 11 (1 February 1945): 246-49.

"Comments on the Fifth Statement: Pattern for Peace; 5. International Institutions to Maintain Peace with Justice Must Be Organized." *World Affairs* 107 (March 1944): 34-37.

"Conceptions and Misconceptions Regarding Intervention." *The Annals of the American Academy of Political and Social Science* 144 (July 1929): 102-104.

"The Dawes Report and the Peace of Europe." *The Independent* 112 (26 April 1924): 218.

"Developing Bipartisan Foreign Policy." *The Department of State Bulletin* 22 (8 May 1950): 721.

"A Diplomat and His Faith." *The Christian Century* 69 (19 March 1952): 336-38.

"Discussion of Greek Problem." *The Department of State Bulletin* 19 (14 November 1948): 607-11.

"Door to Peace." *Vital Speeches of the Day* 17 (1 November 1950): 39-42.

"Essentials of a Peace with Japan." *The Department of State Bulletin* 24 (9 April 1951): 576-80.

"Europe Must Federate or Perish." *Vital Speeches of the Day* 13 (1 February 1947): 234-36.

"Far Eastern Problems: Defense through Deterrent Power." *Vital Speeches of the Day* 18 (1 June 1952): 493-95.

"A First Balance Sheet of the United Nations." *International Conciliation* 420 (April 1946): 177-82.

"Foreign Policy: Ideals Not Deals." *The Commercial and Financial Chronicle* 165 (20 February 1947): 996ff.

"The Free State versus the Police State." *Vital Speeches of the Day* 13 (15 September 1947): 719-20.

"Free World Unity." *The Department of State Bulletin* 26 (21 January 1952): 91-92.

"Freedom and Its Purpose." *The Christian Century* 69 (24 December 1952): 1496-99.

"Freedom through Sacrifice." *The Commercial and Financial Chronicle* 163 (30 May 1946): 2912 and 2955.

"The Future of the United Nations." *International Conciliation* 445 (November 1948): 579-90.

"The General Assembly." In *The Foreign Affairs Reader*. Edited by Hamilton Fish Armstrong. New York: Harper and Brothers, 1947.

"How to Take the Offensive for Peace." *Life* 28 (24 April 1950): 120ff.

"How Work for World Peace?" *Freedom and Union* 4 (April 1949): 8-9.

"Ideals Are Not Enough." *International Conciliation* 409 (March 1945): 131-41.

"Importance of Initiative in International Affairs." *Vital Speeches of the Day* 18 (15 March 1952): 333-35.

"Improving Relations with Russia." *The U.S. News and World Report* 27 (8 July 1949): 30-33.

"The Interdependence of Independence." *The Department of State Bulletin* 23 (17 July 1950): 91-92.

"Japanese Peace Treaty Viewed as Positive Step in Free World's March toward Peace." *The Department of State Bulletin* 25 (15 October 1951): 616-20.

The John Foster Dulles Oral History Collection. Seeley G. Mudd Manuscript Library. Princeton: Princeton University.

The John Foster Dulles Personal Papers. Seeley G. Mudd Manuscript Library. Princeton: Princeton University.

The John Foster Dulles White House Memoranda. Seeley G. Mudd Manuscript Library. Princeton: Princeton University.

"Korean Attack Opens New Chapter in History." *The Department of State Bulletin* 23 (7 August 1950): 207-10.

"The Korean Experiment in Representative Government." *The Department of State Bulletin* 23 (3 July 1950): 12-13.

"Laying Foundations for a Pacific Peace." *The Department of State Bulletin* 24 (12 March 1951): 403-407.

Long Range Peace Objectives: Including an Analysis of the Roosevelt-Churchill Eight Point Declaration. New York: The Commission to Study the Bases of a Just and Durable Peace, 1941.

"The Meaning of Freedom." *Vital Speeches of the Day* 14 (15 July 1948): 581-83.

"A Militaristic Experiment." *The Department of State Bulletin* 23 (10 July 1950): 49-50.

"Moral Force in World Affairs." *Presbyterian Life* (10 April 1948): 13ff.

"Moral Leadership." *Vital Speeches of the Day* 14 (15 September 1948): 706-708.

"New Aspects of American Foreign Policy." *The Department of State Bulletin* 23 (8 May 1950): 717-20.

"New Phase of American Foreign Policy." *The Department of State Bulletin* 23 (17 July 1950): 88-91.

"North Atlantic Pact." *Vital Speeches of the Day* 15 (1 August 1949): 617-24.

"Not War, Not Peace." *Vital Speeches of the Day* 14 (15 February 1948): 270-73.

"Our Foreign Loan Policy." *Foreign Affairs* 5 (October 1926): 33-48.

"Our Vital Peace Decision." *Vital Speeches of the Day* 12 (15 October 1945): 7-8.

"Peace Is Possible." *Presbyterian Life* 1 (28 February 1948): 3.

"Peace Is Precarious: Can We Keep It?" *The New York Times Magazine* (19 August 1945).

"Peace May Be Won." *The Department of State Bulletin* 24 (12 February 1951): 252-55.

"Peace with Russia." *The Christian Century* 65 (25 August 1948): 849-51.

"Peace without Fear." *The Department of State Bulletin* 24 (7 May 1951): 726-31.

"Peace without Platitudes." *Fortune* 25 (January 1942): 42.

"Peaceful Change." *International Conciliation* 369 (April 1941): 493-98.

"A Policy for Peace Insurance." *The Department of State Bulletin* 22 (29 May 1950): 862ff.

"A Policy of Boldness." *Life* 32 (19 May 1952): 146ff.

"The Political Cost of Peace." *International Journal of Religious Education* 20 (October 1943): 3.

"The Problem of Peace in a Dynamic World." *Religion in Life* 6 (Spring 1937): 191-207.

"The Question of Formosa." *The Department of State Bulletin* 23 (4 December 1950): 911.

"The Reparation Problem." *The New Republic* 26 (30 March 1921): 133-35.

"Report on Moscow Meeting of Council of Foreign Ministers." *International Conciliation* 432 (May 1947): 449-59.

"Reputation and Performance in World Affairs." *Vital Speeches of the Day* 15 (15 May 1949): 465-68.

"A Righteous Faith." *Life* 13 (28 December 1942): 49-51.

"Road to Peace." *The Atlantic Monthly* 156 (October 1935): 492-99.

"San Francisco Address." *The U.S. News and World Report* 32 (10 October 1952): 102-104.

"The San Francisco Charter: A People's Document." *The Commercial and Financial Chronicle* 162 (5 July 1945): 113.

"The Search for a Bond of Fellowship between the Free East and the Free West." *The Department of State Bulletin* 25 (17 December 1951): 973-77.

"Securities Act and Foreign Lending." *Foreign Affairs* 12 (October 1933): 33-45.

"Security in the Pacific." *Foreign Affairs* 30 (January 1950): 175-87.

"Seven Nations to Unite and Keep the Peace." *The Department of State Bulletin* 23 (30 October 1950): 687-91.

"Should Economic Sanctions Be Applied in International Disputes?" *The Annals of the American Academy of Political and Social Science* 162 (July 1932): 103-108.

"Six Pillars of Peace." *Vital Speeches of the Day* 9 (15 April 1943): 405-407.

Six Pillars of Peace: A Study Guide Based on "A Statement of Political Propositions." Edited with an introduction by John Foster Dulles. New York: Commission to Study the Bases of a Just and Durable Peace, 1943.

The Spiritual Legacy of John Foster Dulles. Edited by Henry P. Van Dusen. Philadelphia: The Westminster Press, 1960.

"State-Control versus Self-Control." *Vital Speeches of the Day* 12 (15 July 1946): 593-95.

"Statement of Guiding Principles." *Biennial Report of the Federal Council of the Churches of Christ in America* (1942) 42-45.

"Strategy for the Pacific." *The Department of State Bulletin* 24 (26 March 1951): 483-85.

"Summary of Pacific Treaty Developments." *The Department of State Bulletin* 25 (15 October 1951): 620-21.

"Sustaining Friendship with China." *The Department of State Bulletin* 24 (28 May 1951): 843-45.

"The Task of World Peace." *The Commercial and Financial Chronicle* 166 (21 August 1947): 727ff.

"Thoughts on Soviet Policy and What to Do about It." *Life* 20 (3 June 1946): 112ff. and (10 June 1946): 118ff.

"To Save Humanity from the Deep Abyss." *The New York Times Magazine* (30 July 1950).

"Toward World Order." In *A Basis for the Peace to Come.* Edited by Francis J. McConnell. New York: Abingdon-Cokesbury Press, 1942.

"Tribute to U.S. Armed Forces in Korea." *The Department of State Bulletin* 23 (6 November 1950): 728.

"United Front against Red Aggression." In *Representative American Speeches: 1950-1951.* Edited by A. Craig Beard. New York: The H. W. Wilson Company, 1951.

"United States and Russia Could Agree but for Communist Party's Crusade." *The U.S. News and World Report* 26 (21 January 1949): 32-36.

The United States and the World of Nations. New York: Federal Council of the Churches of Christ in America, 1940.

"Uniting for Peace." *The Department of State Bulletin* 23 (23 October 1950): 651-55.

"U.S. Views on Trusteeships." *World Report* 1 (19 November 1946): 45-47.

War or Peace. New York: The Macmillan Company, 1950.

War, Peace and Change. New York: Harper and Brothers, 1939.

"What I've Learned about the Russians." *Collier's* 123 (12 March 1949): 25ff.

"What Shall We Do with the United Nations?" *The Christian Century* 64 (3 September 1947): 1041-42.

"What the United Nations Is and Might Be." *The New York Times Magazine* (24 October 1948): 10ff.

"What Will Happen Now in Japan?" *U.S. News and World Report* 30 (27 April 1951): 30-34.

"Why the Communists Really Believe Their Own Lies." *The Reader's Digest* 58 (May 1951): 130.

"World Brotherhood through the State." *Vital Speeches of the Day* 12 (1 October 1946): 743-46.

"World Organization: Curative and Creative." *Biennial Report of the Federal Council of Churches of Christ in America* (1944) 135-37.

Index

MUP *The Transformation of John Foster Dulles*

Designed by Alesa Jones
Composition by MUP Composition Department

Production specifications:
    text paper—60-pound Warren's Olde Style
    endpapers—Multicolor Antique Dove Grey
    covers (on .088 boards)—Holliston Crown Linen 13407
    dust jacket—100-pound enamel printed 2 colors:
        PMS 181 (grey), PMS 453 (rust); and varnished

Printing (offset lithography) and binding
    by Penfield/Rowland Printing Company, Inc., Macon, Georgia

DATE DUE
